Composing Cultures

Cultural Frames, Framing Culture

Robert Newman, *Editor*

Composing Cultures

Modernism, American Literary Studies,
and the Problem of Culture

ERIC ARONOFF

University of Virginia Press
CHARLOTTESVILLE AND LONDON

University of Virginia Press
© 2013 by the Rector and Visitors of the University of Virginia
All rights reserved
Printed in the United States of America on acid-free paper
First published 2013

9 8 7 6 5 4 3 2 1

LIBRARY OF CONGRESS CATALOGING-IN-PUBLICATION DATA

Aronoff, Eric.
Composing cultures : modernism, American literary studies, and the problem of culture / Eric Aronoff.
    pages   cm. — (Cultural Frames, Framing Culture)
Includes bibliographical references and index.
ISBN 978-0-8139-3483-9 (cloth : alk.)
ISBN 978-0-8139-3484-6 (pbk. : alk.)
ISBN 978-0-8139-3485-3 (e-book)
    1. American literature—History and criticism. 2. Popular culture in literature.
3. Literature and society—United States. 4. Culture in literature. 5. Modernism
(Literature)—United States. 6. Anthropology in literature. I. Title.
PS169.P63A76   2013
810.9'3552—dc23

2013004998

A book in the American Literatures Initiative (ALI), a collaborative publishing project of NYU Press, Fordham University Press, Rutgers University Press, Temple University Press, and the University of Virginia Press. The Initiative is supported by The Andrew W. Mellon Foundation. For more information, please visit www.americanliteratures.org.

For Yael
You make my life a heaven

Contents

	Acknowledgments	ix
	Introduction: The Problem of Culture	1
1	Van Wyck Brooks and Edward Sapir: Divided America and the Form of Genuine Culture	23
2	Possessing Culture: Willa Cather's Aesthetic of Culture in *The Song of the Lark* and *The Professor's House*	57
3	Cultures, Canons, and Cetology: Modernist Culture and the Melville Revival	85
4	Recovering the Whole: Culture, Region, and Poetry in the Literary Criticism of John Crowe Ransom and Allen Tate	136
	Conclusion: Composing Critical Cultures	181
	Notes	195
	Index	219

Acknowledgments

Over the course of this project's development, I have benefited from the conversation, advice, and support of many colleagues and friends. I would particularly like to thank Eduardo Cadava, Brad Evans, Scott Herring, Myra Jehlen, Walter Johnston, Jack Kerkering, Walter Benn Michaels, Steve Rachman, Guy Reynolds, Eric Santner, Leif Sorensen, Michael Warner, and Glenn Wilmott, each of whom in their own ways contributed to the substance and form of this book. I would especially like to thank Marc Manganaro, who has helped me work out these ideas since their inception, and who has been a mentor and friend at every stage of my academic career. I would also like to thank Steve Esquith, Anita Skeen, David Sheridan, and my colleagues in the Residential College in the Arts and Humanities at Michigan State University for making possible the vibrant, creative intellectual community where my passion for teaching and research could be brought together, and this book brought to fruition. Thanks also to Lauren Hall and Linda Benson for their help editing the manuscript.

Portions of chapter 2 previously appeared in "The Kingdom of Culture: Culture, Ethnology and the 'Feeling of Empire' in *The Song of the Lark*" in *Willa Cather's "The Song of the Lark,"* ed. Debra Cumberland (New York: Rodopi Press, 2010), 127–49, reprinted with permission of Rodopi Press; and in "Possessing Culture: Willa Cather's Aesthetic of Culture in *The Song of the Lark* and *The Professor's House*," *Genre* 43 (Spring/Summer 2010): 61–90. Portions of chapter 3 first appeared in "Cultures, Canons, and Cetology: Modernist Anthropology and the Form of Culture in Lewis Mumford's *Herman Melville*," *ESQ: A Journal of the American Renaissance* 58, no. 2 (Summer 2012): 185–217, and are reprinted with permission from Washington State University. Portions of chapters 1, 2, and 4 appeared in "Anthropologist, Indians, and New Critics: Culture and/as Poetic Form in Regional Modernism," *MFS: Modern Fiction Studies* 55, no. 1 (Spring 2009): 92–118, and are reprinted with permission from Johns Hopkins University Press.

    I couldn't have done this without my family. Thank you to my father and mother, Jan and Marika Wallach, who always encouraged me to follow my interests; and to Mike and Rita Aronoff for being both family and great friends. My children, Maya and Aidan, have grown along with this book; thank you, guys, for all your patience, and the joy you have brought to my life. (Yes, daddy's done with the book!) And most of all, to Yael, my soul mate: you make everything else possible; you make life more joyous, fulfilling, and fun than I ever imagined it could be.

Composing Cultures

Introduction: The Problem of Culture

In their recent survey of the state of literary studies, William B. Warner and Clifford Siskin argue that the time has come—as their title proclaims—for "stopping cultural studies."[1] For Warner and Siskin, the reason is straightforward: "culture *is* the problem with cultural studies" (104, emphasis in original). Before cultural studies, they claim, literary study struggled under the limitations of "literary history, author-centered study and various species of formalism (genre theory, close reading, rhetorical analysis)" (94). With the rise and triumph of cultural studies from the 1980s through the early twenty-first century, however, literary critics learned to "inscribe literature into the amorphous but expansive term 'culture.'" Embedding works of literature within "discourses of knowledge" and "the effects of power," cultural studies made literature (and therefore literary studies) politically relevant (94). But while they admit this movement gave literary critics valuable new ways of looking at literature through the lenses of gender, race, and class, Warner and Siskin argue that "the strategic vagueness of the term and concept of 'culture'" is the problem (95): it is a "Teflon category" in which we "totalize" all the activities of every people, period, and group, and this "totalizing indifference" leaves us "floundering" (104). If, as they claim, culture is equally and indifferently everything, then it tells us nothing.

In lamenting the problem of culture, Warner and Siskin engage in what has become a ritual jeremiad from within anthropology as well as within literary studies in the past twenty years, as culture has become ubiquitous in both literary studies and everyday language. On the one hand, culture is everywhere, used to explain what people do or do not do, or what they can or cannot do. "Corporate culture" gets the credit for success or is the culprit for misbehavior.[2] Culture is the prize in the "war" between red states and blue states and has been used to frame real war between the United States and Muslim groups in the Middle East as a "clash of civilizations." "Culture wars" and debates over multiculturalism make clear the stakes in the competition over what counts as culture: culture marks who belongs in what group, and how. In the wake of the 9/11 attack and the war on terrorism, some lamented the supposedly postmodern emphasis on multiculturalism in the 1990s, and in turn renewed calls to define a shared American culture—even while those proclaiming "we are all Americans" were hard pressed to define what exactly that shared American culture might be.[3] And if culture is used to imagine what counts as American identity, it is also central to traditional definitions of "the human" itself—definitions that have been challenged by recent claims by biologists that nonhuman primates and dolphins have culture.[4]

What it means to "have (a) culture" is likewise hard to define. Culture includes everything a designated group does; everyone is part of "a culture." But that omnipresence is coupled with fragility, as groups are said to "lose their culture" in the face of assimilation or the forces of globalization. At the same time, culture remains closely associated with particular kinds of artistic and intellectual activities (the *New York Times*, for example, features a series called the "Cultured Traveler"). Thus everyone possesses (or is possessed by) a culture; at the same time, some groups or individuals seem to possess (or be possessed by) culture more than others.

Simultaneously, despite (or perhaps because of) its ubiquity, attempts to define culture founder on several overlapping, contesting, and contradictory traditions of thinking about what counts as culture. As Warner and Siskin note, cultural studies scholars themselves have difficulty in trying to—and indeed seem to see no urgency to—identify their object of analysis: as one landmark anthology in the field put it, "Cultural studies is an interdisciplinary, transdisciplinary, and sometimes counterdisciplinary field" that simultaneously works between "both a broad, anthropological and a more narrowly humanist conception of culture."[5] The construction is telling, suggesting that there are two distinct conceptions of culture—the "humanist" and the "anthropological"—and that these two conceptions might be separated (if cultural studies theorists wanted to). Opening themselves to Warner and Siskin's charge of totalization, they go on to assert their "commit[ment] to the study of the entire range of a society's arts, beliefs, institutions, and communicative practices."[6]

Interestingly, while literary critics like Siskin and Warner have only lately begun to advocate a turn from culture, the term has been in crises within anthropology—the discipline for which it has been the defining conceptual term—for several decades, coinciding nicely with its rise in stock within literary studies. In what critics like Susan Hegeman have identified as a "veritable 'writing against culture' genre," anthropologists like James Clifford, George Marcus, Renato Rosaldo, Lila Abu-Lughod, and others have argued that the anthropological version of culture is deeply imbricated in the structures of racism and imperialism, which it, in many ways, was historically conceived to combat.[7] For these postmodern anthropologists, the idea of culture as a "whole way of life" "incarcerates" those subordinate, non-Western Others to whom it is applied within essentialized, homogenized, localized, and/or dehistoricized identities.[8] The culture concept's imperialism is, these critics argue, embodied in the genre of the ethnography itself, which imagines "natives" naively inhabiting "a culture" that can be made visible only by the expert ethnographer and the coherent text s/he composes. Thus, even as literary studies have made culture a central term, some anthropologists have been trying to imagine "anthropology beyond culture" or to "forget culture" altogether as a concept too weighted with baggage.[9]

As in postmodern anthropology, the problem of culture seems recently to have reached a critical mass within literary studies, as Warner and Siskin's argument attests. For some like Walter Benn Michaels, the modern idea of cultural identity, from its inception in the modernist period, has really been grounded in race, rather than replacing it.[10] At the same time, critics reacting to cultural studies' "intellectual imperialism"—in which the techniques of literary criticism are deemed sufficient to read any culture, or conversely whose all-encompassing definition of culture erases the distinction between text and context—have begun to argue for a (re)-turn to thinking about "form," or as a recent issue of *American Literature* has put it, "aesthetics and the end(s) of cultural studies."[11] Critics within American Studies have likewise suggested that the discipline's recent agonizing over the shape of the field is linked to the problem of culture: as some scholars have struggled to imagine American Studies from a transnational, global, or comparative perspective, critics like Hegeman have suggested that "what may be particularly haunting the concept of culture" in American Studies "is its close relationship to constructions of nationalism"; to speak of America, for some, is to automatically invoke an idea of national culture.[12] In response, Americanists like Russ Castronovo and Wai Chee Dimock have suggested a return to concepts of the aesthetic, as precisely the kind of transnational concept that can replace ideas of "nation" and "national culture" in American literary studies.[13]

In their narrative of the rise of the problem of culture within literary studies, Warner and Siskin contrast the limits of aesthetic formalism and close reading to the expansiveness of culture—a narrative that is echoed in the various calls to return to aesthetics and formalism cited earlier. Imagining a once-upon-a-time before culture was a problem for literary studies, Warner and Siskin invoke a common characterization of literary studies "pre-postmodernism," that is, in the modernist period when the New Critical reading methods developed from the 1920s through the 1950s came to dominate the field. Modernist New Criticism, this argument goes, treats the text as an autonomous aesthetic object and thereby "severs it irretrievably" from history and culture.[14] But was there ever such a moment when culture, form, and aesthetics were separate categories—when culture was not a problem for literary studies?

In contrast to this narrative, *Composing Cultures* argues that American modernism, especially in the period from 1915 to 1941, is precisely the period in which culture becomes the problem for literary studies—or to put it another way, the period culture becomes the problematic, the cluster of orienting questions, around which literary studies, anthropology, and the Americanist literary canon organize themselves as they achieve their modern disciplinary form. Beginning with the rise of the "Young Americans" in the first decade of the twentieth century, whose particular brand of progressive nationalism was epitomized by Van Wyck Brooks's *America's Coming of Age* (1915), and ending with John Crowe Ransom's *The New Criticism* (1941) and F. O. Matthiessen's *American Renaissance*, it is this period in which the two movements that together determined the shape of American literary criticism come to fruition. One was the professional, aesthetic criticism embodied in the methods of the New Criticism; the other was the establishment of American literature as an academic discipline, with its roots in the practices of literary history—two trends that are brought together in Matthiessen's synthesis of New Critical methodology and Americanist literary history.

These critical trends are of course inextricably intertwined with the production of modernist literary texts themselves, as artists and critics shared common social and aesthetic concerns—indeed, in which many key figures were both artists and critics, who then articulated the critical approaches that constructed the canon we retrospectively call "modernism." At the same time, it is also the period in which anthropology achieves its modern disciplinary forms, around precisely these questions about the nature of culture and its representation. Finally, it is in this period that the writing of members of certain ethnic and regional groups—most notably, the work of the Harlem Renaissance and African Americans—come to be seen as literatures; in short, it is in this period that the concept of "multiculturalism" develops.

This book argues that in all of these fields—anthropology, literary criticism, Americanist literary history, and imaginative literature—culture emerges in this period as a defining problem. Far from being, as Warner and Siskin narrate, a moment when formalist criticism cordons literary studies off from the concept of culture, I argue that modernist conceptions of culture and modernist ideas of literary form—or, how to "read" a culture and how to "read" a text—are inextricably intertwined. Tracing the contours of this problematic of culture and form as it shapes modernist literature, anthropology, literary criticism, and canon formation, I make several interlocking arguments. One is that the modernist problematic of culture was not developed within anthropology and then disseminated or applied by other disciplines; rather, it emerged in a thoroughly interdisciplinary conversation, involving figures who crossed the boundaries between what later became literature, literary criticism, anthropology, linguistics, and social science. This shared problematic, in turn, did much to shape the terms of the particular arguments that developed within each discipline.

New ways to conceive of culture, I also argue, became new ways to conceive of the literary text and how to read it. One powerful model of culture crucial in shaping the discourse across disciplines was the conception of culture as a spatial whole—that is, as an internally coherent structure of meaning, imagined as an object in space. In this way, from the outset, the modernist conception of culture was always an aesthetic, formal concept. These new versions of spatialized culture in turn became—in the hands of critics who were crucial to both the reconstruction of the Americanist literary canon and the practice of literary criticism—new versions of the poetic text, conceived of as itself a structured, spatial whole. Moreover, this spatial reimagining of culture made possible reimagining the physical or conceptual space upon which culture would be mapped—the "unit" of culture. While some critics imagined culture as coextensive with the state and argued for both a national culture and a literature that would map it, others—both progressive and reactionary—imagined the unit of culture as both a geographic region and a transnational global culture, with culture in each case bypassing the space of the nation-state. This argument, of course, is crucial in reexamining the supposedly national(ist) origins of American Studies, in order to think through current calls for making American Studies transnational. In effect, this book suggests, cultural studies begins in the 1920s and 1930s, and understanding the ways in which the problem of culture shaped literature, literary criticism, and Americanist canon formation in turn illuminates the current problem of culture in literary studies.

"The Meaning of Culture for Poetry": Self, Region, and Nation

The interconnected questions of culture and form engaged by *Composing Cultures* might best be introduced by turning to a critic much like the kind Warner and Siskin might have had in mind as they imagined literary studies before the problem of culture: Allen Tate, one of the founders of the New Criticism. At the center of a 1932 essay on Emily Dickinson, for example, Tate gives a close reading of "The Chariot." Claiming that it is "one of the perfect poems in English," he explicates its formal features, highlighting the terms of tension and unity that would come to typify New Critical aesthetics. Thus, the "pattern of suspended action" in the poem is "charg[ed] with movement" by the rhythm; "every image is precise" and "extends and intensifies every other ... fus[ing] into a single order of perception" the apparently heterogeneous elements of the poem.[15] But far from bracketing the poem's aesthetic form from culture, Tate's close reading is embedded within, and serves to elaborate upon, a broader contemplation of the relation between form and culture: the essay is entitled "New England Culture and Emily Dickinson." Tate is above all interested in the question of the relation between these two terms. "What," he asks, "is the meaning of culture for poetry?"(163).

In exploring that question, Tate begins by positing at least two definitions of culture. There is, he says, "what we popularly call culture," which designates "the material" that "great poets" leave behind: "We study [the great poets] to acquire it." Here, Tate seems to draw on Matthew Arnold's famous definition of culture as "the pursuit of ... perfection by means of getting to know ... the best that has been thought and said in the world."[16] But the "source of a poet's true culture," Tate goes on to suggest, "lies back of the paraphernalia of culture." In contrast to this first version of culture, "a culture" is defined as "an available source of ideas that are imbedded in a complete and homogeneous society"; as a complete, taken-for-granted system of ideas, it "cannot be consciously created" (163).

By invoking this version of culture—shifting from the mass noun "culture" to the count noun "a culture," and imagining culture as a complete or whole way of life "imbedded" in the worldview shared by a particular community—Tate of course draws on an idea of culture that was at that very moment becoming central to the new discipline of anthropology as it emerged in its modern form. This sense of culture is, for Tate, what gives rise to poetic form: "This world order is assimilated . . . to the poetic vision" of great poets like Dickinson and, while for the poet herself these ideas must be an "unconscious discipline, . . . they give form and stability to [her] fresh perception of the world" (163). Moreover, Tate argues, the "perfect literary situation" is formed when "a culture" is just at the beginning of "breaking up": located at the "equilibrium of an old and new order"—Shakespeare and Donne at the end of the medieval system, Dickinson at the end of the Puritan system—the poet can "probe the deficiencies of a tradition" but still "has the tradition to probe." Thus—in language that tellingly echoes the key terms by which Tate defines the great poem, and the role of the New Critic in revealing that greatness—culture gives "form and stability" to the poet's "perceptions." The poet, in turn, is able to "[exhibit] the structure, the internal lineaments, of his culture by threatening to tear them apart" (165).

Engaging these two senses of culture, and the question of the meaning of culture for poetry, Tate raises a number of conceptual tangles. Defining culture as "an available source of ideas" embedded "in a complete and homogeneous society," he makes culture descriptive, insofar as there can be multiple cultures, one of which is particular to New England. At the same time, the concept is normative, insofar as culture must be "complete and homogeneous"; otherwise, it does not count as culture. The poet (Dickinson) is representative, insofar as she assimilates the world order that characterizes her culture, but she is also exceptional—a "great" poet or genius. While I will return to the intricacies and implications of these formulations later, my point for now is that in Tate's essay, we do not find Warner and Suskin's version of formalist literary studies before the problem of culture; instead, Tate reveals the way in which he—and the modernist literary criticism of which he is a founding figure—was always concerned with the meaning of culture for poetry.

When in this essay Tate invokes culture as a relative, whole way of life, he is of course invoking a version of culture that had become the central concept of the emerging discipline of anthropology during the previous two decades. Tellingly, at around the same time that Tate wrote that essay, one of the chief theorists of culture in that discipline also turned to Emily Dickinson to work out his version of the question "What is the meaning of culture for poetry?" In the May 1925 issue of Harriet Monroe's *Poetry*, alongside Monroe's review of Ezra Pound, Edward Sapir published "Emily Dickinson, a Primitive," his review of the recently released *Complete Poems of Emily Dickinson*. Sapir, by 1925, had already established himself as one of the most important students of Franz Boas, who, from his Department of Anthropology at Columbia University, led the reshaping of American anthropology around new conceptions of culture as plural, relative systems of meaning.[17] Sapir was a brilliant linguistic anthropologist who had performed groundbreaking work analyzing Native American languages. He was also a poet, literary critic, and public intellectual who frequently contributed articles on a wide variety of intellectual issues—from literary criticism to analyses of immigration and race, to reviews of the latest works on psychology and sociology—to the major publications whose pages shaped American modernism, such as *The Dial*, *The New Republic*, and *The Freeman*.

Interestingly, the anthropologist who would be instrumental in making Tate's version of "a culture" central to anthropology does not deploy this sense of culture in his review of Dickinson. When culture appears, it is as that from which Dickinson was free—a remarkable statement, it seems, for an anthropologist to make, and one that signals the complicated terrain of culture in the modernist period. Echoing the common critical focus on Dickinson's seclusion, Sapir argues that "she was not 'in the swim' of anything, she had but casual contacts with the culture of her day"; even more forcefully, Sapir imagines that Dickinson was able to "discover herself" because she "drank very sparingly ... of the stream of literary culture."[18] In imagining the distinction between culture and the self, Sapir invokes Tate's sense of culture as "the paraphernalia," the bits of literature and learning that are acquired, and therefore inessential. This division between external culture and one's whole "self"—which for Sapir includes both the intellectual and the spiritual faculties—is, characteristic of what Sapir calls the "material age": focusing on the "externalized world," Sapir argues, the "bulk of contemporary verse ... gives us ... subtle explorations of the intellect, but curiously little spiritual life" (100). Culture in the material age, it turns out, is "external," split from the self, while also splitting the self by dividing intellect from spirit.

Sapir's diagnosis of Dickinson's success, however, echoes Tate's in crucial ways: where Tate imagines Dickinson as part of a "complete and homogeneous society," Sapir imagines her a complete "self." Her poetry succeeds because it is "protected from the slightest alloy of sham"; in contrast to the materialism that would divide intellect from spirit, Dickinson's "life was all of a piece"—and so, thus, was her poetry (98, 105). It is in this sense of a prelapsarian unity of self that Dickinson is, as Sapir's title suggests, "a primitive." For Tate, a culture provides a poet like Dickinson with the "form" that unites the "purely personal" and the "intellectual," so that "there is that unique focus of experience which is at once neither and both" ("New England Culture," 164); Dickinson thus inhabits a unified structure of "a culture." For Sapir, she is a unified structure of "a self." For both, this unity is reproduced in the "essential significant form" of her poetry ("Primitive," 104).

As critics like Richard Handler have argued, Sapir's theory of the integral self and poetic form is part of his "anti-romantic romanticism," in which Sapir constructs "freedom in form" as the antidote for both the externality of a material age and the excesses of the unrestrained self he associates with Romanticism. While Sapir here imagines the formal unit of this integrity to be the self, elsewhere, as I will suggest later, he, like Tate, imagines that unit to be a regional culture.[19] What is important here is that for Tate and for Sapir, writing at the moment when literary studies and anthropology emerge in their modern disciplinary form, culture and aesthetics are part of a common conversation, and the subject of intense debate. Literary studies is, in the modernist period, already cultural studies; culture is already about aesthetics.

Their contemplation of culture and form, moreover, takes place amid a broader debate over culture in yet another sense: whereas Tate imagines the unit of culture as the region (New England, in the case of Dickinson), others in the period imagine it as the nation. Writing within a few years of Tate's analysis, Van Wyck Brooks also turns to Dickinson in relation to culture, but for Brooks, that culture is national, rather than (solely) regional. When Brooks elaborates on "the meaning of culture for [Dickinson's] poetry," he was already (as I will examine in detail later) one of the founding fathers of the movement of Young Americans, who, taking inspiration in his call for "America's Coming-of-Age" in 1915, had undertaken the modernist critique of American life. In *New England: Indian Summer, 1865–1915*, Brooks seems to echo Sapir's conclusion that Dickinson was an isolated, individual genius. Dwelling on the details of Dickinson's reclusive life while lauding her poetry, Brooks suggests that "her style, her stamp, her form were completely her own."[20] The volume of which this account is a part, however, suggests that Dickinson's "form" is not "completely her own," but in a complex way, is a national form.

Indian Summer was the second volume of Brooks's three-volume attempt to reconstruct "the literary history of the United States," begun in 1936 with *The Flowering of New England, 1815-1865*.[21] And while, as the volumes' titles suggest, Brooks begins by thinking about culture at the regional level—he describes New England as exemplifying a "culture cycle," with the development, growth, and expression of "the thoughts and feelings of the people" (*Flowering*, 527)—that culture becomes in Brooks's literary history "American" culture. The move from Dickinson's "own" form to national form is encapsulated, for example, by Brooks's pronouncement later in the volume that she was a "unique and original American poet," a label that is repeated through the volume (373). On the one hand "unique," she is also crucially representative; unlike for Tate, she is not representative (merely) of a region, but of "America." She is, Brooks claims, part of the "main stream" along with Hawthorne, Thoreau, and Emerson, in which the "local and parochial [New England] mind, which had always been universal, proved to be also national" (*Flowering*, 530-31).

As with Tate's and Sapir's formulations, Brooks's idea of culture raises questions of the form of culture; the form of poetry; and the unit of culture as individual, regional, national, and/or universal (to name just a few possibilities). For Brooks, Dickinson thus becomes part of a recomposed American literary history, and canon formation becomes the means to constitute a culture that it then could be said to reflect. Brooks's "Makers and Finders" series enacts his project to create what he elsewhere called a "usable past."[22] That "usable past" is composed in turn in order to work (as he titled an earlier essay) "Toward a National Culture."[23] For Brooks, then, the meaning of culture for poetry might be said to be reversed: poetry, or literature more broadly, becomes the bearer of a culture that is properly national. And the literary critic who "discovers" the canonical authors through "effort and insight" takes on the crucial role of being, paradoxically, both a "maker" and a "finder" of culture.

Culture, Cultures, and American Cultures

This book argues that the interlocking questions raised by Warner and Siskin were the very questions that were central to American artists, critics, and anthropologists like Tate, Sapir, and Brooks in the years

1915–41: what is culture, what is the unit of culture, and what is the relation between culture and aesthetics? As many scholars have observed, American artists and intellectuals in the years leading up to World War I, and especially in the decades after the war, sought with renewed vigor to redefine a specifically American identity and culture. Americans experienced the pride and economic prosperity that came from their emergence from World War I as a world power, while also struggling with the social and philosophical questions about the very nature of modern industrial civilization the war brought with it. At the same time, unprecedented waves of immigrants from Southern and Eastern Europe reached U.S. shores, and new social and political movements—labor unions, socialism and communism, the reemergence of the Ku Klux Klan in the South—created a sense of social instability and rapid change. In response to what were perceived as new conditions, writers, artists, politicians, and social scientists sought new ways—from the Immigration Act of 1924 to Van Wyck Brooks's calls to find a "usable past"—to define what was specifically "American" about America. Along with this rising interest in things American came an increased interest in redefining—or, as critics such as Waldo Frank would call it, rediscovering— American literature, rescuing its study from what a new generation of critics considered genteel Victorian-age pedants who looked to England for their literary standards of excellence.

But even as American critics and artists in the 1920s and 1930s attempted to redefine the content of a particularly American culture— embodied, in part, in a newly reformed American literary canon—the form of "culture" as a concept, what counted as culture, was itself undergoing radical transformation and becoming the subject of intense debate. As Raymond Williams famously noted, the term "culture" has always involved a complicated and layered set of interrelated, and often logically incoherent, ideas.[24] Through the nineteenth century, the term could mean, variably, a general process of self-development and spiritual and mental improvement; the related notion of Culture, designating the highest artistic and intellectual achievements of a given society, most often associated with Arnold's "the best that has been thought and said"; and the Romantic idea, beginning in the work of Johann Gottfried Herder, of culture as an inner, spiritual growth linked to national or racial gifts. Herder and those who followed proposed this word specifically in opposition to, and as a critique of, the term "civilization," which in the eighteenth century and most of the nineteenth carried a connotation of teleological progress toward European industrial society. Though the Herderian notion of plural national cultures could be seen as an opening move toward relativism and pluralism, in fact, both the Herderian version of culture and high Culture were universal and hierarchical concepts: cultural achievements of different societies or historical periods could ultimately be measured against a single set of standards and compared, with cultural products being either higher or lower on the scale.

The notion of culture as embracing all aspects of a group's social and material life—a whole way of life—was not decidedly crystalized until the late nineteenth century, in Edward Burnett Tylor's *Primitive Culture* (1871).[25] Even here, however, Tylor's version of culture, while encompassing more than just the fine arts, was decidedly universalist, informed by an evolutionary idea of progress. As stated in the title, and implicit throughout his text, culture is singular, with individual civilizations having more or less culture, occupying higher or lower positions on the scale of evolution.

In the 1910s and 1920s, however, this constellation of definitions of culture became even more complex, as artists, intellectuals, and social scientists articulated new versions of the term, and its use proliferated across a wide variety of disciplines. These shifts in the meaning of culture have been most thoroughly examined by anthropologists telling the history of their own discipline. The debate over culture, in what George Stocking has called the "classical period" in American anthropology, became the central question around which the discipline defines itself through the modernist period.[26] Rather than seeing individual elements within a society as distinct entities, comparable with similar elements in other societies in order to place them on an evolutionary scale as Tylor had done, anthropologists such as Bronislaw Malinowski and Franz Boas, and the latter's students Edward Sapir and Ruth Benedict, began arguing that cultures must be understood as whole systems, the individual elements of which could be understood only in relation to one another. Only by viewing a culture from the inside, seeing the integration of its various elements as a functional whole, could any one element—be it a religious practice, a grammatical structure, or a moral value—be properly understood. Implicit in this version of cultures as wholes is a theory of pluralism. Since individual practices can be understood only in relation to other practices within a culture, they are rendered logically unavailable for comparison to similar elements in other cultures. Rather than particular practices being "better" or "worse," "higher" or "lower," they can only be "different."

This shift in conceptualization, from evolutionary progression to relative wholes, is reflected in the different characteristic forms of representation the two versions called for: Tylor, for example, compiled encyclopedic volumes, arraying similar elements from different societies—say, a particular type of tool or a religious practice—side by side on a comparative evolutionary scale. The ethnography—the detailed rendering of all the various elements of one culture, as analyzed by the inside position of the participant-observer—came to be the emblematic text of the modern anthropologist, epitomized in the work of Bronislaw Malinowski. This shift toward cultures as relative, synchronic wholes was itself a gradual, ambiguous, and uneven one. Even theorists such as Boas and Malinowski, who made the functional-organic view of culture the center of their theoretical models, persisted at times in viewing individual practices, and indeed whole cultures, in evolutionary terms.

Composing Cultures

Although the story of the rise of this anthropological version of culture and its relation to literary modernism has often been told—with anthropology at the center, and with critics and artists applying these anthropological conceptions to literature—*Composing Cultures* decenters anthropology as the source from which new conceptions of culture were disseminated. Rather, I argue that these new conceptions of culture arose from a thoroughly interdisciplinary debate in the period, involving social scientists, literary critics, philosophers, artists, and anthropologists alike, often with key individuals fulfilling several of these disciplinary roles at once. Indeed, I will suggest, this debate might even be seen as a pre-disciplinary debate, in which the lines between these disciplines are fluid and blurred, and that it is through this debate and around the ways in which culture is deployed by different figures to different materials that these disciplines—anthropology, literary criticism, American Studies, literary history—define their modern identities.

My approach here is not a study of influence, with a unified, coherent "culture concept" passed directly between specific individuals, but rather Foucauldian, in which the figures involved share a problematic, or an orienting cluster of unresolved problems, each understanding the terms differently and working them out in various disciplinary forms, but nonetheless responding to one another as part of a common debate. At the same time, specific points of contact and dialogue among these figures abound. This interdisciplinary debate, I will suggest, in many ways occurred in the key "little magazines" and intellectual journals of the modernist period, such as *The Dial, The New Republic, Seven Arts, The Freeman*, and *The Nation*, on whose pages essays by public intellectuals from a variety of backgrounds and training would jostle side by side, forming a common conversation around key terms like "culture," even if their ostensible topics seemed unrelated. And this story is in many ways a "New York" story, as intellectuals from all of these backgrounds met and traveled shared circuits within the city—from Columbia University and Harlem uptown, to Greenwich Village and the New School of Social Research downtown, and to the publishing houses and journal offices scattered throughout Manhattan—even as the city became a central node in a common circuit of travel beyond the city, to what became key sites of culture for anthropologists, artists, and social and literary critics alike, most notably the Pueblo Southwest and the Deep South.

Seeing this reconceptualization of culture as arising from a broader interdisciplinary conversation makes visible how the contours of that debate in turn structure debates within each discipline. Within literary studies, new ways to think about culture(s) produce new ways to define (and read) the literary text itself. From liberal critics such as Van Wyck Brooks and Lewis Mumford seeking to redefine "American" literature to reactionary critics such as Allen Tate and John Crowe Ransom seeking to resist the idea of "national" literature as such, the aesthetics of culture as a meaningful whole is transposed into a theory of the text as a self-contained, meaningful structure.

Conversely, I will argue, seeing the anthropological versions of culture—particularly the versions deployed by the students of Franz Boas, such as Edward Sapir, Ruth Benedict, and Margaret Mead—as arising from within this interdisciplinary conversation reveals the ways in which these versions of culture are themselves aesthetic concepts. Conceptions of culture turned on issues of form, and these formal issues were often most visible in these anthropologists' writings about literature and poetry in the period. A key term that circulated within these interdisciplinary conversations is "experience," a term that, for various thinkers, stood as a unifying term overcoming the perceived divide between "theory" and "practice." Experience, and its relation to the idea of culture as a formal whole, structures key shifts within both anthropology and literary criticism, as it reconceives who had the authority to represent and interpret the objects of analysis ("cultures" and "texts"). In anthropology, this meant a shift in authority from the "armchair anthropologist" to the scientifically trained "participant-observer," who could enter the structured whole of a culture, see it from both within and without, and then embody that cultural whole within the ethnographic text (itself a formal "composition," a genre whose rules bring harmony and structure to the otherwise disparate pieces of data assembled by the ethnographer). This shift finds its parallel, I argue, in literary criticism, with the rise of the professional poet-critics T. S. Eliot, Tate, and Ransom, who could derive their authority from their roles as both participants and observers of modernist literature.

These new conceptions of culture, in turn, enable a wide variety of positions for critics, social scientists, and artists seeking to redefine America. Conceiving cultures as unified wholes entailed new metaphors of value: instead of practices or artifacts being ranked higher or lower, now entire ways of life could be termed "whole," "unified," or "divided." Suddenly, in contrast to the cultural wholeness anthropologists found in Native American and South Sea Island societies, American "civilization" could be described as divided or fragmented—a diagnosis many of the works seeking to define what Van Wyck Brooks called an American "usable past" were explicitly supposed to correct. Such terms lay behind, for example, Raymond Weaver's, Van Wyck Brooks's, and Lewis Mumford's contributions to the Melville revival of the 1920s, which decisively reshaped the Americanist literary canon.

Furthermore, the idea of cultural wholes became not just a question of unity versus disunity or division, but what kind of unity that culture constitutes. From this question springs two of the most important lines of argument that run through this book. First, the idea of culture as spatial form emerges as crucial in shaping modernist conceptions of culture and aesthetics. Rather than imagining culture as a temporal process—of evolutionary development, or technological sophistication, or even patterns developed over time—key figures begin to imagine culture as a synchronic, spatial structure, characterized by "meaning" constituted through the relation of elements in the structure. This spatial aesthetic, I argue, in turn shapes new conceptions of the meaningfulness of literary texts as spatial forms.

Second, this idea of structural bounded culture(s), in turn, is deployed in debates over national and/or regional cultures. At what level is genuine unity to be found, as opposed to, on the one hand, division and fragmentation, and on the other, the attempt to force a unity where no such wholeness "naturally" exists? Which is the site of "authentic culture"— the region or the nation? And what is the relation of each of these terms to the state? And what is the relation between these conceptions of region, nation, and state with the idea of a cosmopolitan or transnational culture or civilization? Finally, what are the implications for these kinds of identities for aesthetic form? For anthropologists like Edward Sapir, to writers like Willa Cather, to key architects of the reformation of the Americanist canon like Lewis Mumford, to critics like Tate and Ransom, the unit of culture becomes the geographic region, in explicit tension with the idea of a national culture, where culture is coterminous with the state. In these cases, the region becomes both a geographic and an aesthetic concept, as regional culture—like the well-wrought poem—is marked by the achievement of "form."

Approaching the problematic of culture in this way, I argue, reveals continuities between critical movements that have often been seen as antithetical and complicates what are often seen as the politics of culture, literary formalism, and canon formation. In accounts of modernism, critics have tended to see anthropological versions of cultural pluralism as inherently producing a leftist politics, as opposed to the conservative hierarchies of the Arnoldian versions of high Culture.[27] Thus, scholars of modernism like Ann Douglass tend to array the "good" modernists—pluralist, democratic, progressive—against the "bad" modernists—reactionary, elitist, universalist, usually with the New Critics as the paradigmatic examples.[28] Similarly, critics of canon formation such as Paul Lauter and David Shumway tend to see the dominant ideology at work in the institutionalization of American literature as reactionary, formed in order to suppress the voices of women, minorities, and the working class. One of the outcomes of this project, I believe, will be to reveal how the anthropological version of culture, in its several complex forms, could be mobilized to support a wide variety of political and ideological positions, and indeed how the circulation and deployment of the culture concept in the 1920s and 1930s complicates this opposition between high Culture and anthropological culture. What critics like Douglass and Lauter overlook are the related conceptions of cultural wholeness and recovery that underpin both sides of their ideological coins, underwriting the New Critical emphasis on textual wholeness *as well as* the celebration of African American culture as a culture, and the idea of American literature and culture as a distinct entity to be studied in the 1920s *as well as* the project of critics like Lauter and Shumway to bring the literatures of minorities, women, and the working class into the canon as distinct cultures deserving a place of respect in academia.

Christopher Douglas has brilliantly analyzed the circulation of concepts of culture among anthropology and sociology and the rise of several minority literatures (African American, Asian American, Native American, Latino) to construct a "unified field theory" that ties together these multicultural literatures—which have generally been treated as separate phenomena—across time through the twentieth century to the present.[29] In a similar way, this project seeks to create a "unified field theory" of modernist disciplines. But rather than tracing this field diachronically through the twentieth century, as Douglas does, I trace it synchronically, tracking the way in which debates over culture, in the relatively circumscribed frame of American modernism, shaped the emergence of disciplines and approaches that are generally seen as at odds or even antithetical politically: anthropology and aesthetics, formalist literary criticism and literary history, regionalism and nationalism, progressive politics and reactionary conservatism.

Composing Cultures builds on critical work undertaken on the circulation of the culture concept between anthropology and literature in the modernist period and extends these discussions in several ways. Walter Benn Michaels has uncovered the way in which discourses of culture and cultural pluralism served nativist constructions of an American cultural identity in the 1920s. Culture, Michaels has shown, often served not to debunk ideas of race so much as to replace them, as cultures became something one "inherited," "lost," or "recovered," based on an essential identity that is ultimately racial.[30] More closely allied with the approach of this book, Susan Hegeman and Marc Manganaro have each excavated the ways in which discourses of culture circulated among anthropologists, social critics, and artists in the modernist period. Hegeman focuses on American anthropology and literature, tracing the emergence of various ideas of American or national culture, and in particular the spatialization of the culture concept, wherein sites of "genuine culture" could be geographically grounded in specific regions, with various relations to metropolitan centers.[31] Manganaro examines the circulation of the culture concept more widely in the Anglo-American context, while also tracing the relation between Boasian anthropologists like Ruth Benedict and Zora Neale Hurston and New Critics like Cleanth Brooks and Kenneth Burke.[32] As noted earlier, Christopher Douglas also examines the interdisciplinary circulation of the culture concept, with particular attention to the relationship between the cultural pluralism of Boasian anthropology, the sociology of Robert Parks with its emphasis on processes of assimilation in the mid-twentieth century, and the rise of multicultural literatures through the 1990s.

My argument in *Composing Cultures* is situated at the interstices created by these important works, by focusing particularly on aesthetic form—the form of culture and the form of texts, canon formation, and the relation of both to questions of national and regional cultures and literatures. Michaels is particularly interested in the relationship between cultural and racial identity contained in the idea of culture as "purity" or as "heredity," in ways that make it a covert substitute for "race." Douglass similarly focuses on culture and racial identity, arguing that ideas about what counts as the literature of a particular group (African American literature, Native American literature, and so on) have been grounded in debates over who counts as members of that group—ideas that have always rested on race. Neither scholar attends to culture as itself "form," or its significance for the idea of literary form. I instead focus on the idea of culture as whole, as an aesthetic object. Hegeman's idea of spatial culture differs crucially from my use of the term "spatial." For Hegeman, that spatialization is primarily a geographic concept, referring to the ways cultures are arranged relative to one another in space (in peripheral regions, remote from the metropole); I am interested in the spatialization of culture as an aesthetic concept, in which cultures are conceived as spatial structures themselves, which are then mapped onto those geographic regions. Hegeman thus does not deal with the New Critics or the concept of literary form. Manganaro, in contrast, addresses culture and literary criticism, but given his interest in the Anglo-American circuits of culture (dealing extensively with Eliot, Joyce, and Malinowski), he does not situate this discussion within debates over the unit of culture—universal, national, or regional—that I shape the particularly American context of the debate I trace. None analyze the connection between these debates over culture and the reformation of the Americanist literary canon (via Melville) and the debates over national, regional, and cosmopolitan culture they involve. In sum, my project is unique in its contribution to understanding the relationship among culture, literary form, and canon formation in the period, and the corresponding implications these have for debates over cultural and literary studies in the early twenty-first century.

This project, then, will examine the interplay between culture and cultures, and the interplay among anthropology, literary criticism, and imaginative literature, to tease out how debates over culture structure ideas of national, regional, or individual identity on the one hand and aesthetic value on the other. The chapters are organized to establish the contours of the problematic of culture and to trace the working out of these lines of debate in modernist literary texts, in the formation of the Americanist literary canon, and in the regional aesthetic and poetic theories of modernist literary criticism. I will analyze a wide variety of texts—from anthropological texts attempting to theorize culture to novels, magazine pieces, and literary criticism. Each of these texts, directly or symbolically, thematically or formally, is engaged in working out the problem of culture and form.

I begin in chapter 1 by laying out the intellectual, social, and political context within which the modernist culture concept emerges in the United States in the 1920s. Focusing on figures who cross the borders between social science and modernist art—in particular, the anthropologist and linguist Edward Sapir and literary and social critic Van Wyck Brooks—I examine their shared project of overcoming the perceived "dissociation" of modern secular society by trying to conceptualize a whole way of life, each aspect of which—economic, artistic, philosophical, scientific—was integrated in a meaningful way. Brooks and Sapir help lay out the key terms in the discourse of culture, opposing a "divided" American civilization to an idea of "genuine" culture as an aesthetic whole. Brooks's *America's Coming-of-Age* (1915) sets the terms in which the problematic is conceived, imagining an America without culture, divided between highbrow idealism and lowbrow pragmatism, and pointing to the intertwined issues of immigration, labor, nationhood, and aesthetics around which the discourse of culture circulates. Edward Sapir in turn articulates, in his "Culture, Genuine and Spurious," the solution of genuine culture—a solution whose key terms (and the complications they entail) become paradigmatic for other critics of culture in the period. In particular, I argue, Sapir articulates a theory of culture as a "meaningful whole," conceived of as spatial structure: culture is a synchronous structure in which the meaning of each element arises in relation to every other element in the structure. The unit of culture, in turn, is the geographic region as well as the transnational, cosmopolitan globe; in both cases, genuine culture stands in contrast to the "spurious" culture of the nation-state. This formulation of culture as a spatial, aesthetic whole both arises out of Sapir's interest in poetic form and is part of a similar spatialization of culture at work in both the restructuring of the Americanist canon and the rise of the New Criticism. In straddling a normative and a descriptive definition of culture, Sapir's version is symptomatic of the conceptual difficulties inhabiting the discourse of culture. In his roles as anthropologist, linguist, poet, and literary critic engaged in the modernist debates over language and aesthetics, Sapir also embodies the interdisciplinary (or pre-disciplinary) nature of the debates over culture.

In the chapters that follow, I trace these debates, and in particular the idea of culture as spatial form, as they work themselves out in literature, in the formation of new literary canons and literary criticism. In chapter 2, I analyze Willa Cather's shifting deployment of Native American art and artifacts in her novels *The Song of the Lark* (1915) and *The Professor's House* (1925) to argue that these shifts both participate in and are paradigmatic of debates over culture in the 1920s. As critics of American culture sought alternative models, the figure of the Indian emerged for many as a key location for genuine culture. Putting Cather's novels in dialogue with both late-nineteenth-century paradigms of primitive culture and Sapir's deployment of the Indian in "Culture, Genuine and Spurious," I counter arguments that have seen Cather's novels merely as two parts of a single pluralist argument about culture and art, inspired by Cather's journeys to the Southwest in the early part of her career. Instead, I argue that Cather's shifting deployment of Indian art in the two novels is in fact paradigmatic of the tensions in the debate surrounding culture occurring in that period. In *The Song of the Lark*, Cather constructs a universal, evolutionary model of culture in which the primitive but essential desire embodied in Native American art reaches its culmination in the refinement and self-possession of Cather's protagonist. In contrast, in *The Professor's House*, Cather imagines the meaningful whole of culture itself as an art object. Picking up Sapir's definition of genuine culture as a self-contained, meaningful whole, Cather imagines the sculptural remnants of the Cliff Dweller civilization—its architecture, its pottery—as a synecdoche of the composed, whole way of life of which they are a part. Cather's theory of culture as a spatial "composition" is in turn linked to her theory of narrative composition, and her regionalism. Imagining both a culture and a narrative as whole, spatial objects, Cather provides a transition between modernist anthropology and the New Criticism.

New versions of culture, I argue, in turn produce new ways to read and value texts. Thus, in chapter 3, I turn to a case study in criticism and canon formation in the 1920s, arguing that key moments in the revival and canonization of Herman Melville in this period are shaped by the debates over culture. From the early revival of interest in Melville's South Sea tales to the elevation of *Moby-Dick* as an "American" masterpiece, the shifting terms of Melville criticism can be seen as symptomatic of shifting ideas of culture and literature. Melville criticism and Americanist canon formation more broadly in turn become a field in which these debates are prosecuted. I begin by tracing the connections between the epistemological and aesthetic concerns of Raymond Weaver's *Herman Melville: Mariner and Mystic* (1921), Van Wyck Brooks's essays on Melville in *The Freeman*, Bronislaw Malinowski's *Argonauts of the Western Pacific* (1922), and Sapir's "Culture, Genuine and Spurious." Critics like Weaver, I argue, emphasize Melville's access to and depiction of a whole way of life that, only in the 1920s, could be seen as a culture. Melville, in his position as participant-observer—one who combines both imagination and experience—could in turn assume the representational authority required by this new conception of culture. This cultural wholeness could then, of course, be turned into a critique of one's own divided culture.

This standard of cultural wholeness in turn becomes, in Lewis Mumford's *Herman Melville* (1929), a standard of aesthetic wholeness embodied in *Moby-Dick*. Placing Mumford's biography of Melville in the context of Mumford's essays on culture, regionalism, and the state, Mumford's Melville becomes the embodiment of the genuine regional culture of the "golden day" of the American 1850s, in his person as a poet-whaler and author uniting the practical and the artistic, and in the very form of his writing. For Mumford, the wholeness of regional culture and the wholeness of Melville's life translate into the wholeness of the text itself: *Moby-Dick*, uniting divergent genres, realms of experience, and philosophies into one "mythic" whole, becomes a synecdoche for the whole regional culture in which it was produced. Further, in canonizing *Moby-Dick* as essentially the product of a regional culture, Mumford complicates the idea of a national novel even as he promotes it. This reading of *Moby-Dick* reveals a set of assumptions shared with reactionary critics such as John Crowe Ransom and Allen Tate, commonly viewed as the liberal Mumford's political opposites.

In chapter 4, I pick up the themes of regionalism and aesthetic form that emerge in the previous chapters to argue that Allen Tate's and John Crowe Ransom's New Critical theories of poetic meaning are also shaped by the debates over culture. Bringing together Southern Agrarian writings like *I'll Take My Stand* (1930) with essays on poetry in *The World's Body* (1938) and *The New Criticism* (1941), I suggest that the New Critical poem, with its emphasis on organic, atemporal wholeness, serves as a synecdoche for a genuine regional culture that is by definition whole and meaningful. The terms in which Tate and Ransom conceive culture in turn become the terms by which they judge poetry. Taking Tate's infamous criticism of Hart Crane's *The Bridge* (1930) as a paradigmatic example, I show how Tate's contrast between an authentic, regional unity and the false unity of the state becomes an argument about poetic form: poetry that, like Crane's epic, aspires to embody America must "fail" to be "unified," because for Tate there is no such thing as a unified American culture. Finally, I examine the parallel issues of professional authority—for the participant-observer, for the poet-critic—that arise from the intertwined ways the New Criticism and modernist anthropology conceive their "objects" of analysis as spatial, meaning-generating structures.

In conclusion, I offer some thoughts about how the history of debates over culture in the 1920s and 1930s might illuminate current debates over whether we are "beyond culture" or should forget it, and the implications of the "aesthetic turn" in cultural studies. In contrast, I suggest that rather than forgetting culture, we engage in what I will call "critical culturalism," in which we continue to deploy culture in a way that is provisional and aware of its own history. Thus, the aesthetic turn in literary studies is not so much a turn away from culture, but part of an ongoing interrelation between culture and aesthetics that coalesces in the modernist period.

1 / Van Wyck Brooks and Edward Sapir: Divided America and the Form of Genuine Culture

This chapter sets the context for what I argue is the interdisciplinary debate over culture in early American modernism, and it lays out several key contours of that debate—contours that will in different ways in different disciplinary arenas structure debates within modernist anthropology, literary criticism, and "Americanist" canon reformation. Specifically, I reveal the way in which the interdisciplinary journals of politics, arts, and opinion that in many ways shaped the contours of modernism were also important organs through which the debate over culture circulated, as articles by anthropologists, literary critics, social scientists, and artists formed what Richard Brodhead has called a "concerted textual program" constituting the problematic of culture.

Van Wyck Brooks and Edward Sapir, I argue, were two key participants in this program, articulating different but complexly related versions of culture that together chart the contours of the debate. Brooks, I argue, makes "culture" itself the issue for "American" national identity: in contrast to a nineteenth-century idea of high Culture, Brooks articulates a model of cultural pluralism, wherein "culture" is defined as a unified "whole"; that whole, in turn, is organic in form and national in scope. In contrast, Sapir articulates a model of culture that is likewise plural and whole, but whose form is imagined as spatial, structural, and semiotic. Rather than the elements of "a culture" being organically related, they are connected structurally to create "meaning." The "unit" of this spatially conceived culture, moreover, is the region, which stands in explicit contrast to a "spurious" national culture. Together, the contours of this debate—what is culture, what is the unit of culture, and what is the relation of culture to form—will in turn structure, each in their disciplinary-specific terms, the debates within anthropology, literature, criticism, and canon formation.

I begin by citing two moments, each well known in the disciplines with which they have traditionally been associated. The first is the publication in 1915 of Van Wyck Brooks's *America's Coming-of-Age*. A former student of Harvard professor Barrett Wendell, and a disciple of romantic Irish artist and nationalist John Butler Yeats, Brooks by 1915 had already established his reputation as a literary critic, first writing in London and New York and then teaching literature at Stanford. Brooks wrote *America's Coming-of-Age* during a year in London, where he was teaching literature courses in the socialist Worker's Educational Association and immersing himself in the radical working-class politics and literary life of that city. When the outbreak of World War I forced his return to the United States, Brooks moved to the Upper West Side of Manhattan near Columbia University to teach and write—and thereby placed himself at the center of the growing ferment of literary, artistic, and political activity that would, with Brooks's participation, come to characterize modernist New York.[1]

In *America's Coming-of-Age*, Brooks articulates what would become the classic formulation of "Young America's" critique of the "genteel tradition" of the nineteenth century. Americans, Brooks argues, labor under a "peculiar dualism": "on the one hand a quite unclouded, quite unhypocritical assumption of transcendent theory ('high ideals'); on the other a simultaneous acceptance of catchpenny realities."[2] This now-famous divide between the "Highbrow" and the "Lowbrow," between ideals and practicality, results in both the pragmatic "atmosphere of contemporary business life" and "the fastidious refinement" of American writers, whose detachment from everyday life results in "the final unreality of most contemporary American *culture*" (9, emphasis added).

For Brooks, then, the problem of America is a problem of culture. His solution is to redefine culture itself: in place of passive preoccupation with high Culture, Brooks calls for a new definition of culture that would fuse these two realms, the practical and the ideal, into a whole, or what he calls elsewhere a "living, active culture," a "fabric of ideas and assumptions, of sentiments and memories and attitudes which make up [a] civilization."[3] Thus Brooks seeks to replace the "culture of industrialism" with what he calls, in an article in *The Dial* three years later, a "national culture."[4]

Brooks's call for a new American culture—indeed, for a new definition of culture as such—has long been regarded as a foundational moment in the disciplinary history of American literature and American Studies, a status granted almost immediately by the young intellectuals who first read it. Inspired by the essay, Waldo Frank, James Oppenheim, and Paul Rosenfeld invited Brooks to join their new journal *Seven Arts*—the journal that became, despite its short life span, one of the most influential venues for the Young Americans modernist revolt against the "genteel tradition." Included among its contributors and associates were Randolph Bourne, Lewis Mumford, and a remarkable array of literary critics, poets, and public intellectuals who came to define American modernism.

Brooks, however, was far from the only intellectual seeking to redefine the idea of culture in this period, and his *America's Coming-of-Age* might be fruitfully set next to a second document that has become equally well known within the history of American anthropology. Writing only a year after Brooks's call for a national culture and appearing in the same journal—*The Dial*—anthropologist, linguist, literary critic, and poet Edward Sapir published "Civilization and Culture," an analysis of American life that would form the core of Sapir's more famous article, "Culture, Genuine and Spurious," published in the *American Journal of Sociology* in 1924. Like Brooks, Sapir contrasts a divided and fragmented American "civilization" with a definition of culture as a "whole." Modern America, Sapir suggests, is a "spiritual hybrid of contradictory patches, . . . watertight compartments of consciousness that carefully avoid participation in a harmonious synthesis." Divided between utilitarian economic activity and abstract ideals, "part of the time we are dray-horses; the rest of the time . . . we are listless consumers of good that have received no least impress of our own personality."[5]

In a single, compact definition, Sapir shifts the axis of culture from the nineteenth-century hierarchy of "high" and "low," to "fragmentation" and "wholeness." In contrast to fragmented, "spurious" culture, Sapir defines "genuine culture" as "not of necessity either high or low; it is merely inherently harmonious, balanced, self-satisfactory. It is the expression of a richly varied and yet somehow unified and consistent attitude toward life, an attitude which sees the significance of any one element of civilization in its relation to all others. It is, ideally speaking, a culture in which nothing is spiritually meaningless" (233). Rather than "hybrid patches" and "water-tight compartments" separating different elements of life, genuine culture is characterized by "the firmness with which every part of that life—economic, social, religious, and aesthetic— is bound together into a significant whole" (235).

Sapir here articulates a model of cultural pluralism that comes to be identified as the "anthropological" concept of culture. Rather than being measured on a single, universal scale, multiple lifeways can count as culture. Moreover, rather than specifying the content of the values that make up a culture, Sapir instead defines culture by its *form*—what counts as culture is not the set of values themselves, but the way they hang together to create a "unified," "harmonious" structure. Sapir's genuine culture, then, takes the division diagnosed by Brooks and suggests a solution. Specifically invoking Brooks in the 1924 version of the essay, Sapir suggests that "if signs of a genuine blossoming of culture are belatedly beginning to appear in America, it is . . . America *coming of age*."[6]

Culture Contexts: The "Textual Program" of Modernist Publications

I will return to the specifics of Brooks's and Sapir's theories of culture later. Along with the generative terms they employ, however, their essays are also exemplary in the way they index the broader, interdisciplinary context in which this debate takes place—an interdisciplinary conversation indicated, for example, by the anthropologist Sapir's reference to the literary critic Brooks in an essay published first in a modernist journal of arts, politics, and social criticism and then later in a specialized journal of sociology. As historians of anthropology like George Stocking have argued, the modernist "revolt" against Victorian ideals exemplified by Brooks and his *Seven Arts* circle and the redefinitions of culture undertaken by Franz Boas and his students to remake American anthropology cannot be seen as separate projects. Instead, they were part of a common intellectual conversation that circulated from Columbia University to Greenwich Village, from Harlem to the offices of the little magazines and journals through which these conversations were conducted in print. As Stocking has put it, in the "classical period" of the 1920s, the concerns and personalities of "cultural criticism overlapped that of cultural anthropology to an extent that we may not appreciate today, when the boundaries between academic anthropology and the outside world are more sharply imagined."[7]

It is very likely, as Sapir's citation of Brooks's work indicates, that the two men were familiar with each other's work, and almost certainly had met. Both Sapir and Brooks were frequent contributors to the new intellectual journals like *The New Republic*, *The Nation*, and *The Dial* (which in 1918 moved its offices from Chicago to New York to become one of the most important journals of modernism). Brooks was a contributing editor at *The Dial* at the time Sapir's "Civilization and Culture" appeared. In the 1920s, Sapir regularly contributed reviews on poetry, fiction, psychology, and linguistics to *The Freeman*, for which Brooks was the literary editor. More broadly, there were numerous connections between the Young Americans (Waldo Frank, James Oppenheim, and particularly Randolph Bourne and Lewis Mumford) who, along with Brooks, were closely associated with the *Seven Arts* and the circle of anthropologists around Franz Boas. Brooks was well acquainted with several of Sapir's colleagues in the Columbia anthropology department, such as Elsie Clews Parson and Robert Lowie, who collaborated with Brooks and other rebellious intellectuals in their efforts to counter the perceived division of modern America, most famously in the series of symposia organized by Brooks and Harold Stearns in 1920. Gathering together in Stearns's apartment, the group of intellectuals—including Mumford, H. L. Mencken, John Macy, J. E. Spingarn, and Conrad Aiken, as well as Brooks, Stearns, Parson, and Lowie—intensely debated the current state of "American civilization."[8] Parsons and Lowie, like Brooks and Sapir, contributed frequently to *The New Republic* and *The Nation*, as did Franz Boas.

Sapir himself was perhaps the strongest example of this interdisciplinary circulation of ideas. He published literary and music reviews, poetry, and social criticism in a wide variety of the little magazines of the period—in addition to those mentioned earlier, in *American Mercury*, Harriet Monroe's *Poetry*, and others—and published a volume of his own poetry, *Dreams and Gibes*, in 1917.[9] Sapir even experimented with converting ethnology directly into literature, contributing, along with Boas, Lowie, and others, to Parson's *American Indian Life*, an anthology of fictional narratives, written by each anthropologist and centered on each one's Indian tribe of expertise. Indeed, Sapir himself reviewed the anthology in the *Dial* of November 1922—the same issue in which T. S. Eliot's *The Waste Land* first appeared.[10] Thus, the modernist project to revolutionize Victorian ideas of art and morality, exemplified by the social and artistic challenges posed by Brooks, Bourne, Mumford, and the many modernist artists who appeared on the pages of the *Seven*

Arts and its successors like *The Dial*, must be seen as intertwined with American anthropology's revision of basic categories of the civilized and the primitive through the redefinition of culture, led by Boas and his students. They are intertwined both through personal interaction and collaboration and through a dialogue taking place on the pages of influential journals of modernist thought.[11]

The figures that I trace in this project, then, are engaged in a debate over culture that crosses disciplinary lines, forming a common conversation around a common problematic. While the interdisciplinary nature of this debate is illustrated by the conjunction of key figures in journals of the period, the broader contours of the problematic of which this debate is a part—the concerns and problems that the debate over culture could be seen as an attempt to address—can likewise be seen in these journals. In linking the concerns of particular articles that explicitly engage debates over culture (and, more broadly, the authors of those articles) with the concerns of seemingly unrelated articles with which these articles are juxtaposed on the page, I draw here on Richard Brodhead's analysis of the place of late-nineteenth-century regional fiction within "high Culture" periodicals. As Brodhead argues, the meaning of a genre is in part determined not just by the content of that genre alone, but by the "adjacent and complementary genres" with which it is rhetorically and physically linked (here, within the pages of a journal). Genres, he argues, that we see as freestanding were not in fact "autonomous in their original cultural production but formed mutually supportive parts of a concerted textual program."[12] The "concerted textual program" of these journals, of which debates over culture are a part, is the modernist response to the broader political, social, and economic dislocation that marked the first decades of the twentieth century, which caused many to question the nature of modern, industrial civilization and the ideas of progress. While there have been numerous attempts to define the range of issues involved in and the precise nature, extent, and historical timeline of the breakup of Victorian values and the modernist reaction in America, several key interlocking problems are especially important.

In the years approaching the war and after, one source for the perception of social instability was the wave of immigrants who were arriving on U.S. shores in numbers that had profound impacts on the urban areas in which they settled. Between 1901 and 1910, almost 8.8 million immigrants arrived in America, 70 percent from Southern and Eastern Europe, most of them Catholics and Jews. Between 1911 and 1920, 5.7 million immigrants arrived, 59 percent from Southern and Eastern Europe.

By 1910, 40 percent of the population of New York City was foreign born.[13] Xenophobia and debates over the proper ways to integrate—or reject—the immigrant reached their highest intensity during the war.

In the same year that Brooks pronounced "America's coming-of-age," D. W. Griffith announced the advent of a very different America with his widely popular film *The Birth of a Nation*, whose narrative of the "birth" of the (white) racialized nation-state out of the ashes of the Civil War inspired the rebirth of the Ku Klux Klan in the South. The concerns over the possible degenerative effects of immigration and the state of American culture were rhetorically linked on the pages of journals like *The Dial*, where a survey entitled "American Immigration—Past and Present" might be found alongside articles lamenting America's "Laxative Literature."[14] Brooks himself points to immigration as one source for the supposed fracturing of American culture: "The generation that has gone by" since the mid-nineteenth century, he suggests, "has ... destroyed the coherence of the old American circle of ideas, and left us at the height of the second immigration among the chaotic raw material of a perhaps altogether new attitude of mind" (*Coming-of-Age*, 40). The "plain, fresh, homely, impertinent, essentially innocent old America" is like Rip Van Winkle, he suggests, and Hendrick Hudson and his men "have been miraculously changed into Jews, Lithuanian, Magyars, and German socialists," the sound of whose bowling is transformed into "the movement of peoples, the thunder of alien wants." When after twenty years Rip awakens again and returns home, Brooks asks, "will he be recognized?" (*Coming-of-Age*, 40).[15]

This "chaotic ... thunder of alien wants" in turn raised the question of the relationship between a group's way of life—its language, traditions, arts, religion—and the nation, the state, and the nation-state. Through the Progressive era, intellectuals, politicians, and reformers debated whether immigrant groups should be—or even could be—"Americanized," and if so, what precisely this Americanization would look like. What characteristics of language, of behavior, of belief, of taste, if any, defined "an American"? Were "Americans" a "race" defined by genealogy? Was America a "nation" unified by language, traditions, and values (as well as, perhaps, by genealogy)? On the other hand, could other lifeways and value systems make important contributions to the country? If so, then how could the United States be conceived of as a nation? And what was the relationship between this (potential) American "nation" and the "United States"? Was citizenship, for example, a purely political identity, distinct from national identity? More broadly, what was the relation between the political power structures of the state on the one hand, and the nation on the other?

These questions were only sharpened by the Great War and its aftermath. For many intellectuals, the war highlighted precisely the discontinuity between the institution of the industrial state and the lifeways and interests of groups living within that state. Thus, in the months surrounding the appearance of Sapir's "Civilization and Culture" in *The Dial*, one could find numerous articles analyzing (as an article by Lewis Mumford put it) "The Status of the State," trying to define (with Franz Boas) "nationalism," or predicting (along with Thorstein Veblen) "The Passing of National Frontiers" in the international economic order that must follow the war.[16] While opinion about these questions was by no means monolithic, many liberal intellectuals concluded, along with Mumford, that the state is an authoritarian structure whose unity is imposed from above, for the economic interests of a few, and antithetical to local or even authentic national identities.[17] These critiques of the state frequently expressed a tension among an emphasis on the local/regional, the national, and the international, desiring both self-determination for smaller nationalities and regions and "the passing of national frontiers" in favor of international cooperation. These creative tensions between the local and the cosmopolitan, the regional and the global, structure discussions of culture for many of the figures considered in this project, from Brooks's and Sapir's theories of culture, to Mumford's attempts to reimagine American literature while also working on regional planning, to Allen Tate's and John Crowe Ransom's transition from Southern Agrarians to New Critics.

While immigration and the war and the related questions of nationalism and the state formed part of the sense of dislocation in this period, so too did the new, complexly related forms of industrial organization and consumerism that arose in these decades and the labor crises that resulted. Although labor unrest was a constant through the first decades of the century, the year Sapir published "Civilization and Culture" was particularly chaotic. In the atmosphere of the Red Scare inspired by the Bolshevik revolution in Russia, more than four million workers participated in strikes in 1919, including a general strike that shut down Seattle for an entire week and a police officers' strike in Boston that was followed by riots and the deployment of the National Guard.[18]

Intellectuals from both the left and the right lamented the alienating effects of routinized industrial labor on the worker. Thus, the *Dial* issue that followed and contained Sapir's essay was entirely devoted to "the labor crisis." Sapir himself, in "Civilization and Culture," points to the relationship between the current labor crisis and the need to rethink culture by making the "telephone girl"—a position that could be seen as a symbol of both rapid technological progress and the accompanying social shifts that saw increasing numbers of women enter the workforce—the epitome of spurious culture. The telephone girl, "for economic reasons, lends her capacities . . . to the manipulation of a technical routine that has an eventually high efficiency value but that answers to no spiritual needs of her own"; as such she represents "an appalling sacrifice to civilization" at the expense of culture. "The present world-wide labor unrest," he goes on to say, "has as one of its deepest roots . . . the cultural fallacy of the present form of industrialism" (235). Moreover, to many, the economic expansion and centralization of industrial activities and networks—the railroad, the electrical grid, increased urbanization, efforts to standardize and routinize—were seen as part of the coercive power of the state. Thus, liberal critics like V. L. Parrington described the economic integration of the western states into the nation as a kind of imperialism, as the consolidation of the United States' "inland empire."[19]

The concerns discussed earlier—immigration; the relation among culture, nation, and the homogenizing industrial state—came full circle in the debates over the question of culture and Americanization, which for some intellectuals represented just another version of the centralization and standardization Parrington saw in the westward consolidation of state power. Liberal journals like *The Dial* and *The New Republic* frequently contained articles speaking out against the "melting pot" ideal, calling, as Randolph Bourne most famously put it, for a "transnational" America made up of diverse ethnic groups, each with its own traditions and ideals, opposed to the homogeneity of Americanization and the threat of mass entertainment like the cinema and the popular press.[20] These concerns come together, for example, in one reviewer's account of the immigrant experience in America: the melting pot ideal, he argues, represents "mechanical uniformity," as opposed to the "utmost possible differentiation through mental and psychic cross-fertilization, to attain to a high level of humanity." Moreover, he argues, "cultural cross-fertilization" through immigrant absorption goes hand in hand with the U.S. role in the international community, preparing the United States to "assume our duties in the League of Nations" and for "the internationalism that is coming."[21] This resistance to the melting pot and the revaluing of traditional immigrant or regional cultures are in part supported by numerous articles focusing on these groups *as* cultures, with distinct values and aesthetics. In journals like *The Dial*, *The Nation*, and *The New Republic*, alongside articles criticizing the coercive power of the government, expressing disillusionment over the betrayal of the war aims, and examining the labor crisis, one could find articles entitled "Negro American Literature," or "The Folk Culture of the Kentucky Highlands," or "The Irish Renaissance—Renascent," linking these seemingly diverse political, social, and aesthetic issues into "mutually supportive parts of a concerted textual program."[22]

Finally, if ideas of industrial progress and civilization came under fire in this period, so too did the scientific epistemologies upon which they are founded. On one hand, the ideal of objective, practical knowledge derived by reducing experience to certain abstract physical laws gained prestige, as these techniques were applied from everything to assembly-line efficiency to the study of human behavior. On the other hand, this "abstract," partial, "mechanical" way of knowing came increasingly under attack, even from within the scientific community, as philosophers of science like Alfred North Whitehead searched for more "whole" ways of knowing phenomena, and as the discoveries of physicists like Einstein, Bohr, and Heisenberg undermined the certainties of the Newtonian universe.

In this context, the conditions for, or even the possibility of, communication and "meaning" itself came under question, as philosophers, anthropologists, linguists, and literary critics searched for new ways to understand language. As Warren Susman puts it, "There was a growing concern among writers, philosophers, and students of language about the relationship between language and reality.... The question was not only what could and ought one communicate, but also *how* could one communicate at all?"[23] This question motivates the linguistic research of anthropologists and literary critics alike, from I. A. Richards, C. K. Ogden, and Bronislaw Malinowski (who publishes his "Meaning in Primitive Language" as a supplement to Ogden and Richards's *The Meaning of Meaning* [1924]), to Edward Sapir (who publishes a favorable review of *The Meaning of Meaning* in Brooks's *Freeman*), to John Crowe Ransom and Allen Tate, whose theories of poetic language are formulated in part as a reaction to those of Richards and Ogden.[24]

It is within the context, then, of a sense of dislocation and (as T. S. Eliot put it) "dissociation of sensibility" that the debate about culture becomes central for anthropologists, literary critics, and writers alike.[25] Indeed, the search for a particularly American culture that occupied critics like Brooks, Mumford, and the Young Americans in this period was only possible within the context of this debate over culture *itself*, and the tensions and contradictions it generated. Most critics have seen this movement as a period of "cultural nationalism"—the emphasis on nationalism relegating the search for culture to merely a reflection of the increased political, economic, and military assertiveness of the state. Nevertheless, the idea that "America" could have its own, self-contained, and internally consistent set of values and practices, and that such a way of life could be called "a culture," was itself a new and contested idea. This conception of culture in turn undergirds the search for Brooks's "usable past" that produces, in part, the canonization of a new pantheon of "American literature" by the end of the 1920s. And it is on the pages of the journals discussed above that the "concerted textual program" formed by these concerns can be seen.

Van Wyck Brooks: Divided America and "Living Culture"

If in many ways America in the years leading up to World War I was, as Susan Hegeman has put it, a society "divided against itself," then Van Wyck Brooks was perhaps the most influential diagnostician of those divisions, and of culture as the antidote.[26] Brooks himself was from a family that in many ways epitomized the dislocations of the changing economic order. His father was a failed businessman; his mother was from a wealthy family whose means served as Brooks's introduction into the charms of European art. Rebelling against this genteel upbringing, Brooks joined the Young Americans Randolph Bourne, Waldo Frank, James Oppenheim, Paul Rosenfeld, and Lewis Mumford to write against what they saw as the rampant materialism, irrelevant idealism, and jingoistic nationalism that characterized modern life. Instead, they posed a utopian vision of what Bourne called a "beloved community," united by democratic, egalitarian social ideals and individual self-expression.[27]

Brooks worked out his definition of culture, and in particular of *American* culture, through *America's Coming-of-Age* and a series of articles that appeared in the *Seven Arts*, the most important being "Toward a National Culture" and "The Culture of Industrialism." As I suggested earlier, from the outset of *America's Coming-of-Age*, Brooks diagnoses American society as divided at a variety of levels between the crudely materialistic and the ineffectually idealistic, between the "highbrow" and the "lowbrow." This duality in turn has hampered the growth of American literature, "resulting in the final unreality of most contemporary American culture" (9), as writers from Longfellow to Emerson to

Hawthorne retreated into an idealism designed, at worst, not to interfere with material and commercial progress and, at best, to speed it on its way.

This image of unreal culture divorced from practical business is only one example of a broader set of tropes Brooks uses to describe American culture as characterized by division—of surface from depth, outside from inside, part from whole. Indeed, in these instances, culture itself is a problem, as one diminished part of a shattered whole. Brooks employs culture, in these essays, to designate "airy" ideals and superficial refinement. In *America's Coming-of-Age*, culture is likened most often to the movement of goods in the capitalist marketplace, the equivalent of conspicuous consumption. As Brooks puts it, "The acquisition of culture and the acquisition of money—'highbrow' and 'lowbrow'—are equally impersonal, equally extraneous to the real matter" (182); culture becomes "a jealous possession ... an investment which might have been a yacht, a country-house, or a collection of Rembrandts instead" (116). In this context, even the "importation of radical ideas" is harmless, because divorced from "real life" they "have ... the pleasing remoteness of literature[;] ... they become admirably safe [and] even delightful. In the American mind Nietzsche and A. C. Benson—the lion and the lamb—lie down quite peacefully together, chewing the cud of culture" (162).

In characterizing culture as superficial refinement, Brooks engages what Lawrence Levine and John Henry Raleigh have shown was one of the most influential traditions of thinking about culture in the period: the high Culture of Matthew Arnold. For Arnold, culture was a universal and hierarchical concept, designating only the "best which has been thought and said in the world"; the goal of the production and consumption of culture was "the pursuit of ... perfection."[28] Taking up Arnold's terms, and making Arnold himself the "Apostle of Culture," many Victorian Americans, individually and through such institutions as museums, universities, theaters, and orchestras, emphasized the distinction between high Culture and low or mass entertainment, which was the antithesis of culture.

Thus, in his essay "The Culture of Industrialism," Brooks specifically names this pejorative, external culture as the "Arnoldian doctrine about 'knowing the best that [sic] has been thought and said in the world,'" which Americans believe requires only that they be "passively cultivated," able to "share vicariously in the heritage of civilization" without being distracted from their business interests (658). "Our industrial conception of culture," he argues, assumes that "by a process of injection from the outside, by means of indiscriminate lecturing and the like, the fact that life is a miraculous and beautiful thing can somehow be pumped into the middle of [our] soul" (665). The result is a culture that is impersonal and, in a word that will reverberate through much of the criticism on culture in general and Melville in particular, "abstract" (663).

In contrast to the external cultivation he associates with Arnold, Brooks posits another kind of culture, familiar from the Romantic tradition extending from Coleridge, through Carlyle, Ruskin, and Morris (who was a particular influence on Brooks): an organic or "living, active culture" (655). In contrast to a particular set of exemplary ideas one has to acquire to know, Brooks's culture is a taken-for-granted horizon of living, the "fabric of ideas and assumptions, of sentiments and memories and attitudes which make up [a] civilization" (655). As opposed to American dualism, in a living, active culture, the "ideas and assumptions" are knit to everyday practices, to form a coherent "fabric," or, in his most common metaphor, a "living" relation that can "motivate the American scene and impregnate it with meaning" (658).

This specifically organic relation between the ideals and practices of a society and between the individual and that collection of ideas and practices is captured in the metaphor of oyster culture with which Brooks begins his essay "Toward a National Culture." Quoting a "Report on the Oyster Industry," Brooks plays on the various connotations of the term "culture," in a metaphor that is both a pun and a serious description of "cultivation": "When first hatched they are free-swimming, microscopic creatures, but in a few hours they fall to the bottom and are lost unless they can adhere to a firm, clean surface while making their shells and undergoing development."[29] As is made clear in this metaphor, Brooks's organic understanding of culture contains a version of both group culture and individual cultivation: the "free-swimming individual" needs a "firm surface"—that fabric of "ideas and assumptions[,] ... sentiments and attitudes and memories" —that enable an individual's development or cultivation. Thus, culture is both the development of the individual and the set of beliefs and practices that *enable* that development, or what he calls elsewhere that "all embracing organism" of which those cultivated individuals are a part (*Coming-of-Age*, 64). To put it another way, *self*-culture is only possible in *a* culture.

Moreover, a key term in Brooks's living culture—and one that will become, as we shall see in chapter 3, a key term in the Melville revival of the 1920s, of which Brooks is a crucial figure—is "experience." While at times Brooks uses the word to designate empirical encounters with the material world (as opposed to "airy ideals"), experience more specifically is the fusion of bodily and emotional responses with intellectual comprehension, or encounters with materiality that have a corresponding set of ideas and ideals through which to integrate them. Experience produces the organic connection between an individual's—and a people's—practices and beliefs. "Ideals," he writes, "are healthily born midway in the evolution of a people; they spring from a certain level of experience that has been attained by all in common" ("National Culture," 542). Experience as a "general touchstone" (542) here functions as that "firm, clean surface" Brooks describes, to which "free-swimming" individuals must adhere and "develop," or be lost. It is that which makes both everyday events and complex ideas "meaningful." As he puts it, "To the catholic, Dante, to the aristocrat, Nietzsche, to the democrat, Whitman, inevitably *means* more than any of them can mean to the scholar who merely receives them all through his intellect without the palpitant response of conviction and a sympathetic experience" ("Industrialism," 659). At the culmination of that essay, Brooks's alternative to the culture of industrialism places experience at its center, as that which brings together the "fabric" of culture: the elements of a "national existence" are there, "but they are not grouped in the right order; and so they have no cumulative effect. As soon as the foundations of our life have been reconstructed and made solid on the basis of our own experience, all these extraneous, ill-regulated forces will rally about their newly found center; they will fit in, each where it belongs, contributing to the essential architecture of our life" (666). Experience here forms the "center" around which the divided elements of American life will achieve form, as we will see later.

In analyzing Brooks's deployment of Arnoldian culture, it must also be noted that Matthew Arnold himself saw culture as the antidote to the ills of modern, external "civilization," and Brooks's reading of Arnold as the prophet of the culture of industrialism is in some ways a *mis*interpretation, albeit one shared both by those early-twentieth-century critics who advocated Arnoldian high Culture and by those young modernists who, like Brooks, railed against it. Arnold's culture is universal and hierarchical and has one standard—the "best which has been thought and said in the world"—such that individual elements from anywhere in the world might fit in that category; this culture is a distinct subset of objects and activities, different from all other elements in the life of a people that are "not culture." But, like Brooks, Arnold imagines culture as the antidote precisely to the external and mechanical civilization of industrialism.

As Arnold puts it in *Culture and Anarchy*, culture is an "inward condition of the mind and spirit... *at variance* with the mechanical and material civilization in esteem with us" (33, emphasis added). And, far from being invested merely in the stockpiling of elite knowledge for its own sake, Arnold's culture requires attention to the larger society: "Perfection, as culture conceives it, is not possible while the individual remains isolated. The individual is required... to carry others also with him in his march towards perfection, to be continually doing all he can to enlarge and increase the volume of the human stream sweeping thitherward" (33). Thus, culture for Arnold requires "a *harmonious* perfection, developing all sides of our humanity; and... a *general* perfection, developing all parts of our society" (9, emphasis in original). More important, rather than reifying this hierarchy of achievement into a permanent order, Arnold sees culture as the prerequisite for a restless curiosity that questions that order. Arnold finishes the famous quote by stating that culture is "getting to know... the best which has been thought and said in the world, and, through this knowledge, turning a stream of fresh and free thought upon our stock notions and habits" (5). Thus, while crucial distinctions remain between Arnold's universal, hierarchal version of culture and what I will argue is Brooks's organic pluralism, in many ways Brooks's romantic turn to culture as an antidote to modern alienation draws on Arnold despite himself, and as Susan Hegeman has suggested, Brooks's attempt to diagnose and reconcile the highbrow and the lowbrow could be seen as "an American version of... *Culture and Anarchy*."[30]

Returning to *America's Coming-of-Age*, for Brooks, writing in 1915, the fabric of "living culture" is literally embodied in one American artist: Walt Whitman. Whitman, he argues, "precipitated the American character. All those things that had been separate, self-sufficient, incoordinate—action, theory, idealism, business—he cast into a crucible, and they emerged, harmonious and molten, in a fresh democratic ideal, which is based upon the whole personality" (118). Whitman's ability to merge the "separate" aspects of American life into a "harmonious" whole is in part due to his "experience": "Having the ideas of New England... he came from the other side with everything New England did not possess: quantities of rude emotion and a faculty of gathering humane experience almost as great as that of the hero of the Odyssey. Living habitually among world ideas, world emotions, world impulses and having experienced life on a truly grand scale, this extraordinary person... became... a man of the world in a sense which ambassadors are not" (113). Citing a passage in *Specimen Days* in which Whitman describes his work with troops in the Civil War—binding wounds, reading passages of the Bible aloud, playing "twenty questions"—Brooks admires the breadth and variety of Whitman's activities, the "ways that he gained his experience, [and the] ways that he shared it" (115). Whitman thus embodies Brooks's theory of culture as the synthesis of experience and values.

Crucially, the terms by which Brooks describes this Whitmanian fusion—and the terms by which he describes this living culture as such—are in metaphors of organic and artistic "form." Citing Coleridge's theory of a "point of rest," the point "upon which the harmony of a work of art is founded and to which everything in the composition is more or less unconsciously referred," Brooks characterizes Whitman as just such a "focal center" for the nation. He is "that secure and unobtrusive element of national character, taken for granted, and providing a certain underlying coherence and background of mutual understanding [that] radiates outward and articulates the entire living fabric of a race" (119). Thus, in the concept of the "focal center," Brooks articulates the interconnecting organicisms of the poet, the literature he or she composes, and the culture that he or she expresses (and *of which* he or she is the expression), all in terms of organic form. In its "coherence" as an "entire living fabric," a genuine national culture achieves "the harmony of a work of art" and itself can be described as an aesthetic object (119). In short, the organic form of a work of art (and the body of the artist) is a synecdoche for the form of a society, while at the same time providing the focal center around which a society might be formed.

Thus, Brooks consistently refers to the problem of American culture as a problem of organic form. American life does not constitute a culture precisely because it is form*less*: it is, he describes, "a vast Sargasso Sea.... All manner of living things are drifting in it,... gelatinous, unformed, flimsy, tangled, rising and falling, floating and merging... everywhere an unchecked, uncharted, unorganized vitality like that of the first chaos. It is a welter of life which has not been worked into an organism" (*Coming-of-Age*, 164). Although here the analogy is to an organism, it is also, simultaneously, to a work of art—a simultaneity captured in the phrase "*worked* into an organism." Brooks's metaphors for the particular order and composition constituted by a living culture, as illustrated in the passages quoted earlier, are often to the work of art or the "architecture of our life." And if here America is not yet an organism, it is also not yet a great work of art: "Our life," he suggests elsewhere, "is like a badly motivated novel, full of genius but written with an eye to quick returns; a novel that possesses no leading theme, in which the style alternates between journalese and purple patches, and every character goes its own arbitrary way, failing of its full effect."[31] Under Brooks's aesthetic of organic culture and form, a nation without a "living culture," then, is analogous to a bad work of art. Conversely, unformed American life in turn results in unformed literature. It produces writers like Dreiser who "memorialize" the "chaotic, unmotivated world . . . of things" in a "prodigious pile of language built of the commonest rubble, and cohering, in the absence of any architectural design, by sheer virtue of their weight and size" ("National Culture," 541). Harmonious works of art can be created only within a "living culture," and a "living culture" in turn requires those works of art to form its focal center, around which it can achieve form.

As the example of Whitman indicates, the artist is the key figure for both making and reflecting the order of Brooks's culture. Cultures in this theory can be composed, like works of art: the elements "which really make the life of a society do not spring spontaneously out of the mass. They exist in it—a thousand potential currents and cross-currents; but they have to be discovered like principles of science, they have almost to be created like works of art. A people is like a ciphered parchment which has to be held up to the fire before its hidden significances come out" (*Coming-of-Age*, 177). The artist is he or she who can articulate and make formal the "significances" that are "potentially" already there.

This, of course, raises a tension that will characterize not only Brooks's formulation of culture, but anthropological theories of culture *and* theories of poetry through the 1920s and 1930s: the complicated, even contradictory relationship between the cultivated individual, the work of art (or cultural object), and *a* culture. This problematic is exemplified in the tension between Brooks's analogies that national culture is "discovered like science" and "almost created like . . . art." Are the elements of a national culture "out there" for the perceptive artist (or anthropologist) to find and articulate? Or are they composed by the artist (or anthropologist), given form through the work of art (or ethnography), and then become retroactively a (formally whole) culture? Does the artist form a coherent way of life that only then can be seen as a culture? Or does the coherent way of life form the artist? On the one hand, Brooks suggests that "the mind is a flower that has an organic connection with the soil it springs from," and the artist "can only express the better intuitions and desires of his age and place" (*Coming-of-Age*, 33). National culture is at times the essence of identity, as "the more . . . organically you feel the pressure of society," he argues, "the more... you become yourself" (99). On the other hand, Brooks articulates that the role of the artist (and the critic) is to *transform* a society: Whitman, in his prime example, takes a series of attributes that were "incoordinate" and coordinates them into organic form—literally in his own person—for the first time. Brooks likewise assigns this role as maker of culture to the critic, who "*make[s]* a situation of which the creative power can profitably avail itself" ("National Culture," 547, emphasis added) and provides, like Whitman, a model of "fusion" for others to follow. This, of course, produces a paradox: how does a Whitman, who runs contrary to the dominant ethos, arise if "the mind is the flower of the soil from which it springs"?

While this tension between culture and form, the individual and the group, remains unresolved in Brooks's theory, the unit of culture, the level at which a living culture achieves aesthetic harmony, is the "nation," which is coterminous with the political boundaries of the United States. For Brooks, to realize a national culture—to constitute "a society which is an all-embracing organism"—regional and ethnic differences must be minimized. In describing the obstacles preventing a common American culture, for example, Brooks laments that "we are incongruous at once in blood and in culture" and indeed seem to live in different historical eras, which he identifies by region. "There are," he describes, "centers of our civilization where nothing is real but the future," while there are "tenacious outposts of culture in Tennessee and Kentucky where the speech of the people remains unchanged from the time of Queen Elizabeth." He concludes that "we are a population at sixes and sevens, holding among all classes and at all stages of development scarcely any common conviction."[32]

Likewise, when Brooks optimistically predicts the emergence of such a "common conviction," it will coalesce at a national level, with the subordination of regional differences to national "life in common." Through the ferment of criticism and inquiry by the "younger generation," he suggests that

> somehow America has become under our eyes a living entity, visibly in the process of developing a third dimension.... Americans, north, south, east, and west, have ceased... to be merely Texans and Kentuckians and Californians and New Englanders, satisfied, so far as the art of writing is concerned, with the dialect and local color of a "Kentucky literature," or what not. They have become, to our imagination, human beings, and human beings faintly flushed

with that desire for a higher life that implies a life in common. They have *manifested* themselves in a way that may lead to a "national culture." ("National Culture," 546–47, emphasis in original)

Thus, regionalism becomes a necessary stage on the path to national culture, but one that will be transcended in favor of "the aims and hopes we have in common" (546).

While for Brooks culture is a national concept, it is also *plural*. It is *a* culture, a common set of experiences and values, but one among many possible sets of experiences and values that might belong to other nations. This pluralism is evinced, for example, in Brooks's essay "On Creating a Usable Past," where Brooks contrasts the (mistaken) universalism of the English Matthew Arnold against the nation-based pluralism of the French Sainte-Beuve. Arnold, Brooks narrates, "once objected to Sainte-Beuve that he did not consider Lamartine an important writer, [to which] Sainte-Beuve replied, 'Perhaps not, but he is important *for us*.'" In shifting the scale of value from "what is important" to "what is important *for us*," Brooks thereby moves from a universal scale of value to a relative one.[33]

At the same time, Brooks's conception of a relative, national culture exists alongside, and potentially in some tension with, a conception of Culture, a set of values (aesthetic, philosophical, ethical) that are cosmopolitan and international. Indeed, for Brooks—in a move that will be repeated, with variations, by key figures in a variety of disciplines engaged in debates over culture—national culture is the necessary, but not sufficient, condition for partaking in this cosmopolitan Culture. Brooks laments, for example, that Americans are "unable to think and feel in international terms"—specifically, to deeply comprehend the more disturbing and radical ideas of the European literary tradition. But the ability to enter this international culture, it turns out, is predicated on a grounding in a national culture. "The very essence of being cultivated," he argues, "is to have developed a capacity for sharing points of view other than our own" ("Industrialism," 659). But this ability to share points of view that are not ours is predicated, he suggests, on the individual having his or her own "point of view" first—and that, it turns out, is available only through "experience." Having a "point of view," one can in turn "share in the experience of others" and be "cultivated"; to be cultivated is in turn to be cosmopolitan, to think internationally. Thus, Brooks concludes, because Americans have "no national fabric of spiritual experience, . . . we are . . . unable to day to think and feel in international terms" ("Industrialism," 659). Having a national culture is, in turn, a necessary stage through which one can comprehend the culture of others and think internationally.

In Van Wyck Brooks's early writings on culture, literature, and America, then, he articulates some of the key contours of the problematic of culture that I argue shape the debate within anthropology, literary criticism, and the reformation of the Americanist literary canon. The debate includes these questions: What is the proper form of culture? What is the relation between individual and group culture? What is the relationship among the artist, the work of art, and culture, and how does one properly "know" (or change) one's culture once it is defined as the "taken for granted" horizon of living? Brooks's *America's Coming-of-Age*, I have suggested, articulates the paradigmatic modernist diagnosis of American culture as divided, at a variety of levels, between idealism and materialism, economic effort and spiritual life. In the process, Brooks posits a new way to define culture as such: the idealism and refinement that have been called "culture," Brooks argues, are symptoms of the problem, and what is needed to remedy this dualism is a new kind of culture, whereby culture constitutes an organic whole way of life, grounded in experience uniting practice and ideals, highbrow and lowbrow, and literature and society. Crucially, Brooks's key terms for describing this organic culture often involve the achievement of "form": "a culture" is both an organism and, as he puts it, "like a work of art" (especially a sculpture or a poem), and the form of a society's literature is both a symptom and a shaper of that culture's form (or lack thereof). Finally, for Brooks, the proper unit of the culture he hopes to call into existence is the nation. This national, organic model of culture, I suggest, is countered by Edward Sapir's regional, spatial, and semiotic model of culture.

Edward Sapir: Regional Culture as Spatial Form

While Van Wyck Brooks's *America's Coming-of-Age* sets the terms for diagnosing the problem of a "divided" America as a problem of "culture," Edward Sapir's "Civilization and Culture" takes up Brooks's terms and offers a new definition of culture. Where Brooks imagine a culture being "birthed" over time into organic form, Sapir imagines culture as existing in synchronic "space," as an aesthetic structure. While Brooks sees the potential for a living culture to arise out of the American "welter of life," Sapir offers a model of genuine cultures already existing within American borders—specifically, the cultures of Native American tribes. Where

Brooks imagines culture as national, Sapir sees it as properly regional and fundamentally antithetical to the state. These terms of Sapir's redefinition of culture, I argue, in turn structure debates over literature, literary criticism, and the Americanist canon, on both the political left and right, for the next several decades, as ways to read culture are transposed into a way to read literature and poetry.

By the time he wrote " Civilization and Culture" in 1919, Sapir was already recognized as one of Franz Boas's most brilliant students, and he went on to become the most influential linguistic anthropologist of his generation. Born in Prussia, the son of an orthodox cantor, Sapir immigrated to the United States with his family at the age of six and grew up on New York's Lower East Side. Intellectually gifted, he first won a Pulitzer scholarship that allowed him to study at the prestigious Stuyvesant High School, and later to gain entry to Columbia University. At Columbia, Sapir studied linguistics (in particular, Germanics, which involved the most rigorous methods of philology); in his last years as an undergraduate, he encountered Boas and his work on Native American languages. Sapir's graduate work turned to linguistics and anthropology and, under Boas's influence and guidance, he began to record and study Amerindian languages. Through the 1910s and 1920s, he performed and published groundbreaking ethnographic and linguistic work on Wishram, Takelma, Yana, and other Pacific Coast tribes.[34]

At the same time, Sapir was intensely interested in art, literature, and literary criticism. As anthropologist David Mandelbaum has put it, "Science and art were combined in Sapir in unusual degree. He as a meticulous linguist, disciplined in linguistic detail.... Yet he was a humanist and artist as well, sometimes predominantly so."[35] Around 1916, as Richard Handler has shown, Sapir's interests shifted from Boasian anthropology and linguistics to aesthetics and criticism—and, most crucially, the relation between these fields. As discussed earlier, Sapir was intensely engaged in the broader artistic and intellectual circuits of postwar New York, publishing essays, poetry, and criticism in a variety of journals including *The Dial*, *Poetry*, *The Nation*, *The New Republic*, and *The Freeman*.[36] For example, between 1917 and 1929, Sapir published twenty-two pieces in *The Dial* alone, including articles on culture, education, and religion; book reviews on both literary and sociological texts; letters; and even three poems.

In both "Civilization and Culture" and the later "Culture, Genuine and Spurious," Sapir brings together anthropology and aesthetics to articulate a theory of culture as aesthetic form. Sapir begins by echoing

Brooks's description of a fragmented industrial civilization: American civilization, he argues, is made of a "spiritual hybrid of contradictory patches, of water-tight compartments of consciousness that avoid participation in a harmonious synthesis" ("Genuine," 315). Like Brooks's division of highbrow and lowbrow, Sapir emphasizes the separation between values and practices, or "patches" in American life. Most acutely, he points to the division between the needs and interests of the individual and their economic role in a civilization that prizes "efficiency" above all. Modern American civilization, he suggests, tends to regard "the individual as a mere cog, as an entity whose sole raison d'être lies in his subservience to a collective purpose that he is not conscious of or that has only a remote relevancy to his interest and strivings" (315). As cited earlier, Sapir's paradigmatic example of this alienated position is "the telephone girl who lends her capacities ... to the manipulation of a technical routine that has an eventually high efficiency value but that answers to no spiritual needs of her own" (315–16).

In contrasting the "efficiency" of modern "civilization" to the spiritual needs of the individual, Sapir here echoes both Brooks and Arnold. Like them, Sapir separates "culture" from external, mechanical "civilization," which denotes "the ever increasing degree of sophistication of our society and of our individual lives [but is] a merely quantitative concept" that sets the conditions for culture. Decisively separating the two concepts, Sapir argues that "civilization, as a whole, moves on; culture comes and goes" (317).

In contrast to "contradictory patches" of incongruent values and practices, Sapir's genuine culture is "inherently harmonious, balanced, self-satisfactory. . . . Richly varied and yet somehow unified and consistent," a genuine culture is one in which "nothing is spiritually meaningless," and in which "the significance of any one element of civilization [arises from] its relation to all others" (314–15). If, for Sapir, genuine culture is "unified" and "meaningful," Native Americans' traditional way of life is the paradigmatic genuine culture. "The American Indian," he writes,

> who solves the economic problem with salmon-spear and rabbit-snare operates on a relatively low level of civilization, but he represents an incomparably higher solution than the telephone girl of the questions that culture has to ask of economics. The Indian's salmon-spearing is a culturally higher type of activity than that of the telephone girl or mill hand simply because there is normally no sense of spiritual frustration during its prosecution ... because it

works in naturally with all the rest of the Indian's activities instead of standing out as a desert patch of merely economic effort in the whole of life. (316)

Indian culture is genuine precisely because of "the firmness with which every part of that life—economic, social, religious, and aesthetic—is bound together into a significant whole" (318).

In these passages, several key elements of Sapir's definition of culture emerge. First, rather than a universal process unfolding in time toward a specific end, Sapir's culture is a self-referential system existing in space. In both the evolutionary definition of culture as "technically used by the ethnologist" (308) and the definition of culture as "individual refinement" popularized by Arnold (309)—to cite the two traditions of thinking about culture against which Sapir sets his theory of "genuine culture"—culture is a single process measured on a universal standard existing outside the system. For Arnold that standard was "perfection," against which "the best which has been thought and said in the world" could be measured, regardless of where "in the world" that cultural element might originate. For late-nineteenth-century ethnologists, that standard was "progress" or technical sophistication: as Sapir puts it, "From this standpoint... all human groups are cultured, though in vastly different manners and grades of complexity. For the ethnologist... 'higher' and 'lower'... refer not to a moral scale of values but to stages, real or supposed, in a historic progression or in an evolutionary scheme" (ibid.). In both Arnold's and the ethnologist's definitions, individual elements of culture could be compared and ranked, low to high, on the scale of culture, whose horizon is "perfection" or "progress."

In citing the definition of culture "technically used by the ethnologist," Sapir most likely had in mind E. B. Tylor, the most influential proponent of cultural evolution in late-nineteenth-century ethnology. In his landmark *Primitive Culture* (1871), Tylor defines "culture or civilization" as "that complex whole which includes knowledge, belief, art, morals, law, custom and any other capabilities and habits acquired by man as a member of society."[37] But despite his language of culture as a "complex whole," that whole is not plural, made of a series of self-contained "wholes," but is singular, a universal process in which "various grades may be regarded as stages of development or evolution," with the highest stage represented by European civilization. Crucially, for Tylor the job of the ethnologist was to "classify" and "arrange" the *individual* "phenomena of Culture" "stage by stage, in a probable order of evolution." Rather than studying the various elements of a group's way of life in relation to *each other*, "a first step in the study of civilization," he argues, "is to dissect it into details, and to classify these in their proper groups"—say, weapons, farming implements, or religious ideas—to demonstrate the progressive development of that class of elements *across* civilizations "with little respect... in such comparisons for date in history or for place on the map."[38] Using this comparative method, the ethnologist could reconstruct the universal, evolutionary stages of development of any category of artifact or practice.

In contrast to both Arnold's "perfection" and Tylor's "development," forming teleological narratives unfolding in time, Sapir's culture is above all *self*-referential, held together in space: genuine culture is "self-sufficient," "inherently harmonious," with meaning arising from each element's synchronous "relation to all others" within the system. While both Sapir and Arnold describe culture as internal, spiritual processes that are whole and harmonious, the results of these elements are crucially different. For Arnold, they refer to and lead one toward a standard outside the system—perfection; for Sapir, wholeness and harmony instead generate a self-referential meaning or significance. As a self-referential, closed system, Sapir's culture is thus plural and relative—culture*s* rather than Culture. And in contrast to Tylor's culture, wherein individual elements of a civilization are available for abstraction and comparison with artifacts of the same type from another civilization, in Sapir's genuine culture individual elements can be connected only to other elements in the "whole" to establish meaning or significance.

A diachronic, comparative narrative of cultural evolution and Sapir's synchronic, spatialized model of culture in turn produced different *forms* by which these concepts could be expressed or displayed. One early embodiment of these formal differences was in the debates between Sapir's mentor Franz Boas and one of the curators of the Smithsonian museum, Otis T. Mason, over the proper mode of ethnographic display.[39] Boas's own work had long implied a synchronic, spatial model, although he had not explicitly theorized it in the way his students like Sapir would in later years. Through the late nineteenth century, American museums translated the then-dominant narrative of cultural evolution into visual terms by organizing artifacts in display cases according to apparent function (say, baskets, fish hooks, or cooking implements) and arranging them in supposed order of sophistication or level of technical ability, to display the evolutionary progress of technology over time (leading to the modern industrial age as the highest stage of that progression). Boas argued in a series of articles that artifacts should instead be regarded in the context (geographical, historical, material) of the group life in which they are found. "We have to study," he argued, "each technological specimen individually in its history and in its medium. . . . By regarding a single implement outside of its surroundings, outside of other inventions of the people to whom it belongs, and outside of other phenomena affecting that people and its productions, we cannot understand its meaning."[40] Boas proposed the "tribal arrangement of specimens," with artifacts placed in "life group displays" or dioramas, thus creating an artifactual representation of the idea of cultures as relative wholes.[41] This formal difference, discussed in chapter 3, will be crucial in understanding the narrative practices of modernist authors like Willa Cather.

Sapir's formulation takes the relationship between cultural part and whole that was implicit in Boas's practice and writing and makes it explicit as a theory of culture as such. As Hegeman and others have pointed out, the central theoretical tenets of Boasian anthropology have to a large degree been defined in retrospect, and often through the work of his students, such as Sapir.[42] Boas's thinking about culture, while it retained certain core elements, shifted in emphasis over time, and he was notoriously reticent to abstract his particular observations about individual cultures into a theory of culture as such, often to the frustration of his own students.[43] In many ways, as historians like Stocking have argued, Sapir's "Culture, Genuine and Spurious" marks one of the first and most important attempts by Boas's students to formulate such a theory.[44]

At the same time, by articulating a theory of culture, Sapir's formulation itself marks a decisive shift, bracketing Boas's emphasis on the historical processes of culture in favor of culture as a spatialized, bounded object. While Boas emphasized the importance of placing individual artifacts or practices in the context of the "whole" culture, he was less interested in defining that whole at any particular moment in time. For Boas, that context included complex historical processes of "diffusion" in which elements migrated and shifted across time and space through contact between peoples; the whole within which an individual element was located was thus always partial and provisional.[45] Sapir here elevates the idea of the whole to a theoretical principle: individual elements make up a structure in space, rather than being diffused across time, and form a discrete whole, the boundaries of which are reified by the "firmness with which every part of that life [are] bound together."

Sapir's spatial model of culture, finally, has an aesthetic that arises out of its semiotic structure: that is, it is harmonious and unified through the structural relationship of elements that, in their relation to one another, have "meaning," rather than having a "function" within a machine or constituting parts of an organism (to cite metaphors drawn upon by some other anthropologists or critics such as Brooks). The "meaning" that Sapir identifies with genuine culture does not refer to any particular *content* of that meaning, but rather the *structure* of values that creates that meaning: he is, in short, interested not in *what* a particular element means, but *how* it has meaning, in its relation "to all others."

The structural nature of Sapir's genuine culture links "Culture, Genuine and Spurious" to Sapir's work in linguistic anthropology, for which he was perhaps most famous. Through his groundbreaking analyses of American Indian languages, Sapir developed a theory of language that saw each language as a structure, made up of a unique set of phonetic patterns that formed a unified field of possibility—a unity that lay beneath the specific content of whatever one might say in that language. "The outstanding fact about any language," he argues, "is its *formal* completeness. . . . The world of linguistic forms, held within the framework of a given language, is a complete system of reference, very much . . . as a set of geometrical axes of coordinates is a complete system of reference to all points of a given space."[46] Self-contained and internally complete, each language constitutes its own world. The structural or formal unity of (a) language, then, becomes the formal unity of (a) culture in "Culture, Genuine and Spurious."

Culture thus becomes, in Sapir's formulation, a sculpture (or, as I argue in the following chapters, a modernist poem) rather than a story, whose aesthetic properties arise from its semiotic structure. This concept of culture as a spatialized, meaningful structure forms a central element in the debates over culture and modernist literary criticism and practice in the period. In constructing culture as an aesthetic object, Sapir also raises a tension in the problematic of culture that will bedevil anthropologists for decades to come—a tension already present in Brooks's image of Whitman as "focal point": If culture is an art object, then who is the artist? Do individual artists create the objects and ideas that then organize and unify the group, which then constitute a culture? Or do genuine cultures enable the creation of aesthetic objects that could be said to embody the culture? And what is the relationship of the anthropologist to that aesthetic object? More broadly, what is the ontological and epistemological status of culture? Are cultures objects or systems of meaning that exist out there in the world, independent of the anthropologist's gaze, such that the trained eye of the anthropologist as expert interpreter only makes visible what is already there? Or, conversely, do cultures lack any ontological existence but are instead composed through the active engagement (or interference) of anthropologists, including their attempts to capture it in forms like the ethnography?

In Sapir's formulation, culture is revealed only through the active engagement of the observer in a process he calls—in a term that will resonate with literary modernists like Cather—"selection." Sapir's opening move separating his theory of genuine culture from culture as "technically used by the ethnologist and the culture-historian" is in part one of selection. The ethnologist's culture includes "any socially inherited elements in the life of man, material and spiritual," making them all, "equally and indifferently, elements of culture" ("Genuine," 309). This undifferentiated list of elements Sapir calls "civilization." In contrast, genuine culture for Sapir requires "stressing *selected* factors out of the vast whole of the ethnologist's stream of culture as intrinsically more valuable, more characteristic, more significant in a spiritual sense than the rest" (310, emphasis added). In contrast to the "vast whole" of civilization, genuine culture's meaningful, structured whole is organized around certain characteristic elements, "those general attitudes, view of life and *specific* manifestations of civilization that give a particular people its *distinctive* place in the world" (311, emphasis added). These "specific manifestations" that make a culture "distinctive" are, it seems, "selected" and made visible by the artist/anthropologist who has the ability to see the ideal form amid the flurry of cultural details.

Again, for Sapir, the structure of culture is analogous to the structure of a language. In his popular textbook *Language*, for example, Sapir draws a similar distinction between compiling comprehensive lists of ultimately irrelevant "facts" and apprehending the crucial underlying structure: "The unschooled recorder of language," he suggests, "provided he has a good ear and a genuine instinct for language, is often at a great advantage as compared with the minute phonetician, who is apt to be swamped by his mass of observations."[47] In this formulation, the anthropologist/linguist becomes the artist who both creates (by making visible) and reveals (because it is already there) the aesthetic whole of culture by separating the meaningful from the irrelevant.

Unlike Brooks, who turns to a mid-nineteenth-century Yankee poet for his model of synthesis, Sapir turns to the Indian as a model for genuine culture; in so doing, he indexes a key image around which the interdisciplinary debate over culture in the period will circulate. Sapir's image of the Indian salmon fishing, of course, references Indians of the Pacific Northwest—the subject of his linguistic studies and the work of Boas and others. But as several scholars have pointed out, images of the Native American more broadly were of particular fascination in modernist America, and in new ways. The Pueblo Indians of the Southwest—as will become clear in the following chapters—were particularly fascinating for American modernists, including Sapir's fellow Boasian anthropologists.

Sapir's turn to the Indian as a paradigm of culture marks the intersection of imperialism, anthropology, and modernist aesthetics that characterized the modernist problematic of culture. The growing fascination with Southwest Indian art and life—for anthropologists, artists, and the general public—followed the development of new routes of transportation and commerce that opened these areas to both tourism and scientific exploration. The Atchison, Topeka, and Santa Fe Railroad did not reach Albuquerque, New Mexico, until as late as 1880, and in the years that followed, the railroad penetrated farther into the Southwest, making access easier to areas hitherto accessible only with difficulty by horse and wagon. In the first decades of the twentieth century, then, the region was still in the process of being integrated into the commercial and industrial grid extending from the East—a process that liberal historians like V. L. Parrington would call, writing just three years after Sapir's publication of "Culture, Genuine and Spurious," the consolidation of the "inland empire" of the United States.[48]

As new towns and outposts sprung up along these rail routes, increased numbers of white Americans traveled to the area, both to settle and take advantage of new economic opportunities and to tour this "exotic" area and see its native inhabitants. As Edwin Wade puts it, "For White America, it was a time of personal movement and exploration, and the railway allowed Victorian sophisticates and metropolitan adventurers the experience of meeting in person 'pacified' Pueblo and Navajo Indians in their native habitats."[49] By the late 1890s, passenger departments of the railroads actively began to "mine the landscape for culture," producing handbooks (often written by scholars) describing Indian art, ceremonies, and lifeways (and outlining the paid side trips that could take them there) to lure tourists to the area.[50] By 1924, the Santa Fe Railway was transporting fifty thousand tourists a year to the Grand Canyon and by 1926 had begun specific "Indian Detours" to bring travelers to witness "exotic" ceremonies and performances.[51]

Prominent among the increased number of tourists to visit the Southwest in these decades were both anthropologists and artists. As historians of anthropology have frequently pointed out, the development of anthropological discourse has followed the routes of imperial expansion, as ethnologists and anthropologists follow the colonial administrator or missionary into newly colonized regions. And in the first decades of the twentieth century, and especially from 1915 to 1935, the Pueblo Southwest became a key site at which the most influential American anthropologists of the period developed their theories of culture—anthropologists such as Boas and Sapir's fellow students Parson, Benedict, A. L. Kroeber, and Leslie Spier.[52]

At the same time, more artists came to see the Pueblo Southwest as being both a worthy subject *for* art and a site where a unique kind of art was being produced *by* the indigenous inhabitants. Epitomized by the success of Mary Austin's series of articles and stories about Pueblo Indian art and life—culminating in *The American Rhythm* (1923), in which she argued that Native American rhythms form the basis for American poetry—interest in Southwest Native American art and themes intensified through the 1920s and 1930s.[53] This interest on the part of artists increased through the postwar years into the 1920s, with figures like Mabel Dodge Luhan, D. H. Lawrence, and Laura Gilpin making pilgrimages to the region and making the Indian the subject of their art in their quest for the "primitive" authenticity felt to be lacking in American life.[54]

Sapir's deployment of the Indian as a paradigm of culture is significant, then, in several registers. First, it underscores the way in which debates over culture in modernist anthropology and debates over aesthetics in modernist art must be seen as a common problematic—here illustrated in the way both anthropologists and artists traveled side by side (literally and imaginatively) to Native American sites like the Pueblo Southwest and the Pacific Northwest to find alternative models through which to critique Victorian American life. Second, Sapir exemplifies the ways in which Indians, for some modernist anthropologists and artists, were deployed not as examples of primitive energy lacking in civilization or models of "nature," but as models of "culture"—and even more specifically, culture as aesthetic form.

Finally, Sapir's deployment of the Indian exemplifies the complex intersection of anthropology, imperialism, and progressive critique: while Sapir's and Boasian anthropology's fascination with Native American culture was enabled by and participated in the processes of U.S. imperialism, Sapir deploys his idea of genuine culture precisely to *critique* the power of the imperial state in favor of a theory of regional difference. For Sapir, the level at which culture achieves form is not the nation or state, as it is for Brooks, but instead the geographic region. As Sapir writes, the "geography of culture" is regional, reaching "its greatest heights in comparatively small, autonomous groups [but] rarely remains healthy and subtle when spread thin over an interminable area." Thus, while "the national-political unit tends to arrogate culture to itself," it succeeds "only at the price of serious cultural impoverishment of vast portions of its terrain" ("Genuine," 329). While in the 1920s some like Brooks sought to redefine an "American" culture to match the material and military prestige that followed World War I, others like Sapir argued that the idea of an American culture itself was an oxymoron: "It is in the New World," Sapir writes, "that the unsatisfactory nature of a geographically widespread culture ... is manifest. To find substantially the same cultural manifestations, material and spiritual, often indeed to the minutest details, in New York and Chicago and San Francisco is saddening" (330).

Thus, in contrast to some critics like Richard Brodhead and Amy Kaplan who see literary regionalism as complicit in the imperial project of nation building, Sapir's deployment of regional culture explicitly resists what he sees as the imperialism of national culture.[55] At the same time, however, Sapir's version of regional culture is also not, as other critics of regional modernism contend, a self-contained nostalgia that withdraws from broader cosmopolitan and transnational concerns. For Sapir, the answer to the problem of national culture comes in the form of new modes of economic and political internationalism in the postwar era that weaken the primary role of the nation-state, thereby freeing up regional cultures. "If the economic and political integrity of these large state-controlled units becomes gradually undermined by the growth of international functions," he predicts, "their cultural raison d'être must also tend to weaken" (ibid.). Culture then will flourish in "relatively small social and ... minor political units ... that are not too large to incorporate the individuality that is to culture as the very breath of life. ... Between these two processes, the integration of economic and political forces into a world sovereignty and the disintegration of our present unwieldy culture units into small units whose life is truly virile and individual, the fetich [sic] of the present state, with its uncontrolled sovereignty, may in the dim future be trusted to melt away" (ibid.). Ultimately he imagines a "series of linked autonomous cultures[,] ... each serenely oblivious of its rivals because growing in the soil of genuine cultural values" (331).

Thus, Sapir's theory of regional culture as spatial whole, exemplified in the American Indian, resists the hegemonic abstraction of "national culture": grounded in the region, but integrated in cosmopolitan networks, genuine culture leapfrogs over the industrial state. In this way, Sapir, and modernist anthropological revisions of culture by Boasian anthropologists more generally, participates in the broader critique of the state being prosecuted by many liberal Young American modernists like Randolph Bourne, Waldo Frank, and Lewis Mumford—many of whom Sapir knew personally and whose writings appeared side by side with his articles through the 1920s—*as well as* (as I demonstrate later) reactionaries like Allen Tate and John Crowe Ransom. Sapir's contrast between genuine regional culture and spurious national culture, moreover, is expressed in terms of form: the harmonious, unified spatial whole versus the "thin," "flat cultural morass"—or form versus formlessness.

In the following chapters, I return to both Brooks's and Sapir's formulations of culture: Sapir's theory of regional culture as spatial composition, with the American Indian as its exemplar, will be crucially intertwined with sites as seemingly diverse as Willa Cather's novels of the Southwest and Allen Tate's and John Crowe Ransom's New Criticism, and both Sapir's and Brooks's shifting ideas of culture will play a crucial role in the Melville revival in the 1920s. For now, I want to highlight the ways in which Brooks's attempt to articulate the terms of an organic American culture in *America's Coming-of-Age* and Sapir's attempt to define the structure of regional culture in "Culture, Genuine and Spurious" set contours of the problematic of culture in American modernism—a problematic that will structure the debate within anthropology and literary criticism in the period. First, the conjunction of Brooks and Sapir highlights the interdisciplinary nature of the debate. The publication of "Civilization and Culture" in *The Dial* alongside articles by both Sapir's fellow Boasian anthropologists *and* figures more traditionally associated with literary modernism, such as Brooks and his fellow Young Americans, points to a network of individuals and issues circulating through the pages of these journals, forming a common conversation around a variety of political, aesthetic, and epistemological issues that were in turn expressed through debates over culture. Highlighting this interdisciplinarity counters the conception of an anthropological version of culture emerging in this period that is then "applied" by critics and artists. Instead, it must be recognized that anthropologists, critics, and artists alike focused on a set of common problems of modernity—the solution to which came to be seen as culture.

Second, Brooks and Sapir encapsulate the terms for the debate by articulating the challenging conditions of modernity—including rapid immigration; new forms of state power and centralization; new forms of consumerism, mass entertainment, and communication; and the rising prestige of technological development, even as new theories challenged the certainties of scientific knowledge in terms of fragmentation versus wholeness. In defining culture as "whole," each explicitly contrasts his ideas of culture to what they argue is the nineteenth-century ideal of culture, embodied by either Arnold or ethnologists like Tylor, as universal processes of either perfection or progress; instead, they define culture as plural and relative—multiple cultures, rather than a single Culture. For Brooks, the whole culture is an organic whole, literally embodied in the heroic figure of Whitman; in this formulation, the divide between abstract knowledge and practical reality is overcome by experience. For Sapir, in contrast, the whole of culture is an aesthetic object, the wholeness of which arises out of a spatial structure that generates meaning from the interrelation of parts. Taken together, these new versions of culture formed part of a common project—in many ways the Romantic and antimodern project—of artists, anthropologists, and critics who sought to overcome the perceived "dissociation of sensibility" of modern secular society by conceptualizing a whole way of life, each aspect of which—economic, artistic, philosophic, scientific—was integrated in a meaningful way. This whole comes to be called, as Edward Sapir put it, genuine culture.

Third, as indicated by their analogies between "ways of life" and art, the debate over culture is also a question of aesthetics. Particularly, Sapir's conception of culture as meaningful whole makes culture itself an aesthetic object, defined in spatial terms. Particularly when coupled with a literal grounding in a geographic region, culture becomes spatialized and is perceived to have aesthetic form and structure, like sculpture or architecture. At the same time, art objects—sculpture and architecture, but also, I argue, poetry and novels—produced from within a culture can be seen as embodying in their own form and structure the whole of the culture from which they are produced. The spatialization of culture, for key figures like Mumford, Tate, and Ransom, is matched by the spatialization of poetry and literature, as the literary text is seen as an object itself, a structure in space as opposed to unfolding in time. This spatialization in turn opposes and prioritizes culture over history, myth over narrative, the lyric over the epic. At the same time, the conception of culture as a specifically meaningful whole engenders the search for *how* language and symbols "mean" within a culture, and within a poem. Shifting theories of culture, then, produce shifting theories of literary form-shifts that I argue in the following chapter can be seen in the changing narrative experimentations in Willa Cather's novels between 1915 and 1925.

Fourth, reconceiving cultures as plural wholes in turn generates further aspects of the problematic. On the one hand, the pluralist version of culture enables particular ways of life that had heretofore, under nineteenth-century developmental conceptions of civilization, been seen as primitive or "without culture"—groups like Native Americans and African Americans—as themselves having "a culture." Indeed, this pluralist conception of culture makes possible the search for a particularly "American culture" that occupies critics like Brooks, Mumford, and the Young Americans. On the other hand, as the examples of both Brooks and Sapir illustrate, the discourse of culture is fraught with tensions and unresolved problems, with the new definitions of culture often neither entirely new nor entirely coherent.

While Brooks and Sapir reject one standard of evaluation—that of higher or lower on the basis of technical civilization or progress—the result is not merely a descriptive or analytic version of culture. Instead, a new evaluative criterion is introduced in the requirement of wholeness and unity, a criterion by which modern America could be seen as fragmented, with only "spurious" culture—that is, without culture at all. There might be many more kinds of culture, and many more groups that might lay claim to having a culture—but, as Sapir puts it, "culture comes and goes," with not all groups equally cultured all the time. This tension is especially evident when the normative distinction Sapir makes between "genuine" and "spurious" culture is placed alongside his explicitly analytic theories of language and value. Thus, rather than seeing the story of culture in this period, as some disciplinary histories would have it, as the shift from one definition of culture to another or the triumph of one disciplinary definition over another (variously, the "anthropological" over the "humanist," the relative over the hierarchical, the analytical over the normative), Brooks and Sapir reveal how the discourse of culture in this period is characterized by both of these impulses simultaneously, with the tension between the analytic and the evaluative, the plural and the universal, expressing a problematic that structures both the anthropological and the literary debates over value.

Fifth, another aspect of this problematic is the question of what defines the whole, and the relation of parts to wholes. The idea of cultural wholes became not just a question of unity versus disunity or division, but what *kind* of unity: at what level is genuine unity to be found, as opposed to the attempt to force a unity where no such wholeness "naturally" exists? What is the site of authentic culture, the region or the nation—and what is the relation of each of these to the state? For critics like Brooks, who spent his life trying to define an "American" culture, the unit of culture is national, where the nation is coextensive with (if not identical to) the state. On the other hand, as exemplified by Sapir, for many modernists, the unit of genuine culture is the region, as opposed to the industrial, abstract, centralized, and homogenized nation-state. Thus, for critics like Sapir and others, culture becomes a concept that can be wielded against the state; in this way, modernist regionalism is decidedly different from the regionalism of the late nineteenth century, in which "local color" might be displayed in order to, as Howells puts it, "represent the whole of America."

These tensions structure the literary dimension of debate as well (and indeed, the anthropological and literary debates are inseparable): debates over the structure of culture in turn become debates over how to read literature, and redefining how meaning is constructed within a culture in turn translates into new ways of looking at meaning and language in poetry. Debates over the boundedness of culture become debates over the ways in which literature could be read as national, regional, or universal. Reading cultures as organic wholes also reconceived who had the authority to represent and interpret these cultures. In anthropology, this meant a shift in authority from the "armchair anthropologist" to the scientifically trained participant-observer who could embody the culture within the ethnographic text. In literary criticism, this meant the rise of the professional poet-critic like Eliot, Tate, and Ransom, who could derive their authority as both participants and observers of modernist literature.

Finally, I want to draw attention to the way new configurations of culture as regional and plural make available positions *both* conservative and liberal, progressive and reactionary. Mobilized against jingoistic ideas of national culture and Anglo-Saxonism, the logic of cultural pluralism also underwrites nativism and the defense of the homogenous local community; making available the search for an American culture, it also makes available the idea of Native American, African American, or other ethnic cultures *as* cultures. Indeed, the same position—for example, a regionalist environmentalism that opposes the predations of industrialism—can be found in figures on both the left (Mumford) and the right (Ransom). Attention to the ideological complexities of the culture concept in this period then troubles the traditional "left-right" categories in which the history of modernism in this period is generally told.

2 / Possessing Culture: Willa Cather's Aesthetic of Culture in *The Song of the Lark* and *The Professor's House*

> *Artistic growth is, more than it is anything else, a refining of the sense of truthfulness. . . . That afternoon nothing new came to Thea Kronborg, no enlightenment, no inspiration. She merely came into full possession of things she had been refining and perfecting for so long.*
> —*Song of the Lark* (1915)

> *That was the first night I was ever really on the mesa at all—the first night all of me was there. This was the first time I ever saw it as a whole. . . . Something had happened in me that made it possible for me to co-ordinate and simplify, and that process, going on in my mind, brought with it great happiness. It was possession.*
> —*The Professor's House* (1925)

In 1923, Willa Cather's essay "Nebraska: The End of the First Cycle" appeared in *The Nation* as part of the journal's series "These United States." Despite the editors' possible intention, Cather's description of the "great cosmopolitan country known as the Middle-West" was less a contribution to a unifying vision of "these United States," and more a description of a transnational, polyglot region defined by its differences from the rest of the country. Reflecting what I have been arguing are emerging modernist versions of cultural pluralism—articulated in various ways by humanist critics like Van Wyck Brooks, Randolph Bourne, and Horace Kallen, and literary-minded anthropologists like Edward Sapir—Cather describes the "early population of Nebraska" as "largely transatlantic," with "colonies of European people, Slavonic, Germanic, Scandinavian, Latin, spread across our bronze prairies like the daubs of color on a painter's palette." Each of these "colonies," she describes, had its own arts and traditions, and all were populated by "cultivated, restless young men."[1] In this description, Cather does not describe a unified Nebraskan culture or way of life, but celebrates a mix of unassimilated, variegated cultures.

Moreover, the titular cycle is a cycle of culture. While Cather sees culture as plural, varying across space with the nationality of each "colony," she also, like Edward Sapir, sees it varying across time: in Sapir's words, "culture comes and goes."[2] For Cather, the "end of the cycle" means the European "cultures" of the early settlements have faded: while the "thrift and intelligence" of these early pioneers made the State prosper, that well-being is threatened by the "ugly crest of materialism, which has set its seal upon all of our most productive commonwealths," making the second generation "very much interested in material comfort, in buying whatever is expensive and ugly... instead of making anything" ("Nebraska," 238). Like Brooks and Sapir, Cather's terms link anthropology and aesthetics, the making of artifacts and art: each group has "a culture" or a way of "making" meaningful artifacts, which are implicitly beautiful (because meaningful); the absence of culture is marked by buying things that are "ugly." Cather goes on to hope that future generations will "revolt against all the heaped-up, machine-made materialism about them ... [to] ... go back to the old sources of culture and wisdom." She imagines this culture being transmitted through literal cultivation of the soil: visiting the "graveyards of my own country," reading "on the headstones the names of fine old men I used to know"—names that are significantly Norwegian and Bohemian—Cather hopes that "something went into the ground with those pioneers that will one day come out again ... not only in sturdy traits of character, but in elasticity of mind, in an honest attitude toward the realities of life, in certain qualities of feeling and imagination" (237).

In imagining that "something" to be both plural (in that several different groups have it in different ways) and universal (it is also a general "elasticity of mind"), both regional (located in discrete "colonies") and "cosmopolitan," both ethnographic and aesthetic, both the mark of civilization and the sign of modernity's decline, Cather situates herself within the tensions of the debates over culture that are central to this period. In the previous chapters I have argued that, beginning around 1915 with the publication of Brooks's *America's Coming-of-Age*, the concept of culture emerges as central for American intellectuals from a wide variety of disciplines. New definitions of culture as ways of life that are plural, relative, and above all "whole" and "meaningful" arise in complex tension with nineteenth-century definitions of culture as artistic refinement, spiritual and mental improvement, or evolutionary progress. Literary critics like Van Wyck Brooks and anthropologists like Edward Sapir set the dominant metaphors of fragmentation and wholeness through which intellectuals conceptualized the challenges of modernity. For both Brooks and Sapir, each in different ways, "culture"—both in the sense of individual artifacts and ways of living—is characterized by aesthetic *form*; while Brooks conceived of that form (and the literary canon that might represent it) as national, for Sapir the unit of culture was regional.

In this chapter I suggest that the problematic of culture represented by Brooks and Sapir is also central to Willa Cather's novels. Cather's novels are particularly interesting indexes of the shifting debates over culture and aesthetics in the period given her position as a writer who has been seen as "in between." Cather's second novel brought her literary fame in 1913, and her most famous works were written over the next twenty years. But born in 1873, Cather was significantly older than many of the artists who defined "modernism." Her re-creations of Nebraska pioneer life (like *O Pioneers!* [1913] and *My Ántonia* [1918]) or precolonial Southwest Native American landscapes (*Song of the Lark*, *The Professor's House*, and *Death Comes for the Archbishop* [1929]) are markedly different from the urban, cosmopolitan concerns of many of her modernist contemporaries. Some Young Americans like Randolph Bourne ranked her work "alongside modern literary art the world over"; others, like Hemingway and Granville Hicks, dismissed her work as nostalgic, provincial, and matronly, out of touch with the social and existential crises of the day and the radical literary responses they called for.[3] Cather herself adopted a seemingly antimodern, backward-looking posture when she famously declared that "the world broke in two in 1922 or thereabouts," and declared her allegiance to the values of earlier era.[4]

More recent criticism, however, has established Cather's progressivism and literary modernism, identifying the ways in which Cather's regionalism and romantic nostalgia were themselves part of a tradition of "modernist anti-modernism."[5] And while the settings of her novels were the Mid- and Southwest, she was also rooted in the center of American urban modernism, New York City, where she lived from 1905 on. As, first, the literary editor of *McClure's* magazine, and then as a resident in Greenwich Village, Cather was intimately connected to the New York literary scene. Moving back and forth, physically and in memory, between Greenwich Village, Nebraska, and—most important for our purposes here—the Native American Southwest, Cather in many ways mirrors the movement of modernist American anthropologists who, as I will elaborate later, likewise shuttled between Greenwich Village, uptown

Columbia University, and the modernist "laboratory for anthropology," the Pueblo Southwest.[6] Cather's position "in between"—between romantic nostalgia and modernism, regionalism and cosmopolitanism, aesthetics and anthropology, Eastern metropole and Western periphery—makes her work an index of the complex transitions and tensions in the debates over culture between 1915 and 1925.

Cather's participation in this problematic of culture is perhaps most clearly indicated in her fascination with, and consistent use of, Indian art and artifacts in her fiction. Critics have long noted the centrality of Southwest Indian art for Willa Cather's aesthetic. Encounters with Cliff Dweller artifacts and ruins stand at the center of two of Cather's novels: in *The Song of the Lark*, Cather's semiautobiographical bildungsroman, the budding artist Thea Kronborg retreats from the cold indifference of Chicago to find inspiration among the ruins of an Indian tribe "related to the Cliff Dwellers" in Arizona's "Panther Canyon"; at the center of *The Professor's House* (1925), Cather's family drama of spiritual division and alienation in Middle America, stands "Tom Outland's Story," in which the main character discovers the Mesa Verde–like "Cliff City," and attains a spiritual relation to the Cliff Dwellers themselves by excavating and collecting its art and artifacts.[7]

Critics have largely drawn a direct line from the first novel to the second—often including along the way Cather's 1916 essay on Mesa Verde in the *Denver Times*—seeing each as part of a consistent aesthetic argument extending through Cather's career.[8] They have been read either as representing Cather's desire, like D. H. Lawrence, "to bypass the conscious and intellectual elements in her characters in quest of the instinctual and the unconscious," or as representing a harmonious alternative to the crass commercialism of modern America.[9] Sharon O'Brien, for example, suggests that Cather was attracted to the fact that in "Indian culture . . . everyday life was imbued with order and meaning."[10] In these arguments, changes in Cather's presentation of Indian artifacts are read as the development of Cather's artistic technique, rather than as any fundamental shift in her interpretation of those artifacts.[11]

Rather than teaching the lessons of "Indian culture," I argue that these novels are about "culture" as such, with the Indian as exemplar. Moreover, far from articulating a consistent argument about culture, the novels each construct a different model of culture and literary form, and together represent a shift in Cather's construction of culture as such. These novels thus reflect and participate in the problematic of culture I have been tracing—how to (re)conceive the concept of culture, and how to (re)define literary form—and specifically the ways in which imperialism, identity, and aesthetics are intertwined in these debates. In *The Song of the Lark*, I argue, Cather constructs a model of culture that is universal, evolutionary, and progressive, abstracting Native American artifacts from their context, placing them in a universal, progressive "long chain of human endeavor," of which Indian artifacts form the earliest, most primitive links (and the Wagnerian opera sung by Thea Kronborg, the latest). Cather's theory draws on key elements of two of the dominant constructions of culture in the late nineteenth century—that of the ethnologist E. B. Tylor, and that of Matthew Arnold. This theory of culture as transhistorical, progressive "refinement" is in turn mirrored both in the "cultivation" of the individual artist and in the pioneer's possession and cultivation of the land.

In contrast, by 1925, Cather's construction of culture had shifted from a universal Culture, to a relative, plural conception of culture*s*, in which any artifact becomes significant only in relation to the entire way of life of which it is a part. In defining culture as "whole" and "meaningful," Cather engages the terms of Edward Sapir, whose "Culture, Genuine and Spurious" (1924) likewise constructs "culture" as aesthetic *form*. Cather makes explicit Sapir's aesthetic, conceiving "a culture" as *itself* an art object—and object "designed" by the "selection" of the artist/anthropologist. Cather's new construction of culture makes it possible for one to "possess culture" in new ways: rather than "possessing" one-*self* (through self-"cultivation"), one can possess "a culture," or a cultural identity. Finally, Cather's construction of a spatialized culture reveals the intersection of modernist anthropology, modernist aesthetics, and literary criticism as it will emerge in the New Criticism of the 1930s and '40s—an intersection that also sheds light on the current "aesthetic turn" in literary studies.

Willa Cather in the Laboratory of Culture

In the spring of 1912, Willa Cather made her first trip to the American Southwest, taking a train across America to visit her brother Douglass in Winslow, Arizona. This trip, as many of her biographers have noted, was a turning point in her career. Cather had until recently been managing editor of *McClure's*, and although she had already written one novel while working for the magazine—*Alexander's Bridge* was to come out while Cather was in the Southwest—the trip marked her decision to quit editing and devote herself to writing.

In enthusiastic letters to her friend Elizabeth Shepley Sargent, Cather described her initial resistance to the ugliness of Winslow, which soon changed to fascination with the landscape that surrounded it. The desert, she wrote, was "big and bright and consuming," and seemed to be the setting for "a new tragedy or a new religion."[12] She also visited the cliff dwellings of Walnut Canyon, a national monument several miles outside of Flagstaff, where a collection of some three hundred cliff dwellings about one thousand years old, abandoned in the twelfth century, were preserved in the dry desert air. Cather's letters attest to the emotional impact of these encounters with the desert and the Native American ruins.

This initial encounter with ancient Indian artifacts and ruins was followed three years later by a trip to Mesa Verde itself, the site of the most extensive Indian cliff dwellings in the United States. Traveling with Edith Lewis by rail to Mancos, the closest town to Mesa Verde, Cather went to visit the brother of Dick Wetherill, the rancher who had first rediscovered the ruins, and heard the story of the discovery first-hand.[13] She and Lewis then traveled to Mesa Verde by wagon and spent a week at a government camp, exploring various sections of the complex with a forest ranger and guide, including one whole day in Cliff Palace, which according to Lewis was "the cliff dwelling with the tower, described in the 'Tom Outland' part of *The Professor's House*."[14] They also got lost in the canyons when an inexperienced guide led them astray and had to leave them behind to go for help. Lewis remembered that "the four or five hours we spent waiting here were, I think, for Willa Cather the most rewarding of our whole trip to Mesa Verde. There was a large flat rock at the mouth of Cliff Canyon, and we settled ourselves comfortably on this rock.... We did not talk, but watched the long summer twilight come on, and the full moon rise up over the rim of the canyon." This scene likewise would be replayed in *The Professor's House* (*Living*, 97).

In her turn to the Southwest in general, and sites of Pueblo Indian culture in particular, as spaces of spiritual meaning and new ideas about art and culture, Cather traveled a route—both figuratively and literally—that was already well established by the time of her first trip in 1912, and one that formed a crossroads for imperialism, anthropology, and modernist art. Already in the late nineteenth century, the Pueblo Indians of the Southwest, both living and extinct, occupied a powerful place in American popular culture: as Edith Lewis describes, Cather "and her brothers had thought and speculated about [the Cliff Dwellers] since they were children. [They] were one of the native myths of the American West; children knew about them before they were conscious of knowing about them" (*Living*, 81). Ethnologists like Frank Hamilton Cushing had already promoted public awareness of Indian life and art of the Southwest, and the World's Columbian Exposition in Chicago in 1893 even featured a replica of the Cliff Palace.[15]

As discussed in chapter 1, new routes of transportation and commerce opened the desert Southwest to both tourism and scientific exploration in the early decades of the twentieth century. Railroad companies actively promoted tours to see its "unspoiled" native inhabitants before they "vanished" beneath the tide of modern American civilization, and increased interest in Native American lifeways brought tourists, anthropologists, and artists alike flocking to the region. By the 1920s, as exemplified by Mabel Dodge Luhan's artist's colony in Taos, New Mexico, the Southwest—along with Greenwich Village—soon became one of the main sites for artists and anthropologists alike where alternative models of culture and art could be found (and produced).

Cather's trips to the Southwest, and her subsequent attempts to represent the Pueblo Indian lifeways and artifacts that she encountered, must be seen in this context. Cather's visit to Arizona in May of 1912 came only two months after the territory was made a state; Cather's brother worked on the Santa Fe railroad in Winslow, and took Cather on one of the much-advertised excursions to see the Hopi Snake Dance.[16] Cather knew many of the influential artists who promoted new images of the Pueblo Southwest as uniquely "American," like Mary Austin, and was well situated—both geographically from her Greenwich Village apartment, and professionally from her years at *McClure's*—to be exposed to the revolt against genteel American that was centered in New York, and the new versions of anthropology that were a part of that revolt.[17] Cather's shifting ideas of possessing culture must be seen as part, then, of the larger problematic of culture I am tracing.

The Kingdom of Culture: Culture, Ethnology, and the "Feeling of Empire" in *The Song of the Lark*

Cather's own first encounter with the Cliff Dweller ruins in Walnut Canyon reappears in her strongly autobiographical novel *The Song of the Lark*, as Thea Kronborg contemplates the ruins of a Cliff Dweller settlement in "Panther Canyon." Thea's most profound feelings are stirred by the decorated shards of pottery strewn about the ruins: the "care, expended upon vessels that could not hold food or water any better for the additional labor put upon them, made her heart go out to those ancient potters.... Food, fire, water, and something else—even here, in this crack in the world, so far back in the night of the past! Down here at the beginning that painful thing was already stirring; the seed of sorrow, and of so much delight" (*Song*, 305). These ancient creations reveal to Thea a universal definition of "any art," as the "effort to make a sheath, a mold in which to imprison for a moment the shining, elusive element which is life itself—life hurrying past us and running away, too strong to stop, too sweet to lose" (303–4). This artistic impulse transcends time, linking her firmly to those Indian potters, making her "feel that one ought to do one's best, and help to fulfill some desire of the dust that slept here.... In their own way, those people had felt the beginnings of what was to come. These potsherds were like fetters that bound one to a long chain of human endeavor" (306).

As Christopher Schedler has argued, Cather's construction of culture fits into the dominant mode of ethnology in the late nineteenth century: cultural evolutionism.[18] Cather's "kingdom of art," which includes both Cliff Dweller pottery and Thea's opera, is both universal and evolutionary. It is universal in that "any art," from pottery to opera, has the same desire to freeze "life itself" into form: the Indian women caught the "elusive element" within their jars, while Thea's singing captures it in the "vessel of [her] throat and nostrils" (304). At the same time, this categorical similarity also makes individual art-ifacts available for comparison and arrangement within a hierarchy. This hierarchy is evolutionary and progressive, with earlier, "primitive" creations setting the stage for later, more developed ones. Throughout these passages, Cather's descriptions are charged with a sense of "beginnings" and "promise," pointing toward future fulfillment—presumably in art like Thea's Wagnerian opera. The "long chain of human endeavor" both links Thea *to* the Indians and marks her progress *beyond* them.

While Indian pottery in Cather's description forms one stage in the evolution of art, it is also crucial that these artifacts are *not* seen as parts of a "whole way of life." Key terms that will become central to Cather's argument about culture in *The Professor's House*—"whole," "meaning," and "design"—are largely absent from these passages. Here, the shards of Indian pottery are significant insofar as they represent a universal category—"art"—abstracted from the other elements of Native American lifeways that surround it, and placed within a transhistorical "chain of human endeavor."

In articulating this relation between individual elements of a group's life to the sum of all that group's practices—the relation of "part" to "whole"—Cather draws on a central feature of the dominant, evolutionary paradigm of "culture" in the late nineteenth century and the practices of ethnographic display it entailed. As discussed earlier, the evolutionary paradigm of culture was most clearly articulated by E. B. Tylor in his landmark *Primitive Culture* (1871), in which he defines "culture or civilization" as "that complex whole which includes knowledge, belief, art, morals, law, custom and any other capabilities and habits acquired by man as a member of society." Tylor, like Cather, includes practices and artifacts of "primitive" societies in the category of "Culture." This is in contrast to, for example, Matthew Arnold, who reserved the term for only the highest achievements of civilization. But Tylor's "Culture" is a singular, universal process in which "various grades may be regarded as stages of development or evolution," with the highest stage represented by European civilization.

Similarly, in his *Ancient Society* (1871), American ethnologist Lewis Henry Morgan, like Tylor, established universal "stages" of evolutionary progress along which the artifacts and practices of any group could be plotted, from "savagery," to "barbarism," to "civilization"; at each stage, subsistence arts and technology could be correlated to associated stages of development in government, family, and property.[19] Morgan, of course, worked out his theory of progress through extensive study of Native Americans, who "possess a high and special value" since they "represent, more or less nearly, the history and experiences of our own remote ancestors when in corresponding conditions" (vii).

For both Tylor and Morgan, the job of the ethnologist was not to study cultures as self-contained, relative wholes, but to "classify" and "arrange" the individual "phenomena of Culture" "stage by stage, in a probable order of evolution"; this principle, as I have argued, found its visual expression in the dominant mode of ethnological display practiced in American museums through the late nineteenth century—practices institutionalized by men like Otis Mason, the curator of the Division of Ethnology of the Smithsonian's National Museum, and by the head of the Bureau of American Ethnology, John Wesley Powell, who saw himself as a student of Morgan. This mode of display translated the evolutionary narrative in spatial terms, and classified and arranged objects by type, alongside other objects of the same category in supposed order of evolutionary development.

In detaching Indian pottery from the context of a "whole way of life," and inserting it into a universal, evolutionary "chain of human endeavor," Cather thus replicates the evolutionary narratives that dominated American ethnology through the late nineteenth century—ways that were in fact increasingly under attack by Boas and his students within both museum and academic anthropology by the time Cather wrote *The Song of the Lark*. Cather does not relate the shards of Indian pottery to other aspects of Indian life or artifacts, to create an image of a whole "way of life" (as, I argue later, she will in *The Professor's House*); similarly, Thea's art is not constructed as part of an American "way of life." Instead, Cather arranges Indian art alongside Thea's art, to create an evolutionary narrative of the transhistorical progress of art itself. That progress is in turn mirrored in Thea's own bildungsroman, as her native childhood talent is "cultivated" through the course of the narrative to make her a fully developed, "refined" artist.

While Schedler correctly associates Cather's model of culture with evolutionary progressivism, this account overlooks the complexity of the novel's contemplation of culture and aesthetics. Rather than merely reflecting a Tylorian evolutionism, Cather braids together multiple traditions of thinking about culture, working the tension between ethnology and aesthetics, enlightenment progress and romantic nostalgia. Far from simply celebrating the progress of civilization, Cather often expressed contempt for the shallowness of modern life, and the importance of the "precious, the incommunicable past" in her work.[20] From early in her career, Cather lamented, like many Americans at the turn of the century, the supposed weakness and exhaustion of modern life, countering with a valorization of "primitive" strength, vitality, and violence: "The world is tired; this century has lived too much and too fast," she wrote, "jaded, exhausted, satiated we have come back to nature acknowledging that she is best."[21] Through much of Cather's fiction, art and imagination form antidotes to the cheap commercialism of the modern world.

In her work generally, and in *The Song of the Lark* in particular, Cather locates the sources of art in the intertwined concepts of memory, childhood, nature, and the primitive. In *The Song of the Lark*, childhood memories form a primary source of art. "A child's attitude toward everything," Thea argues, "is an artist's attitude"; as an adult, "the old things are in everything I do" (*Song*, 460). Indeed, art comes from a source prior even to childhood experience, from a pre-linguistic "nature" that is located within Thea, the landscape, and the Indian. Thea has "a nature-voice ... apart from language, like the sound of the wind in the trees, or the murmur of water," in the same way the Colorado landscape imparts a "joyous force, [a] large-hearted, childlike power to love" that "had nothing to do with words" (77, 220). Similarly, the Indian artifacts in Panther Canyon generate "pleasant and incomplete conceptions" in Thea's mind that "had something to do with fragrance and color and sound, but almost nothing to do with words" (299). Thus, each of these categories—nature, landscape, childhood, and Indian artifacts—is valorized as prelinguistic sources of artistic inspiration.

This alignment of Indian artifacts with nature is made even more evident in Cather's account of Mesa Verde after her visit in 1916, published in the *Denver Times*. In describing the Cliff Dwellers' buildings, Cather begins with a familiar romantic critique of American "civilization": "The [Cliff Dweller] architecture is . . . absolutely harmonious with its site and setting. On the way from New York to the Montezuma valley one goes thru hundreds of ugly little American towns, but when you once reach the mesa, all that is behind you. . . . Color, simplicity, space, an absence of clutter, the houses of the pueblo Indians today and of their ancestors on the Mesa Verde are a reproach to the messiness in which we live."[22] This architectural "harmony," and Indian lifeways in general, however, are described as extensions of natural processes rather than human effort:

> They seem not to have struggled to overcome their environment. They accommodated themselves to it, interpreted it and made it personal; lived in a dignified relation with it. In more sense than one they built themselves into it. They lived by hurrying and concentrating natural conditions and processes just a little. They supplemented the rainfall by building reservoirs and irrigating. House building, in those great natural arches of stone, was but carrying out a suggestion that stared them in the face; often they used a great rock that had fallen down into the archway as a cornerstone and anchor for their own lighter masonry. When they felled cedars with stone axes they were but accelerating a natural process; the ends of their roof rafters looked as if they had been gnawed thru by a beaver. ("Wonderland," 87)

"Accelerating natural processes," "hurrying and concentrating natural conditions," the Indians of Mesa Verde—admirably, for Cather—create artifacts that, rather than being the result of supreme efforts (and therefore monuments to culture), just barely seem to remove themselves from the category of "nature," like the work of beavers.

But crucially in *Song of the Lark*, the "primitive" sources of nature, landscape, and childhood memories must be accessed from temporal and spatial distance, *repossessed* and transformed by the artist through progressive "cultivation." In this teleology, these elements are the raw materials, the necessary but not sufficient conditions for the highest artistic achievements. They are repeatedly framed as "beginnings" and "foundations" precisely because they are to be built upon to shape more perfect forms of art. True art, Thea suggests, requires distance from these sources: quoting Wagner, Thea argues that "art is only a way of *remembering* youth. And the older we grow the more precious it seems to us, and the more richly we can present that memory" (381, emphasis added). The child's experience (like nature or primitive art) is just that, a child's experience; to make it "art," memory (of childhood, of nature, of the primitive) must be *re*possessed, *re*membered, by a later self.

This process of re-possession is "cultivation" and "refinement." In the climax of the novel, describing Thea's most fully realized artistic performance, the narrator suggests that "artistic growth is, more than it is anything else, a *refining* of the sense of truthfulness . . . She merely *came into full possession* of things she had been *refining* and *perfecting* for so long" (395, emphasis added). Thea comes to Harsanyi, her first professional music instructor, as a "fine young savage," talented but with "no cultivation whatever" (174). Culture, then, transforms her from a "savage" to a "refined" artist. Crucially, culture here is *self*-culture, the shaping and improvement of the self, rather than the exposure to either "great works" or a "way of life." This process of "cultivation" reveals the progressive teleology of Cather's "long chain of human endeavor." Indian pottery represents the "beginning" of "what was to come"—namely, the "refinement" of Thea's experiences of the Indian artifacts into her art.

Cather, then, constructs a narrative of evolutionary progressivism within the realm of art, but opposes the application of such narratives to modern civilization as a whole. In combining evolutionary progressivism and romantic resistance to modernity, Cather constructs a model of culture that combines in complex ways two distinct, if related, traditions of thinking about culture in the early twentieth century. On the one hand, Cather's placement of Indian art within a progressive history of "human endeavor" draws on the evolutionary paradigm of ethnologists like Tylor—an evolutionary paradigm that, while relegating "primitive" art to a lower stage on the evolutionary scale, nonetheless counted it *as* "culture." On the other hand, Cather's distinction between the progress of the kingdom of art, and the general state of modern civilization, diverges from Tylor. For Tylor and other evolutionary ethnologists, "cultivation" and "civilization" were essentially synonymous, both terms measuring a society's technical and artistic advancement. Thea's artistic "cultivation," however, takes place in opposition to the mediocrity of modern American life: the section describing Thea's life in Chicago before her trip to the Southwest is entitled "Stupid Faces."

In seeing the "cultivation" of the individual artist as distinct from, and in tension with, the progress of "civilization," Cather draws on a romantic tradition that includes Carlyle (whom Cather particularly admired), Coleridge, and, ultimately, Matthew Arnold. As discussed earlier, like Tylor's, Arnold's version of culture as "the best which has been thought and said in the world" is normative and universal, producing a scale of values ascending toward "perfection"; for Arnold, unlike for Tylor (or Cather), "culture" would not include "primitive" art at all.[23] But while Tylor identifies this progress toward perfection with the technological improvements of civilization, for Arnold "culture" is an "inward condition of the mind and spirit . . . *at variance* with the mechanical and material civilization in esteem with us" (*Anarchy*, 33, emphasis added). In *The Song of the Lark*, culture is likewise an inward process: in her climactic performance, Thea enters "within herself," "the inheritance that she herself had laid up" (*Song*, 395). This emphasis on the "internal" operation of cultivation in turn emphasizes the individual as opposed to the social whole—the tradition of the romantic artist who is the bearer of culture, in opposition to the mass of Philistines who have no culture. This distinction between the artist's inward cultivation and the outward "civilization" in which the artist operates in turn is evident in Cather's description of the Cliff Dwellers. Far from the Cliff Dwellers' pottery embodying a collective "whole way of life," it is, like Thea's opera, produced only by a select few: as Henry explains to Thea, "the stupid women carried water for most of their lives; the cleverer ones made the vessels to hold it." The Cliff Dwellers, it seems, had their "stupid faces" and Philistines as well (303).

Cather, then, constructs a model of culture that is both romantic and progressive, moving to re-possess the past to create more "refined" art in the present. This movement, I argue, is in turn an *imperial* movement: Cather's inward operation of *self*-possession has a corresponding outward movement, as the processes of "cultivation" are also connected to empire. The Cliff Dweller artifacts represent for Cather an essential but insufficiently cultivated "desire"; the Cliff Dwellers' failure to move beyond the canyon is one sign of this insufficiency. Throughout the novel, the eagle in flight symbolizes (artistic) desire. Basking in the sun in Panther Canyon, Thea is galvanized by the sudden sight of an eagle soaring high above: "O eagle of eagles! Endeavor, achievement, desire, glorious striving of human art! From a cleft in the heart of the world she saluted it" (321). In contrast to the eagle, Thea thinks of the Indians as "a timid, nest building folk, like the swallows," who "lived their lives between the echoing cliffs and never dared to rise out of the shadow of the canyon walls" (302, 301).[24]

Another group in the novel, however, *is* linked to the eagle, and by extension, to the artist—namely, the pioneer. Early in the novel, Thea is moved to tears by finding the signs of the wagon trains that transported "the Forty-niners and the Mormons" westward across the plains. Recalling the first telegraph message sent across the Missouri River—"Westward the course of Empire takes its way"—Thea in turn links empire with the flight of the eagles: "Thea remembered that message when she sighted down the wagon tracks toward the blue mountains.... The spirit of human courage seemed to live up there with the eagles" (54–55). The eagle as a symbol for courage, achievement, or desire, then, links the pioneer to the "glorious striving for human art."

Both the pioneer and the artist, it turns out, engage in taking "possession"—the pioneer of the land, the artist of herself. For the pioneer, "the course of Empire" entailed an intimate knowledge of the land that equaled possession: Ray Kennedy—a railroad brakeman, and thus an agent of westward expansion and consolidation—"had that feeling of empire; as if all the Southwest really belonged to him because he... knew it, as he said, 'like the blisters of his own hands'" (220). Thea, in turn, became an artist in the moment that she "came into full possession of things she had been refining and perfecting for so long" (477–78). Thus, the pioneer takes possession of the landscape—in novels such as *O Pioneers!* and *My Ántonia*—explicitly in order to "cultivate" it, just as the artist takes "possession" of herself, through "cultivation" or self-culture.[25] Thus, Cather constructs artistic cultivation as a kind of (self) possession analogous to the pioneer's possession of the continent—and conversely, envisions imperial possession of the land as an aesthetic achievement. As Cather revisits her idea of culture in the 1920s, as I will demonstrate, this imperial movement will remain a crucial factor—even as what is "possessed" and how changes.

"More Like a Sculpture Than Anything Else:" Cather's Aesthetic of Regional Culture in *The Professor's House*

When Cather returns to the Cliff Dwellers and Mesa Verde ten years later in *The Professor's House*, the architecture of the Kingdom of Art has changed. At the center of *The Professor's House* stands Tom Outland's discovery of Mesa Verde–like "Cliff City" on the Blue Mesa. Stumbling upon the ruins while chasing stray cows into a canyon in the Mesa, Tom describes the city high up on the cliffs, "asleep. It was as still as a sculpture—and something like that. It all hung together, seemed to have a kind of composition."[26] In the center of the nest of houses stands a stone tower, "beautifully proportioned," "symmetrical and powerful," "the fine thing that held all the jumble of houses together and made them mean something. . . . It was more like sculpture than anything else" (180). As Tom later puts it, the mesa, the buildings, and the individual artifacts he discovers within them form "a whole" (226).

The individual artifacts and, as important, the "sculpture" they collectively constitute, are a whole, meaningful composition. The emphasis on wholes is followed up in Tom's subsequent excavation of Cliff Dweller artifacts. While Thea contemplates only the "fragments of pottery" in *The Song of the Lark*, Tom seems to deal almost exclusively with "whole" vessels: in the village "water jars and bowls stood about unbroken," and beside the city's spring "stood some of the most beautifully shaped water jars we ever found . . . standing there just as if they'd been left yesterday" (186–87). While the potsherds form a link in the diachronic "chain of human endeavor" in *The Song of the Lark*, the whole pots in *The Professor's House* are linked synchronically only to each other, and to the architectural elements of the Cliff City. The whole composition is finally a synecdoche for the entire way of life of the Indians who built it. Unearthing, examining, and cataloguing everything from pottery, to household utensils, to surgical instruments and agricultural tools, Tom constructs a picture of the Cliff Dwellers that reveals the integration of activities—the mundane, the sacred, the scientific, the artistic, and the practical. Just as the tower "held" the city together and "made them mean something," this assemblage of artifacts reveals to the observer what Professor St. Peter will call a "design of . . . life" (240).

In refiguring culture as a way of life that is characterized as whole, and whose individual elements generate meaning in the context of that whole, the novel participates in what I have been arguing is the broader problematic of culture shaping discourse across a wide variety of disciplines—a problematic that is, of course, central to American anthropology's "classical period," when the discipline is redefined around these new conceptions. As I argue in chapter 1, one important articulation of this new version of culture—and one with which I argue Cather is in dialogue—is Sapir's "Culture, Genuine and Spurious." Sapir, I have demonstrated, was firmly entwined within the circuits of literary modernism and periodical publication, and it is worth noting that Cather was clearly connected with figures that link her to Sapir, and to the debates over culture in the period. Cather would have been familiar with Sapir's writings, particularly via journals like *The Dial* and *The New Republic* (in which, for example, Cather first publishes her essay "The Novel Démeublé" in 1922, and in which Sapir's articles frequently appeared). Cather and Sapir also are linked transitively through figures such as Randolph Bourne, who, as I have suggested in chapter 1, was also engaged in the problematic of culture. Both Cather and Sapir were familiar with Bourne's work, and Bourne had similar views of the Middle West as a "transnational America."[27]

Moreover, Cather was familiar with key figures in anthropology, and specifically, linguistic anthropology. Janis Stout has unearthed letters indicating that Cather knew Boas and his wife.[28] Cather is also linked, albeit tangentially, to Boasian anthropology through her knowledge of the work of Dr. Jesse Walter Fewkes, who had led several expeditions to study the Pueblo cultures of the Southwest in the late nineteenth and early twentieth centuries, and who was a member of the Bureau of American Ethnology. Fewkes himself had met Cather on Cather's visit to Mesa Verde in 1915—it was his party that had rescued Cather and Edith Lewis when their guide got lost in the canyon.[29] She was also good friends with folklorist, linguist, and first female president of the Modern Language Association, Louise Pound.[30] The links in this chain seem firm: Cather was connected through a dense web of social and intellectual connections to the emergent fields of linguistics and anthropology in modernist America.

Cather engages, in *The Professor's House*, in the same discourse deployed by Sapir in "Culture, Genuine and Spurious." Sapir's "genuine culture" is above all unified and whole, "inherently harmonious, balanced, self-satisfactory," in which "the significance of any one element of civilization in its relation to all others" ("Genuine," 310). In contrast to the "spurious" culture of modern industrial America, the Native American's traditional way of life is paradigmatic of "genuine culture," with "the firmness with which every part of that life—economic, social, religious, and aesthetic—is bound together into a significant whole" (318). In this formulation, Sapir constructs a self-referential, structural conception of culture, where what is crucial is not *what* a particular element means, but *how* it means, in its relation "to all others."

In characterizing the Cliff Dwellers' architecture and, by extension, their way of life, as a meaningful whole, Cather echoes the major elements of "genuine culture" stressed by Sapir. The Cliff City is a space where the divisions that characterize the Middle American life of the first book of the novel—of Professor St. Peter from his wife and children, of commercial materialism from spiritual and artistic achievement, of ideal friendship from petty social concerns—disappear. Like Sapir, Professor distinguishes civilization from culture, arguing that technological "progress" empties the world of the meaning generated by religion and art. These divisions are resolved in the unified "genuine culture" of Cliff City, where religion, art, and science become virtually indistinguishable. Cliff City's architecture is simultaneously a technical and an aesthetic achievement, and the "beautifully proportioned" tower is also "used for astronomical observations" (*Professor's*, 197). The Cliff City tower unites empirical science, religion, and aesthetics to "make them mean something."

Even more significant is Cather's spatialization of culture as an aesthetic object. The whole constituted by the elements that make up Cliff City—and, by extension, by the way of life lived in them—is "designed" and "composed" like a "sculpture." As such, Cliff City literally becomes the "vessel" Cather describes in *The Song of the Lark*, "a mold in which to imprison for a moment the shining, elusive element which is life itself" (*Song*, 303). The Cliff City defies time, standing in "immortal repose," "preserved in the dry air and almost perpetual sunlight like a fly in amber" (*Professor's*, 180). But where in *The Song of the Lark* this principle is embodied in the pottery itself, in *The Professor's House* it is embodied in the entire city, and, ultimately, in the way of life it shapes and contains. Moreover, the Cliff Dwellers' defiance of the flux of time is secured in their extinction: if the "roving Indian tribe without culture" that "exterminated" them represents the rapid changes of modernity, the Cliff Dwellers' extinction attests to their resistance to those changes. In articulating an aesthetics of culture as an object in space—synchronic and sculptural, as opposed to diachronic and narrative—Cather creates a structural definition of culture that parallels Sapir's structuralist theories of both language and culture.

The Selecting Hand: Cultures and/as Compositions

Thus, at one level, *The Professor's House* revises Cather's conception of culture dramatized in *The Song of the Lark*, and makes explicit the spatial aesthetic of culture articulated by Sapir. At the same time Cather's novel, both thematically and structurally, is also about the ways this bounded sense of culture (which for Sapir is grounded in the region) is "composed" by the artist and anthropologist who represent them. In particular, the novel dramatizes the way the composition of this spatially bounded culture depends on both the selection and movement—even transnational and imperial movement—of artists and objects.

The novel's construction of culture as an aesthetic whole, and the role of composition in this construction, becomes clear in Tom's epiphanic experience of the "whole" mesa. Returning from an unsuccessful fundraising trip to Washington, D.C., Tom finds the collection of artifacts sold; in the argument that follows, Roddy leaves Tom alone on the mesa. Lying on a rock at the bottom of the canyon and gazing up at the Cliff City, the rock walls, and the night sky, Tom for "the first time . . . saw it as a whole": "It all came together in my understanding, as a series of experiments do when you begin to see where they are leading. Something had happened in me that made it possible for me to co-ordinate and simplify, and the process, going on in my mind, brought with it great happiness. It was possession" (226).

In this crucial passage, Cather reveals the ways in which "a culture" both *is* an aesthetic object to be discovered by the perceptive anthropologist/artist, *and is composed by* the anthropologist/artist representing that culture through the shaping process of selection—and in the process puts her finger on the question of the ontological and epistemological status of cultures that has bedeviled modern anthropology ever since. As I argued in chapter 1, in Sapir's model of the cultural whole, the anthropologist does not simply catalogue the potentially infinite number of cultural elements, but selects, from amid the welter of detail of everyday life, the most significant elements for representation and interpretation. For Sapir, this potentially infinite list of details is Tylor's "civilization"; genuine culture in contrast is formed by "stressing *selected* factors out of the vast whole" as "more significant in a spiritual sense than the rest" ("Genuine," 311, emphasis added). This process of "selection" is central to Cather's understanding of culture: as St. Peter observes, it is the artist's "hand, fastidious and bold, which selected and placed—it was that which made the difference. In Nature there is no selection" (*Professor's*, 61). Tom in turn apprehends the whole of Cliff City through precisely this process: only after he has collected and catalogued the artifacts of Cliff City, and then *lost* them, can he "co-ordinate and simplify," and thereby perceive, the whole culture. As he says of the inspired days that followed, he felt that he "had found everything, instead of having lost everything" (227).

This process of selection is in turn central to Cather's theory of composition, and marks the difference between an artistically inferior literary realism and the "novel démeublé." In her 1922 essay of that title, Cather contrasts the "'realism' [that] asserts itself in the cataloguing of a great number of material objects, in explaining mechanical processes," to the use of selected objects in the works of masters like Tolstoi, for whom "the clothes, the dishes, the haunting interiors of those old Moscow houses, are always so much a part of the emotions of the people that they are perfectly synthesized."[31] Tom's collecting and cataloguing of Cliff Dweller artifacts, then, could be seen as an exercise in the "novel démeublé," and his loss of the artifacts and subsequent apprehension of the cultural whole as the enactment of Cather's admonition to "throw all the furniture out of the window" and "leave the room as bare as the stage of a Greek theatre" (*On Writing*, 43). The Sapirian anthropologist and the literary artist compose their objects: *a* culture, like a novel démeublé, forms a whole, whose structure is both revealed (because it is already there) and created (because it is first made visible) by the anthropologist/artist's ability to select the meaningful from the irrelevant. In short, culture is a composition, composed both by the people who live it and by the artist/anthropologist who attempts to "know" and represent it.

The relationship between Cather's aesthetics of culture, literary composition, and ethnography—and, further, the relationship between regional culture and transnational movement—is made particularly clear in Cather's introduction to her edited volume of *The Best Stories of Sarah Orne Jewett*, written in 1925 as Cather was completing her novel. In giving her account of Jewett's literary regionalism, Cather theorizes a relationship between spatial design, narrative composition, and the rendering of a culture *in* writing. Cather significantly begins by praising Jewett's regional fiction in terms of its formal properties of "design": as opposed to the "Chinese junk," the beauty of which comes from "rich ornamentation," Jewett's stories have the "beauty of the modern yacht, where there is no ornamentation at all; . . . every line of the craft is designed for one purpose . . . so that it has an organic living simplicity and directness" (*On Writing*, 58). This organic design enables Jewett to capture a New England way of life that is on the verge of disappearing: with the elegiac note characteristic of what James Clifford has called anthropology's "salvage ethnography," Cather imagines that "the student reading Jewett fifty years from now" will get from the stories "the characteristic flavour, the spirit, the cadence . . . of a New England which will then be a thing of the past" (54).[32] Like, one might say, an anthropologist, Jewett "saw it as it was," was able "to understand by intuition the deeper meaning of all she saw" (54) and was finally able to capture that understanding in writing.

Crucially, however, this "organic living simplicity and directness," is explicitly *not* natural—that is, growing spontaneously from the material—but comes from the designing hand of the artist—that is, it is the hard work of culture. In comparing Jewett's early "first impressions" and her later "almost flawless examples of literary art," Cather argues "one can . . . watch in process the two kinds of making: the first, which is full of perception and feeling but rather fluid and formless; the second which is tightly built and significant in design. The design is, indeed, so happy, so right, that it seems inevitable; the design is the story, and the story is the design" (48–49). Cather suggests that what is natural—"full of perception and feeling"—is explicitly not art, because "fluid and formless"; what the artist adds to nature, then, is design that is "tightly built" and "significant." This process, Cather indicates, is one of unrelenting effort over a long period of time: it requires "persistence, survival, recurrence in the writer's mind," and repeated attempts, just as "a painter tries different lightings and different attitudes with his subject to catch the one that presents it more suggestively than any other" (48, 51).[33] One must, it seems, move away from the immediate impressions of nature into the hard work of design and composition, in order to then capture "life itself," even if the artist is depicting the way of life she herself has lived. In figuring Jewett's natural-seeming depiction of New England life as explicitly the product of artistic design, then, Cather makes Jewett's regionalism "modernist"—both in its depiction of culture as a whole way of life, and in its embodiment of that way of life in textual design.

Looking at Cather's Jewett essay alongside *The Professor's House* is illuminating in several ways. First, Cather's emphasis on composition as labor illuminates the changes Cather made in the descriptions of Indian artifacts between *The Song of the Lark*, as well as her 1916 Mesa Verde essays, and *The Professor's House* ten years later. In those earlier works, Cliff Dweller artifacts are seen as an earlier stage in an evolutionary development of art, in which the Indian lived by "accelerating natural processes just a little." The Cliff Dwellers in *The Song of the Lark* are "swallows" who never explore beyond their canyon; as such, Cather implied, theirs was an "indolent evasion," and this indolence—a product of the very harmony of their lives and art—led to their "extinction" at the hands of a tribe "less comfortable, less satisfied, and consequently more energetic."

Gone are these references to indolence and natural growth in *The Professor's House*. Where the buildings of Cliff City in the 1916 essay are described as "swallows' nests" (with their associations of timidity and lack of desire), in *The Professor's House* they are simply "pale little houses of stone nestling close to one another... with flat roofs, narrow windows, straight walls"; where Cather naturalized Indian workmanship by suggesting that the "ends of the roof rafters had looked as if they had been gnawed thru by a beaver" ("Wonderland," 7), in 1925 "the cedar joist had been felled with stone axes and rubbed smooth with sand," "smoothly polished," and "carefully fitted," thus proving "their patience and deliberation" (*Professor's*, 190). With the shift from the harmony of natural indolence to the harmony achieved by persistent effort, Cather also eliminates the sneaking sympathy for the "energetic" invaders present in 1916: the invaders in *The Professor's House* are simply "some roving Indian tribe without culture or domestic virtues, some horde that fell upon them in their summer camp and destroyed them for their hides and clothing and weapons, or from mere love of slaughter" (*Professor's*, 198). These changes are not just aesthetic refinements, as Roskowski and Slote would have it, nor are they simply changes in attitude or judgment toward Indian artifacts: the aesthetic changes are part of a reorientation in Cather's version of culture as such, in which primitive artifacts are not seen as natural or lower on the evolutionary scale of universal art, but as artifactual representations of the relative, whole way of life in which they are produced. These artifacts are in turn not as seen as natural outgrowths or reflections, but as the designed, composed results of sustained human effort, and the Indian becomes emblematic not of "natural" growth but of *composing* "culture."

Second, the example of Jewett in turn helps complicate the meaning of Tom's "possession" of the Cliff City and of Cliff Dweller culture. In linking Tom's perception of the cultural whole to both science and writing—and calling the results of both "possession"—Cather dramatizes the utility of the idea of cultural wholes for modernist anthropologists. Conceiving culture as a discrete, spatial whole made it uniquely available to the anthropologist/scientist for study, making it quite literally an object of analysis. As a sculpture, both the city itself and—through Tom's careful collecting, cataloguing, and displaying of the artifacts he uncovers—the way of life it embodies are made available for contemplation, both aesthetic and scientific. Cather thus celebrates what later anthropologists will lament about their discipline—that the conceptualization of culture as designed whole participates in a mode of knowledge that is imperial, "taking possession" of the object in the act of knowing it.

The relationship between imperialism and aesthetics is embedded in Cather's later account of the inspiration behind the novel's structure. Cather claimed that she got the idea for inserting "Tom Outland's Story" within the narrative of Professor St. Peter from "an exhibition of old... Dutch paintings," in which "the scene presented was a living room warmly furnished, or a kitchen full of food and coppers": "But in most of the interiors... there was a square window, open, through which one saw the masts of ships, or a stretch of grey sea. The feeling of the sea that one got through those square windows was remarkable, and gave me a sense of the fleets of Dutch ships that ply quietly on all the waters of the globe, to Java, etc." (*On Writing*, 31). Most critics have followed Cather's lead as she goes on to describe her use of this technique in *The Professor's House*—how she made "Professor St. Peter's house rather overcrowded and stuffy with new things," and then opened "the square window and let in the fresh air that blew off the Blue Mesa." But what is crucial for Cather's theory of culture and composition is how this "remarkable" feeling that blows in those windows is the feeling of imperial movement, as the "fleets of Dutch ships... ply... the waters of the globe" in the process of making the Netherlands one of the richest colonial empires in the seventeenth and eighteenth centuries (and empire, of course, of which "Java" was a major colony).

Even Cather's construction of Jewett herself reveals how deeply the interrelation between Cather's theory of narrative and imperial collecting practices in fact runs. In her Jewett essay, the production of regional fiction seems to depend, not on a hermetically sealed provincial culture that Jewett depicts, but on her position within a larger imperial context: Jewett, Cather rhapsodizes, was born "in a beautiful old house full of strange and lovely things brought home from all over the globe by seafaring ancestors" (*On Writing*, 56). This movement of voyage and return (with possessions) repeats in another register Cather's emphasis, in her description of Jewett's work, and of the Cliff Dwellers in *The Professor's House*, on the need to move away from nature in order to return to it in art. One must first be part of a culture to depict it; however, one must double that initial possession through the hard work of culture. Possessing one's culture, it seems, must also be a returning to one's culture.

In linking regionalism, imperialism, and an aesthetic of culture, Cather in fact constructs an argument that in crucial ways provides a counterpoint to the models of genuine culture deployed by Sapir and others in the period. For Sapir, as I have shown in chapter 1, and other critics on both the left and the right—left-liberal critics like V. L.

Parrington and Lewis Mumford, reactionary critics like Allen Tate and John Crowe Ransom, as I will show later—the "unit" of culture is the region, as opposed to the state. If Cather would agree with Sapir as to the imperial nature of the state, she would disagree with his conclusions: for Cather, imperial movement is inseparable from the growth of genuine culture, and from the artist/anthropologist who would compose those cultures. Thus, for Cather the "unit" of culture becomes more complex, as regional, bounded culture becomes dependent on transnational movement, and formally "whole" local culture becomes a model for a national culture that, while "spurious" in the present, might be made "genuine" in the future. For, while Tom Outland's possession of the Cliff City in *The Professor's House* in many ways enacts the dialectic described in her account of Jewett—losing one's (natural) identity in order to regain it (in art)—the identity Tom Outland (re)discovers is his *American* identity, where "American" is identified with both the Indian *and* the state, as the Cliff Dwellers are retroactively made the first Americans. Tom, in his impassioned "Fourth of July talk" to Blake after the relics are sold, argues Blake had no right to sell "the pots and pans that belonged to my poor grandmothers a thousand years ago," since they " belong to the country, to the State, and to all the people. They belonged to boys like you and me, that have no other ancestors to inherit from" (*Professor's*, 219). This, as Walter Benn Michaels has pointed out, coincides with a more widespread shift in white American conceptions of Indians as the "first" or "Native Americans," as reflected in such political developments as the Indian Citizenship Act of 1924, which automatically made all Indians American citizens. It is through this imaginative process that, as Father Duchene puts it, the artifacts of a people whose existence predates the political state and who are unrelated biologically to any of the characters in the novel become an "important point in the history of your country" (199). Coupling "filial piety" for his Indian ancestors with reverence for classic Greek and Latin civilization, Tom stays on the mesa through the summer studying *The Aeneid*: the possession of Indian culture parallels the narrative of the founding of a nation and an empire.[34] And as Tom's "Fourth of July talk" makes clear, to be "American" is a national and political, as well as a cultural, identity, one that unites "the pots and pans that belonged to my grandmothers a thousand years ago," "the State," and "all the people."

Thus, for Cather the unit of genuine culture, and the level at which aesthetic form can be achieved, is *potentially* the nation, and not just the region. The potential for "America"—where "America" is coterminous with "the United States"—to become a genuine culture is attested to by Tom Outland's reaction upon seeing the Capitol dome and the Washington monument: like his apprehension of the whole of the Cliff City and its setting, Tom watches "the white dome against a flashing blue sky, with a very religious feeling," while his reverence for the Cliff City's tower is echoed in his "watch[ing] the Washington monument colour with those beautiful sunsets" (203, 211).

Of course, part of the point of "Tom Outland's Story," and in particular its setting within the frame of the narrative of the Professor and his family, is the difficulty of realizing genuine culture in modern America. Tom's admiration and religious feeling for the architecture of Washington, D.C., stands in stark contrast to his assessment of the petty bureaucrats he encounters there, who, with their obsession with material advancement and appearances, live their lives "like people in slavery, who ought to be free" (211). Tom loves the city—it's the people he can't stand. It is as if, for Cather, Washington, D.C., emptied of its inhabitants might in fact be a Cliff City-like sculpture. This version of American identity is further complicated by the intense localism Tom's visit to Washington simultaneously evokes: like a traveler in a foreign country (or like an anthropologist), Tom spends his time between meetings with officials "trying to find out something more about the kind of people I had come among," and he is intensely interested in the young married couple from whom he rents a room, who are "unlike any people [he] had ever known" (208-9). He returns to the mesa with a renewed sense of rootedness, "like home-sick children when they come home" (217).

In this way, *The Professor's House* enacts a complex answer to the question of regional, national, and cosmopolitan culture posed by Sapir, Brooks, and others in the period: conceiving culture as regional and bounded whole, the novel suggests, relies on a process of selection and composition that depends on imperial and transnational movement; it is through this process that the possibility of a national culture emerges. Tom's ability to "coordinate and simplify," and thereby "possess," the Cliff Dweller culture, and realize the national identity reflected in his Fourth of July talk, is made possible by the transnational circulation of the Cliff Dweller artifacts themselves: Tom is able to select his objects to be "thrown out of the window" (or have them fortuitously selected for him) when those objects move out of the geographic region of their origin and into transnational and even imperial circulation (in this case, moving with a German antiquities dealer to "Old Mexico," to be loaded on a "French boat" bound for Europe [215]). Similarly, the novel itself circulates between a variety of locations through its tripartite structure. *The Professor's House* is, of course, not a regional novel in the manner, say, of *O Pioneers!*, *My Ántonia*, or *Death Comes for the Archbishop*—novels that predominantly take place within the particular region and whose characters are part of that regional culture. Instead, "Tom Outland's Story" could be described as a piece of regional fiction within a broader framing narrative that moves through a wide array of locales, from rural Kansas, to France, to a Midwest college town: the reader, one might say, has to pass through the metropolitan (or suburban) geography of Sapir's spurious culture before arriving at the site of regional culture, and then has to make the return trip. It is only through this movement that a national culture becomes a possibility.

Thus, in the shift from the progressive model of artistic self-culture articulated in *The Song of the Lark*, to the spatialized aesthetic of culture in *The Professor's House*, Cather revises the very idea of what it means to "possess" culture. Tom's possession of the Cliff City both repeats and transforms Thea's self-possession in *The Song of the Lark*. In *The Song of the Lark*, Cather figures one's identity as an artist as both something one is and something one becomes, something that one already has yet of which one must also take possession. This version of artistic identity, it turns out, is a rehearsal of her construction of a complex national identity in *The Professor's House*. Where Thea, in her climactic moment, "comes into possession" of herself as an artist—a producer of high Culture—Tom here comes into possession of *a* culture, i.e., the Cliff Dweller culture that is both an other culture, and "his" by virtue of his be(com)-ing an American. The move from Thea's taking possession of her artistic inheritance, to Tom Outland taking possession of the Blue Mesa and its artifacts, is the shift from personal cultivation to culture as a whole and meaningful way of life. In both versions of culture and identity, imperial movement is crucial to the process of composition.

Finally, the thoroughgoing parallels between Cather's spatial conception of culture and Sapir's structuralist theories of both language and culture in turn reveal Cather's location at the intersection of modernist anthropology, modernist aesthetics, and literary criticism in a new way. Several critics have noted the resemblance between Cather's description of the Cliff City and Keats's Grecian urn—a resemblance reinforced by the fact that the Cliff Dweller pottery is repeatedly referred to as "shaped like those common in Greek sculpture" (*Professor's*, 100).[35] None, however, have then historicized this reading of Keats's poem as itself a "well-wrought urn," to note that Cather wrote *The Professor's House* precisely in the period when that reading of the ode—and of poetry as such—was about to become dominant. Consider, for example, Cleanth Brooks's famous interpretation of Keats's ode in *The Well-Wrought Urn*: in language that echoes Sapir's definition of culture, Brooks argues that a poem (like Keats's urn) is "a structure," not just of mechanical elements like meter and rhyme, but "of meanings, evaluations, and interpretation; and the principle of unity which informs it seems to be one of balancing and harmonizing connotations, attitudes and meanings."[36] Brooks recommends a vision of the poem that would combat the very "fragmentary existence" against which Sapir (and Cather) assert "culture": "If we can see that the assertions made in a poem are to be taken as part of an organic context, if we can resist the temptations to deal with them in isolation, then we may be willing to go on to deal with the worldview, or 'philosophy,' or 'truth' of the poem as a whole in terms of its dramatic wholeness . . . [rather than favoring] some statement of theme abstracted from it by paraphrase."[37] Significantly, Cather asserts that the tower in Cliff City "held the jumble of houses together and made them mean something," but does not go on to try and define what that "something" is—she does not, one might say, commit the heresy of paraphrase. Cather, Brooks, and Sapir, then, are all interested, to use Sapir's words, "not so much [in] what is done and believed by a people [or in a poem] as [in] how what is done and believed functions in the whole life of that people [or in the whole poem]" ("Genuine," 311).

Setting Cather, Sapir, and Cleanth Brooks side-by-side points out the connection between debates over "culture" and what would become the dominant modernist critical method for reading and writing poetry in the next decades. The coalescing of modernist anthropology around a synchronic, structural version of culture, and what Joseph Frank has called the "spatiality of modernism," must be seen as intimately related responses to a common problem.[38] Frank—and I take Frank's interpretation of modernist poetics to be as much a part of this modernist project as a reading of it—argues that the "spatiality of modernism" is an attempt to deny the temporality of language. "Naturalism," he argues, is produced in societies in which man is "convinced of his ability to dominate and control natural forces." On the other hand, "when the relationship between man and the cosmos is one of disharmony and disequilibrium, we find that nonorganic, linear-geometric styles are always produced. To primitive peoples, for example, the external world is an incomprehensible chaos. . . . Accordingly, their will-to-art . . . reduces the appearances of the natural world to linear-geometric forms. Such forms have the stability, the harmony, and the sense of order that primitive man cannot find in the flux of phenomena."[39] This, argues Frank, is the condition to which modernist poetics responds: "If there is one theme that dominates the history of modern culture since the last quarter of the nineteenth century, it is precisely that of insecurity, instability, the feeling of loss of control over the meaning and purpose of life amidst the continuing triumph of science and technics."[40] Thus, modern poetry tries to replace historical sequence with the timeless unity of myth, and make the poem an object in space. In terms that echo Sapir's theory of culture as a self-referential system of meaning, Frank concludes that "since the primary reference of any word-group is to something inside the poem itself, language in modern poetry is really reflexive. The meaning-relationship is completed only by the simultaneous perception in space of word-groups that have no comprehensible relation to each other when read consecutively in time." Instead of making meaning from the sequence of references, experienced by the reader in time, modern poetry makes meaning when "the entire pattern of internal references can be apprehended as a unity."[41] Sapir's own construction of culture as a whole system of meaning, I am arguing, is precisely a response to the perceived condition of fragmentation that Frank describes. In response to this same "crisis," Cather spatializes and aestheticizes Sapir's "whole" culture. As I will argue in chapter 4, New Critics like Allen Tate and John Crowe Ransom take this idea of culture as aesthetic object in space and embody it in a poem.

From *The Song of the Lark* to *The Professor's House*, then, Cather does not "develop" or continue a single argument about art and Native American culture, but rather deploys two complexly related, but distinct, versions of culture. In *The Song of the Lark*, Cather constructs a model of culture as a diachronic "chain of human endeavor," the progressive movement of which is mirrored by the artist's "cultivation" or "refinement" of her raw talents; this cultivation allows one to take possession of one's identity as an artist, in much the same way as the pioneer takes possession and cultivates the landscape. In *The Professor's House*, culture is constructed as a synchronic, spatial design, whose individual elements collectively constitute a self-referential, meaningful whole. In this version, culture does not just designate a creative process, or the pieces of art themselves, but is *itself* an aesthetic object, "a culture," with a "design" composed by the hands of the people who live it—in much the way a sculptor forms a statue and, it turns out, a writer composes a story. As a spatial object, a culture thus becomes available for possession by the artist/ethnographer who can both discover—because it is already there—and create—because his "selection" and "coordination" of the significant elements makes it visible—its meaningful design. In this way the "unit" of culture likewise shifts between the two novels, from "culture" as a universal process, played out in the self-cultivation of the individual, to culture as grounded in the local or regional, but dependent on imperial or transnational movement, which in turn gives rise to the possibility of "national" culture. Attention to these shifts in the meaning of culture both illuminates Cather's shift in style from the narrative bildungsroman of *The Song of the Lark* to the experimental, tripartite structure of *The Professor's House* that resists narrative development in both its plot and its form, and reveals Cather's participation in the debates over culture that occupied intellectuals across disciplines in this period. Marking a transitive position between the semiotic and structural theories of culture emerging from within anthropology, and the spatial aesthetic of what would become New Critical practices of reading and writing poetry, Cather illustrates the way in which the problematic of culture shaped literary criticism as well as anthropology.

Looked at this way, Cather's work also illuminates current debates over culture and "cultural studies," within both anthropology and literary studies. In some ways Cather's work illustrates the problem with culture that haunts postmodern anthropology: despite the progressive impetus behind the concept for those Boasian anthropologists that promoted it (separating race *from* culture, regional ways of life *from* forces of imperialism), in each of these novels, Cather deploys culture as an act of imperial "possession." At the same time, Cather's aesthetic of culture reveals the way in which the "aesthetic turn" marked by the New Critical emphasis on form in the 1930s was not so much a turn *from* culture, as a working out *of* the problematic of culture within literary studies— a problematic with which anthropology has also grappled, in parallel ways, as the two disciplines separated into their distinct disciplinary identities for the next several decades. The interdisciplinarity of cultural studies could be seen as a resumption of a dialogue begun in the 1920s, and the emerging reaction to cultural studies a turn of that same wheel. The current turn toward the aesthetic as an antidote to the "imperialism" of cultural studies might not be such a turn after all, but—because the aesthetic is already intertwined with the idea of culture—another expression of the problematic of culture.

3 / Cultures, Canons, and Cetology: Modernist Culture and the Melville Revival

I have argued that culture formed a central problematic for American anthropologists, writers, and critics in the 1920s and 1930s. Even as American artists and critics attempted to redefine the *content* of a particularly American culture, the *form* of culture was itself under intense debate, as nineteenth-century definitions of culture as a general process of development or refinement intertwined with new competing definitions of culture as "whole," "meaningful" ways of life. As American intellectuals struggled to come to terms with the rapid economic, technological, and social changes of the century's first decades, the dominant metaphors for describing the social scene were those of division/fragmentation and wholeness. In the face of perceived fragmentation on multiple levels, thinkers across a variety of disciplines attempted to locate and define the limits of the meaningful whole—be it a whole poem, a whole nation or political unit, or a whole way of life. In this context, then, this whole, meaningful way of life comes to be, by definition, "culture"—for anthropologists, artists, and literary critics, all of whom I suggest are working on a common project. The tensions within this debate structure both Edward Sapir's "Culture, Genuine and Spurious" and Willa Cather's changing use of the image of Indian art from early novels such as *The Song of the Lark* to *The Professor's House*, and the connections among culture, literary regionalism, and national identity that they articulate.

These debates are also central to understanding the changing ways literary texts were read and received in this period. This includes both the terms in which they were interpreted and evaluated and the construction of the literary tradition or history in which they were placed. Changes in what counts as culture change what counts as literature, and the way that culture is constructed or, to return to Cather's term, "designed," in turn transforms what counts as design in literature. As historians of American literary studies have shown, it is in the 1920s that American literature first became institutionalized in the academy as a separate discipline, and that the modern canon of American literature—with the handful of mid-nineteenth-century writers of what would come to be called the "American Renaissance" at its center—was established.[1] It was also the period in which what would come to be called "American Studies" first appeared.[2] These processes, I suggest, occurred around changes in the meaning of both "American" and "literature"—changes reflected in, and in some ways enabled by, changes in the meaning of culture.

If the category of American literature underwent a major shift in this decade, then the revival and canonization of Herman Melville in this same period could be said to be the paradigmatic example of this shift. Coming into the 1920s as a brief mention under a section entitled "Cooper and His Contemporaries" in the *Cambridge History of American Literature*, Melville ends the decade as the subject of three major biographies and several articles in the first year of the new journal *American Literature*, and being proclaimed as one of the representatives—along with Emerson, Thoreau, Hawthorne, and Whitman—of what Lewis Mumford would call America's "Golden Day," a pantheon whose status would become permanently enshrined in F. O. Matthiessen's *American Renaissance* in 1941.[3] The Melville revival and canonization of the 1920s, then, was located in an almost unique confluence of literary, cultural, and institutional histories. While other authors underwent reevaluation in this period, no other author's canonization has paralleled so closely the development and institutionalization of American literary studies in the academy through the twentieth century and thus has registered the complexities of the ideological debates that surround it.

The study of Melville studies, then, could be said to be the study of American literature as a discipline. And if, as Lionel Trilling puts it, criticism is the "dark and bloody crossroads where literature and politics meet," the critical reception of Herman Melville is a major intersection where the body count is particularly high.[4] Critics promoting the revival during the 1920s denounced their predecessors' Anglophilic, genteel rejection of Melville; mid-century New Critics and myth critics in turn critiqued the 1920s "liberals" for making his books "*directly* relevant to their concerns and interest"—namely, their post–World War I critique of American materialism and conformity.[5] With the rise of new historicism, poststructuralism, and cultural studies in the past three decades, New Americanists such as Lauter and William Spanos have targeted the conservative consensus politics of early Americanists, arguing that the Melville revival was "part of an ideological conflict which linked advocates of modernism and of traditional high cultural values ... against a social and cultural 'other,' ... portrayed as feminine, genteel, exotic, dark, foreign, and numerous." As a bulwark against the perceived threat of women, immigration, and a restive working class, they argue that "a distinctively masculine, Anglo-Saxon image of Melville was deployed as a lone and powerful artistic beacon against the dangers presented by the masses."[6] In perhaps the latest sideswipe in this intersection, Clare Spark takes to task the modernist "liberals" *and* "radical" New Americanists, arguing that both perpetuate a "conservative Enlightenment" reading of Ahab as an overreaching monomaniac who represents the forces that led to Hitler (for critics in the 1930s to the 1960s) or U.S. imperialism and racism (for New Americanists). Spark in turn charges that these readings themselves are committed to "corporatism" and "ethnopluralism"— philosophical positions rooted in German Romanticism and leading to, surprisingly, Hitler.[7] A bloody intersection indeed.

The example of Melville is a crucial one. Interest in Melville has increased at an astonishing rate since the beginning of the revival—the number of articles written on him nearly doubling every decade through the 1980s—until Melville has become one of the most written about authors in the American canon. As Myra Jehlen has shown, Melville has remarkably weathered, even thrived on, the major shifts in critical approaches that have occurred in the past twenty years.[8] With four major biographies written in the previous twelve years, several best sellers on subjects directly related to Melville, two television miniseries dramatizations (one starring Patrick Stewart and the other William Hurt, sure signs of "greatness"), several musical and theatrical interpretations of his works, and two new graphic novel versions in the last eight years, interest in Melville shows no signs of letting up.[9]

I would like to complicate accounts of the Melville revival and, by extension, the relationship among modernism, American literary canon formation, and American Studies by positioning the revival within the problematic of culture that I have been tracing. The changing terms by which Melville, and *Moby-Dick* in particular, was read and valued and the larger restructuring of the Americanist literary canon of which this revival was a central feature must be understood in the context of both the rise of the "anthropological" version of culture as relative, whole systems of meaning and the modernist fascination with the literary text as spatial form, which culminated in the reading practices of the New Criticism. Seen in this way, the Melville revival engages the problematic of culture and its key questions—what is culture, what is the "unit" of culture, and what is the relation between culture and form—and works those questions out in terms of how one reads a literary text. Questions of the boundedness of culture become questions of the boundedness of the text, and questions of regional, national, or universal culture become questions of canon formation, as canons (re)define the categorical relationships among the texts that make them up. Melville and new readings of *Moby-Dick*, I argue, become exemplars of new ways to understand and "read" cultures, new ways to understand and "read" texts, and new ways to configure textual canons to represent these new cultures.

To make this argument, I focus on several authors whose works on Melville in this period were crucial to his canonization—Raymond Weaver, Van Wyck Brooks, and Lewis Mumford. I begin by briefly reviewing the terms under which Van Wyck Brooks launched the quest for what he called a "usable past," articulated in works like *America's Coming-of-Age*, and which will become key terms in the Melville revival. I then turn to the Melville revival itself, beginning with Raymond Weaver's centenary Melville essay and, more important, his biography *Herman Melville: Mariner and Mystic* (1921). Focusing particularly on Weaver's treatment of *Typee*, I argue that Weaver engages the problem of culture in two ways. First, he makes Melville a symptom of Brooks's divided, essentially culture-less America, with Melville playing the heroic artist in contrast to a Philistine public unable to appreciate him. Second, he lays the groundwork for a way of reading Melville as synthesizing oppositions (romance and realism, science and imagination, artist and empiricist), which, in Brooks's and Mumford's later accounts, will become the hallmark of Melville's mid-nineteenth-century "genuine culture." More importantly, Weaver's emphasis on Melville's "experience" as an observer of the South Sea natives engages the epistemological concerns that were very much at the center of the debate over culture, and the appropriate methods to perceive and record that culture. This debate is expressed within anthropology most clearly in Bronislaw Malinowski's groundbreaking *Argonauts of the Western Pacific*, published a year after Weaver's biography.

I then turn to Van Wyck Brooks's "Reviewer's Notebook" essays on Melville in *The Freeman* in 1923, which help shift the terms under which Melville is received in the period. Brooks's initial evaluation of Melville's artistic failures, set in terms of division and incompleteness, give way to his revaluation of Melville's success in terms of an artistic "wholeness," which in turn represents cultural wholeness—or, more accurately, culture *as* wholeness—as articulated in his earlier essays.

Turning finally to Lewis Mumford's *Herman Melville* (1929), I place this biography of Melville in the context of both Mumford's arguments about culture, regionalism, and the state and Sapir's spatial aesthetic of culture as articulated in "Culture, Genuine and Spurious." Mumford, I suggest, constructs Melville as the embodiment of Sapir's "genuine culture," an entire, regionally based "way of life" in which all elements constitute a "meaningful whole." For Mumford, as for Sapir, this spatially conceived culture is characterized by "form"—an aesthetic form epitomized by *Moby-Dick* and grounded, not in the nation, but in the region. Placing Mumford's *Herman Melville* in dialogue with Sapir and Boasian anthropology reveals that the restructuring of the Americanist canon in this period was not merely a struggle to construct an "American culture" but part of a larger debate over the idea of "culture" itself, which was carried out *across* a range of disciplines and structured key terms of debate *within* each discipline in specific ways.

Examining this common context is thus mutually illuminating: fully unpacking Mumford's argument about *Moby-Dick* as literary form requires acknowledging the connection among culture, form, and region most clearly articulated by Sapir; similarly, recognizing Mumford's contemplation of culture in his literary criticism decenters anthropology as the prime locus in which theories of culture were being worked out in the period. Situating Mumford and the Melville revival in this way, moreover, complicates existing ideological readings of the revival, revealing common conceptual models that unite disciplines and movements generally seen as politically opposed. Far from proceeding under the banner of "traditional high cultural values" against the "social and cultural 'other,'" Mumford's construction of Melville arises in the context of an emerging model of cultural *pluralism*; rather than an expression of nationalism, Mumford's *Moby-Dick* emerges as an expression of a regionalism that resists the nation-state.

Weaver, Melville, and Malinowski: Heroes of Culture in the South Seas

If Van Wyck Brooks set the initial terms by—or against—which culture in the 1920s would be redefined, then he also early on made

Herman Melville a part of his program for American culture. In 1918, a year before Melville's centenary which launched the revival of the 1920s, Brooks singled out Melville as a possible source for a "usable past": "Englishmen," he states, "will ask you why we Americans have so neglected Herman Melville that there is no biography of him"; the "real task for the American literary historian, then," is to ask questions like "what happened to Herman Melville?"[10] A year later, the Melville centenary resulted in a spate of articles in American and British journals memorializing the author; by 1921 Brooks's wished-for biography was published: Raymond Weaver's *Herman Melville: Mariner and Mystic*.[11] Weaver, an instructor in English at Columbia University, had been approached by Carl Van Doren with the idea of a Melville biography; Weaver responded with an article in *The Nation* for the Melville centenary. That article (published only one month before Sapir's "Civilization and Culture" appeared in *The Dial*), along with Frank Jewett Mather's two-part article in *The Review*, served as the most influential opening salvos of the revival.[12] By 1921 Weaver had finished his biography, drawing on hitherto unknown letters and manuscripts obtained from Melville's daughter.

Weaver's biography of Melville was engaged in the problematic of culture as it was debated in the 1920s, both within the discipline of anthropology and in the writings of literary and social critics like Brooks, and this interconnection was part of a pattern that occurred throughout Melville criticism in the 1920s. Unlike Mumford, for whom culture is a central concept, Weaver does not theorize about culture explicitly. Indeed, while Weaver draws on Brooks's diagnosis of a divided America for his explanation of Melville and his career, Weaver never invokes Brooks's alternative of "organic" culture that places Brooks at the heart of the debate over culture in the period. Rather, Weaver's account of Melville—in particular his emphasis on Melville's experience with and representation of the Typees—engages several of the orienting questions that make up the problematic of culture. Specifically, Weaver makes Melville the exemplar of an epistemology and mode of representation that serve as critiques of the modern divide between pragmatism and idealism, at the very moment that these same epistemological and narrative concerns—and the tensions and contradictions that accompany them—are being debated within anthropology and find their most powerful expression in Bronislaw Malinowski's ethnography of the South Seas, *Argonauts of the Western Pacific* (1922).

Melville among the Philistines: Weaver's Arnoldian Culture

From the outset, Weaver's assessment of Melville's grandeur and his diagnosis of Melville's failure echo Brooks's description of American society as divided between vacuous idealism and crass materialism, with a genteel and commercially oriented public looking to literature primarily as entertainment or as a soporific to ease the way toward commercial gain. In an interpretation that would become commonplace in Melville criticism for the rest of the 1920s and 1930s, Weaver casts Melville as the romantic, rebellious artist whose genius could not be appreciated by the genteel and commercial standards of his time. In terms that recall Brooks's lowbrow mentality, Weaver sees the rumors of Melville's insanity in his later years as the defensive reaction of a Philistine public: "The dull and decent Philistine," he argues, "justifies his sterility in a boast of sanity. The America in which Melville was born and died was exuberantly and unquestionably 'sane.' Its 'sanity' drove Irving abroad and made a recluse of Hawthorne. Cooper alone throve upon it. And of Melville, more ponderous in gifts and more volcanic in energy than any other American writer, it made an Ishmael upon the face of the earth" (*Mariner*, 18).

In Weaver's "Philistine" and "sane" America, the artist is fated to rebel against and fall victim to the materialism of his or her age. Reiterating Brooks's narrative of division and artistic alienation—a narrative Brooks himself pursued in his biographies of James and Twain even as Weaver was writing his biography—Weaver claims that "Melville's warring and untamed desires were in violent conflict with his physical and spiritual environment," and his career was "an attempt to escape from an inexorable and intolerable world of reality." Here, "reality" means the materialism and commercialism of Melville's (and Weaver's) America: Weaver sees Melville "held closer to reality by financial worry and the hostages of wife and children," and quotes Melville's now-famous letter to Hawthorne lamenting how "dollars damn me...., What I feel most moved to write, that is banned—it will not pay. Yet, altogether write the *other* way I cannot. So the product is a final hash, and all my books are botches" (*Mariner*, 321, emphasis in original). Like Brooks, Weaver condemns the highbrow "culture of industrialism's" concern for formal perfection, which prevents the recognition of Melville's "complexity and versatility" and the strength of his "imagination." *Moby-Dick*'s defects, he argues, are "formal rather than substantial," and genteel America's "overweening concern for formal impeccability is a fatal sign of weakened vitality."

Instead, Weaver argues, "intensity of imagination... is an infinitely rarer and more precious gift than technical sophistication" (28).

While Weaver takes up Brooks's diagnosis of a divided America that thwarts the efforts of the true artist, he does not take the next step to imagine Brooks's alternative, organic culture uniting artist and society. Weaver instead rests on the distinction between the artist's genius and the "herd" of unappreciative Philistines, a situation ameliorated only by an elite readership (like Weaver) that is able to understand Melville's "complexity and versatility" and sympathize with his rebellion against genteel conventions. In both his centenary article in *The Nation* and his Melville biography, Weaver emphasizes the exclusive nature of an appreciation for Melville: "Neither 'Lycidas' nor 'Moby-Dick,'" he says, "should be read by philistines or pragmatists" who will be unable to appreciate their innovative elements; "the 'popular mind'"—implicitly opposed to critics like Weaver—is unable to see Melville as anything but "an obscure adventurer in strange seas and among amiable barbarians" (*Mariner*, 21). In emphasizing this split between the "popular mind" and those who have sufficiently sophisticated taste to understand Melville, Weaver constructs a normative theory of culture that is closer to a nineteenth-century Arnoldian version of culture than to that of Brooks: art is not the expression of a "whole way of life" but is the product of individual genius, above and separate from the larger society.

"Written from the Inside": Melville, Ethnography, and the Epistemology of Experience

Although Weaver does not enlist Melville as part of a reexamination of culture as such, he does construct Melville as the exemplary model of a Brooksian epistemology of experience, uniting facts with imagination to overcome the dualism of pragmatic materialism and romantic idealism. This kind of experience is embodied above all for Weaver in Melville's South Sea adventures, and their representation in *Typee*. And while Weaver's biographical emphasis on Melville's encounter with the Typees is in many ways typical of Melville's critical reception at the time of the revival (as Melville feared, at his centenary he was indeed remembered best as "a man who lived among the cannibals"), Weaver gives the encounter a new emphasis. Explicitly contrasting Melville's depiction of the Typees to the primitive romanticism of Melville's contemporaries, Weaver emphasizes Melville's ability to gain an "inside" view of Typee life—to be, one might say, a participant-observer of Typee society.

As many critics have pointed out, Melville's rediscovery coincided with, and was in many ways driven by, the fascination with the South Seas, and "primitive" ways of life in general, that characterized both popular and modernist imagination in the 1920s.[13] The year of Melville's centenary, for example, saw the publication of Frederick O'Brian's *White Shadows in the South Seas*; Somerset Maugham's *The Moon and Sixpence*; and the first translation of Gauguin's Tahitian journal *Noa Noa* into English, which, along with his paintings, helped spur this fascination. Indeed, journalists and critics writing on Melville in the early 1920s themselves frequently pointed, either in celebration or with disdain, to the "vogue of the South Seas" as the immediate source of Melville's newfound fame, and Melville was often cited in articles about the South Seas themselves in the early years of the revival.[14]

As the founder of what one reviewer called "the South Sea Style," then, in the early years of the revival, Melville was valued as much for *Typee* and *Oomo* as he was for *Moby-Dick*.[15] Thus, Frank Jewett Mather concludes that "having saved a vanishing charm for posterity, *Typee* may be his most important book"; even into the 1930s, critics like Charles Anderson could write that "the survival value of Melville's reputation lies in the fact that he was the literary discoverer of the South Sea."[16]

Following this pattern, in Weaver's biography, the "most obvious" of Melville's claims to fame is that he was the "literary discoverer of the South Seas"; the less obvious claim is that he, along with Richard Dana, was "the first to lift the hatch and show the world what passes in a ship's forecastle," and the least obvious of all was *Moby-Dick*, "Melville's undoubted masterpiece" (24–25). Reflecting the way many early critics took Melville's novels as autobiographical and saw his later years as tragic decline, Weaver devotes as many pages to the four years between Melville's departure on the whaling vessel *Acushnet* in 1841 and his return on the *United States* in 1844 as to the next forty-seven years until Melville's death; of those pages, as much space is given to a history of colonial involvement in the Marquesas and Melville's supposed four months in the Typee valley, as there is to whaling and *Moby-Dick*.[17]

If in the first two claims to fame in Weaver's list—and indeed, to some extent in the third, as we shall see—Melville is valued as an observer and recorder of heretofore hidden ways of life, then Weaver makes clear that Melville is a particular *kind* of observer. Echoing Brooks's definition of "experience" as the fusion of the objective material world and the subjective emotional or imaginative world, Weaver repeatedly emphasizes Melville's "imagination," which "enrich[ed] the immediate facts of experience." As with Brooks, Weaver's opponent is the "efficiency expert," represented by Benjamin Franklin, for whom the objective gaze of science is for purely utilitarian purposes, who "may indeed bring lightning from the clouds, [but] makes the transfer not to glorify the firmament, but to discipline the lightning and to make church steeples safe from the wrath of God"(73).

Melville's transcendence of the traditional opposition between the objective reality of science and the subjectivity of imagination is made even clearer in Weaver's description of *Moby-Dick*. Describing Melville's mix of "blubber and mysticism" in the novel, Weaver concludes that, while not a "reliable report of personal experience" as he believes *Redburn, Typee, Omoo,* and *White-Jacket* to be, it nonetheless "incidentally... offers one of the fullest, and truest, and most readable history of an actual whaling cruise ever written." Contrasting empirical accuracy to truth, Weaver suggests that "the 'scientific' historian, proudly unreadable, thanks God that he has no style to tempt him out of the strict weariness of counting-house inventories; and in despair of presenting the truth, he boasts a make-shift veracity." Instead, "the truest historians are, of course the poets," and "Melville, writing in the capacity of poet, was licensed in the best interest of truth to expurgate reality" (133). For Weaver, then, "truth," like Brooks's "experience," is found not in the objectivity of pragmatic science, but in the integration of fact with imagination.

The central site of this Brooksian experience is the South Seas, where Weaver differentiates Melville's description of the Typees both from the interested, pragmatic accounts given by missionaries and colonial explorers and from the purely imaginative accounts of "noble savages" given by romantics. Surveying the negative portrayal of the South Sea Islanders in the major explorer and missionary accounts that preceded Melville, Weaver concludes that "one searches in vain among these records for any very vivid sense that the savage and the Christian belong to the same order of nature." Thus, when Melville arrived at Nukaheva, "the Polynesians were without a competent apologist, and the literary possibilities of the South Seas were unsuspected" (203). At the same time, Weaver points to the romantic reaction of "imputing to the unbreeched heathen a touching array of the superior virtues"—the "myth of the 'noble savage'"—and sees this as the product of "a willful backward glance to the vanished paradise of childhood, not a finding of ethnology" (204).

In contrast, according to Weaver, Melville's account is neither that of the pragmatic colonial nor that of the romantic artist writing with no firsthand knowledge. Previous observers of Polynesia, Weaver writes, were men of "insular imagination," whose descriptions succeed in "telling us much of the writer, but never violating the heart of Polynesia" (207). Melville, however, succeeds in "violating its heart" through precisely the combination of experience and imagination his predecessors lacked. His was, Weaver stresses, no "kid-gloved and expensively staged dip into studio savagery," but an immersion in Typee daily life:

> [He] chatted, he smoked, he drowsed [among] the bachelors of the Ti, the men's club of the valley. . . . He witnessed the Feast of the Calabashes when, for the livelong day "the drums sounded and the priest chanted, and the multitude roared and feasted." . . . He entered the funeral fastnesses where the effigies of former heroes eternally paddled canoes adorned by the skulls of their enemies. . . . He heard . . . the clamour of a cannibal feast, and lifted the cover of a tub under which lay a fresh human skeleton. (212)

This combination of experience and imagination, being "the first competent literary artist" who wrote "with authority about the South Seas," in turn produces a new kind of ethnology (15). Melville, Weaver argues, "intuitively understood them, caught their point of view, respected and often admired it" (207). With a combination of firsthand experience and an imaginative sympathy that allowed him to "intuitively" understand the Typee point of view, Melville produces what amounts to an ethnography that is, as Frank Jewett Mather put it, "in a peculiar sense written from the inside," a Typee account of Typee society.[18]

Thus, Melville emerges in Weaver's account not just as an observer of Typee life, but a very particular kind of observer. It must be remembered that in many ways, *Typee*'s success depended from the very beginning on Melville's status as an observer, and on its accuracy as a document. Melville had to swear, for example, that *Typee* was in fact a true story in order to convince his English publishers to print the book. Praise for the novel through the late nineteenth and early twentieth centuries often centered on its accuracy of observation. The documentary accuracy of the novel had in turn resulted by the 1920s in a certain authority within the discipline of ethnology, with Sir James Frazer, for example, citing *Typee* frequently in his accounts of Polynesian tribal practices such as *The Belief in Immortality and the Worship of the Dead*.[19] Weaver's construction of Melville as an ethnographer, however, is precisely not that of Frazer's—that is, an observer accurate and objective enough to provide information that could be compiled and organized by the scholar in the metropole. Rather, Weaver constructs Melville as an observer who combines direct observation based on experience with an imagination—and in particular a "literary" imagination—allowing him to see and represent the native's point of view.[20]

Crucially, however, Weaver argued that Melville's narrative is "written from the inside" only in a "peculiar" sense; that is, it is *not* written from the inside and is *not* a Typee account of Typee society. Melville's "peculiar" status as an observer depends on the tension between—not the resolution of—the two poles of the dialectic, the outside observer and the imaginative participant. At the most literal level, Weaver is careful to make clear that Melville remains ultimately outside the circle of Typee life: he was, Weaver assures us, "never tempted to resign himself to its vacant animal felicity.... While among them, he evinced a desire neither to adopt their ways, nor to change them" (211). This outsider status is most clearly maintained in Melville's refusal to get tattooed, which "was to Melville the outward and visible sign of the lowest degradation" (196). More important, however, is the way this tension is required to give the kind of account Weaver claims Melville makes. While a strictly "objective" account would not "penetrate the heart" of the South Seas, so too a purely empathetic or imaginative identification would also be inadequate. Surrounded by the "taken for granted" quality of a way of life, a Typee could not present an intelligible or analytic account of that life without stepping outside it. As I have shown in the work of Brooks, Sapir, and Cather, it is this central tension—of the relation of part to whole, of immersion in "reality" and the need for "selection," of the listing of traits versus the apprehension of the whole—that characterizes the debate over culture and how to represent it in this period.

The "Imponderabilia of Actual Life": Malinowski, Literature, and the Epistemology of Experience

Weaver's model of Melville as combining observation and imagination to produce the native's point of view, it turns out, is also the model of the new kind of ethnographer constructed by the anthropologist Bronislaw Manliowski in his seminal account of his own South Seas adventure, *Argonauts of the Western Pacific*, published a year after Weaver's biography.[21] As historians of anthropology have long noted, Malinowski's *Argonauts* has come to mark, for those within the discipline as well as for the public at large, the emergence of the modern anthropologist, establishing both the anthropologist's proper methodology—"fieldwork"—and the generic form through which the anthropologist's special knowledge is conveyed—the ethnography.[22] At the same time, critics like Marc Manganaro have situated Malinowski's text within the broader context of Anglo-American modernism, beginning with the fact that *Argonauts* first appears in the same year as Eliot's *The Waste Land* and Joyce's *Ulysses*.[23] Here, I suggest the ways in which Weaver's construction of Melville, and the Melville revival more broadly, engages the same problematic of epistemology, narrative, and culture as Malinowski's ethnographic innovations. Like Weaver's Melville, Malinowski constructs the "ethnographer's magic" as the ability to "grasp the native's point of view, his relation to life, to realize *his* vision of *his* world" (*Argonauts*, 6, 25, emphasis in original). The primary method by which this could be done—the methodological innovation that made Malinowski a model for the next several generations of anthropologists—was the "experience" of fieldwork, which would allow the ethnographer to combine accurate observation with the literary evocation of the "imponderabilia of actual life," in much the manner that Weaver ascribes to Melville (*Argonauts*, 18). Malinowski's theoretical justification for his new methodology of participant-observation, and ultimately the narrative techniques by which he portrays both the whole of Trobriand culture and the mythic role of the anthropologist-as-hero, addresses many of the same epistemological and ideological concerns that lie behind Weaver's construction of Melville and *Typee*.

In connecting Weaver's biography of Melville to Malinowski's ethnography, I am not suggesting that Weaver was directly influenced by Malinowski's work, or vice versa, but rather that both Weaver and Malinowski form part of an interdisciplinary debate over culture, a problematic that structures key questions within each particular discipline. But while the Polish-born, European-educated, and Cambridge-based Malinowski was not as tightly woven into the New York–based network of American modernisms as Sapir and other Boasian anthropologists, he is clearly a part of what Michael North has argued is a more extensive, transnational "matrix of modernism" incorporating a wider variety of disciplines and figures than has generally been considered.[24]

Several critics have articulated some of the complex dialogues between what sometimes have been viewed as two "national traditions": the Americanist Boasian tradition, emphasizing linguistics and historical particularism, and British structural-functionalism. Boas himself began his career working for the British Association Committee on the North-west Tribes of Canada in 1886. His employment marked, as

Stocking notes, the beginning of a shift in British ethnological method toward academically trained natural scientists, who would both collect ethnographic data and formulate theory.[25] Other critics have suggested that both Boas's and Malinowski's common experience of immigration, mobility, and alienation—a condition that applies to many of Boas's students, including Sapir—resulted in their similar theoretical emphases on cultures as "whole."[26] Boasian anthropologists, in later years, asserted that they had been practicing participant-observation all along, and that—as evinced by my earlier discussion of Sapir—the idea of culture as a synchronic, integrated unit contained in Malinowski's functionalism was nothing new. Conversely, as Regna Darnell, North, and Manganaro have shown, Malinowski's interest in ethnographic semantics made him part of the vigorous Anglo-American debate involving anthropologists, literary critics, and philosophers, over meaning and language. Malinowski's essay "The Problem of Meaning in Primitive Language" appeared in C. K. Ogden and I. A. Richard's *The Meaning of Meaning* in 1923, which was reviewed by Sapir in *The Freeman* (which was in turn edited by Van Wyck Brooks) and which was highly influential in the formation of the New Criticism of Allen Tate and John Crowe Ransom (a connection I examine more closely in chapter 4). Ogden, as North has shown, was simultaneously reading the work of another Cambridge colleague, Ludwig Wittgenstein, and corresponding with and publishing the work of Harlem Renaissance poets like James Weldon Johnson and Claude McKay. Thus, in connecting Malinowski and Weaver here, I both situate the Melville revival within the interdisciplinary debate over culture in American modernist anthropology, literary criticism, and canon formation and also indicate the way this debate—over Melville and over culture—is part of a broader debate shaping transnational modernism.

Central to Malinowski's theory of ethnographic knowledge is "experience." Famously uniting what previously had been two separate roles—the data-gathering ethnographer in the field and the metropolitan "armchair anthropologist" who received and organized these data into vast compendiums of cross-cultural comparisons—Malinowski's "ethnographer" derives his or her authority from the central experience of fieldwork, that is, the direct, extended encounter with the people under investigation.[27] The "most elementary" aspect of fieldwork, Malinowski writes, is "to live without other white men, right among the natives . . . by camping right in their villages" (*Argonauts*, 6). In an extended passage that resembles Weaver's catalogue of Melville's access to Typee life, Malinowski describes how the ethnographer begins "to take part, in a way, in the village life, to look forward to the important or festive events, to take personal interest in the gossip and the developments of the small village occurrences; to wake up every morning to a day, presenting itself to me more or less as it does the native.... Quarrels, jokes, family scenes, events usually trivial, sometimes dramatic but always significant, formed the atmosphere of my daily life, as well as of theirs" (7–8).

What is crucial here is the kind of knowledge that "experience" provides. Negotiating between two inadequate sides of an epistemological dualism—much like Brooks's rejection of both highbrow and lowbrow perspectives, and like Weaver's disparagement of both the biased missionary and the idealistic romantic in favor of Melville's lived experience—Malinowski contrasts the ethnographer's knowledge to both pragmatic knowledge and abstract theory. Information obtained from local white residents is "full of the biased and pre-judged opinions inevitable in the average *practical* man, whether administrator, missionary or trader" (emphasis added); here, as for Brooks and Weaver, it is the "practical" nature of the knowledge, that it comes from the desire to "transform or influence or make use of" the natives, that makes it "strongly repulsive to a mind striving after the objective, scientific view of things" (*Argonauts*, 5–6). Malinowski's method equally opposes abstract theory, in this case, the idea of "boundless liberty" associated with the primitive. "In popular thinking," he argues, "we imagine that the natives live on the bosom of Nature, more or less as they can and like, the prey of irregular, phantasmagoric beliefs and apprehensions." Anthropology (under his guidance) "on the contrary shows that their social institutions have a very definite organization, that they are governed by authority, law and order in their public and personal relations.... Indeed we see them entangled in a mesh of duties, functions and privileges which correspond to an elaborate tribal, communal and kinship organization" (*Argonauts*, 10). In language that parallels Sapir's description of the "firmness with which every part of [native] life ... is bound together in a significant whole," Malinowski contrasts the abstract, romantic notion of primitives in a state of nature with natives "entangled in a mesh" of communal meaning and organization—that is, in the mesh of culture. Weaver and Malinowski thus engage similar targets with the epistemology they privilege: in both cases, experience provides knowledge that is neither the practical knowledge of the missionary and colonial nor the purely theoretical constructs of savage "freedom" or economic rationality.

Like Weaver, Brooks, Sapir, and many of the other figures in this study, Malinowski poses "culture" as an antidote to what he and they perceive as modern civilization's mechanistic worldview, where rationalism and efficiency are the measures of value. This common target is exemplified in one particular image that Malinowski is at pains to "explode, once and for ever": the notion of "Primitive Economic Man of some current economic text books.... In popular and semi-popular economic literature," Malinowski contends, the "primitive man, or savage" is taken as a model of rational choice theory, "prompted in all his actions by a rationalistic conception of self-interest, and achieving his aims directly and with the minimum of effort" (60). Intimate study of the Trobriands, however, exposes the inadequacy of this abstraction: in language that echoes Sapir's contrast of the telephone girl and the Indian salmon fisher, Malinowski's native is "prompted by motives of a highly complex, social and traditional nature," and works "toward aims which are certainly not directed towards the satisfaction of present wants, or to the direct achievement of utilitarian purposes" (60). Echoing Cather's theory of art in *The Song of the Lark*, in which the Cliff Dwellers' aesthetic labor was precisely nonutilitarian, Malinowski argues that "work is not carried out on the principle of the least effort. On the contrary, much time and energy is spent on wholly unnecessary effort, that is, from a utilitarian point of view. Again work and effort instead of being merely a means to an end, are, in a way an end in themselves.... All this shows how entirely the real native of flesh and bone differs from the shadowy Primitive Economic man, on whose imaginary behavior many of the scholastic deductions of *abstract* economics are based" (61, emphasis added).[28]

In opposing the abstract, rationalist image of "Primitive Economic Man" with the native whose work is "prompted by motives of a highly complex, social and traditional nature"—that is, by culture—Malinowski echoes many of the figures in this study, for whom the "Economic Man" formed a particularly potent symbol (or straw man). For Brooks, "political economy's" conception of "economic man" epitomizes both highbrow and lowbrow values—highbrow because it is an abstraction incapable of recognizing the "infinitely variegated and everchanging" nature of the "human material" that is its subject, and lowbrow because it abstracts exactly the practical as essential.[29] The mathematician and philosopher of science Alfred North Whitehead, in his influential *Science and the Modern World*, critiques modern science's "attention to *things* as opposed to *values*," a tendency he sees epitomized in "the abstractions of political economy."[30] For John Crowe Ransom, as I will discuss later, economic man constitutes yet another abstraction of science, to be countered with the full particularity of the "world's body," embodied in "a culture" and in the form of the poem. And where for Brooks this nonutilitarian "joy in labor" is called "art," for anthropologists like Malinowski and Sapir, it is "culture," in which economic activity "works in naturally with all the rest of the [native's] activities" and thus has meaning in itself.[31]

My point here is not simply to list similarities, but to suggest that these recurrent images—in this case, the image of the abstract "economic man"—indicate the ways in which Malinowski's epistemology of participant-observation and Weaver's construction of Melville both respond to a similar set of epistemological and social concerns. These concerns were shared by intellectuals across a variety of disciplines, revolving around a perceived split between the material and the ideal, the scientific and the imaginative, or the economic and the artistic. In each case, the response is to imagine modes of knowledge that might reveal the "whole." While Weaver leaves this "whole" unnamed, locating the transcendence of the opposition between fact and imagination in Melville himself, for Malinowski (and Sapir, Brooks, and Mumford), the answer to this condition of dissociation is "culture."

Malinowski most often poses his alternative to pragmatism or idealism as "objective science." This appeal to objectivity, however, is complicated by Malinowski's characterization in other moments of the anthropologist's special knowledge as not merely rational, but bodily and intuitive, and the proper representation of this knowledge as aesthetic. For all his emphasis on scientific objectivity, Malinowski begins his methodological justification on aesthetic grounds: while the trained scientist can use "statistical documentation"—synoptic charts, tables, and so on—to reveal the order governing seemingly chaotic native life, the "best amateur" observers "often excel" in "the presentation of intimate touches of native life [and] surpass in plasticity and in vividness most of the purely scientific accounts" (*Argonauts*, 17–18). This "plasticity" and "vividness," it turns out, are the result of living among the natives for an extended period, allowing the author to "perceive or imagine the realities of human life, the even flow of everyday events, the occasional ripples of excitement over a feast, or ceremony, or some singular occurrence[,] . . . phenomena of great importance which cannot possibly be recorded by questioning or computing documents, but have to be observed in their full actuality." These are, he asserts "*the imponderabilia of actual life*" (18, emphasis in original). Here, the "realities" of life, the "actual," are not available to strictly quantitative measures, or even discrete statements (they cannot be recorded by "questioning"); they must be "observed in their full actuality" by the ethnographer, where that observation is not merely visual, but experiential, in which the ethnographer participates and observes. Malinowski requires the "ethnographer sometimes... to put aside camera, notebook and pencil, and to join in himself in what is going on. He can take part in native's games, he can follow them on their visits and walks, sit down and listen and share in their conversations" (21). The goal here is to become, as Sir James Frazer puts it in his preface to *Argonauts*, "a native among natives" (vii).

The resulting knowledge blurs the traditional subject-object distinction that characterizes most descriptions of objective science. Rather than "facts... scientifically formulated and recorded... by superficial registration of details," Malinowski imagines "penetrating the mental attitude expressed in them," seeing ultimately "the native's point-of-view" (19, 25). And unlike the model of the objective scientist as impersonal—a neutral observer whose objectivity is guaranteed precisely through his impersonality—Malinowski admits that "the personal equation of the observer" is crucial to his method, which depends on the "plasticity" of the ethnographer and his or her ability to fit in with—one might say become—a native. Participant-observation likewise blurs the distinction between the rational, perceiving mind of the observer and his or her body, as Malinowski repeatedly invokes "feeling" (as opposed to seeing) as a legitimate source for knowledge. The observer's "plunges into the life of the natives" leave him or her with "a distinct feeling" that their behavior "became more transparent and easily understandable than it had been before," and this understanding in turn marks itself on the anthropologist's body *as* a "feeling." Describing his initiation into the life of the village, Malinowski describes how he "acquired 'the feeling' for native good and bad manners. With this... I began to feel that I was indeed in touch with the natives" (8). In this moment, the ethnographer literally embodies the traits and practices that before he or she could only observe as "facts... recorded by superficial registration of details." Like Brooks, who imagined "experience" as the common "firm surface" upon which a people's ideals and values grow, the experience of participant-observation gives the ethnographer access to the "good and bad manners" of the native culture that observation alone could not afford.

Moreover, the ethnographer's embodiment of native culture is doubled by Malinowski's characterization of that culture *as* a body. The statistical "survey work" of the merely observing scientist is able to give "an excellent skeleton, so to speak, of the tribal constitution, but it lacks flesh and blood" (*Argonauts*, 17). This "flesh and blood," it turns out, are exactly the "imponderabilia" that are made available to the participant-observer, as is the "spirit—the native's views and opinions and utterances" (made available by the anthropologists' mastery of the native language) (*Argonauts*, 22). Thus, the sum total of the traits and practices that the anthropologist describes—the native's culture—is figured as a person, with a skeleton, flesh, and spirit. More precisely, it is a literary character.

By imagining the experience of participant-observation as allowing the ethnographer to "feel" like a native, and thus have access to his or her vision of his world, Malinowski imagines a kind of knowledge similar to Weaver's description of Melville's "intuitive" understanding of the Typee. In both cases, the combination of experience and imagination, observation and feeling, forms a romantic synthesis of the split between the material (the interested knowledge of the "practical" man) and the theoretical or ideal (the abstractions of the "noble savage"; "primitive economic man"; and, it turns out, the objective knowledge of the merely observing scientist).[32] Critics like Clifford have long pointed to the quasi-mystical nature of Malinowski's version of experiential knowledge: as he puts it, "It is difficult to say very much about experience. Like 'intuition,' it is something that one does or does not have, and its invocation often smacks of mystification.... Ethnographic experience... makes use of clues, traces, gestures and scraps of sense prior to the development of stable interpretations. Such piecemeal forms of experience may be classified as aesthetic and/or divinatory."[33] In this sense Malinowski's naming the ethnographer's work as "magic" is not merely playful, but an attempt to name that element of ethnography beyond the neutral gaze of science, just as Weaver suggests Melville "intuitively" understands the Typees.

At the same time, as discussed earlier, it is crucial for Weaver's construction of Melville that he does not actually become a Typee; the refusal to be tattooed stands as one marker of the mobility (one might say the paradox) of Melville's position as one who is (according to Weaver) both "inside" and "outside" Typee life. Similarly, for Malinowski, it is important that the ethnographer *is* a professionally trained scientist and is still adept at using synoptic charts, questionnaires, and so on—the tools of scientific observations that will allow the ethnographer to perceive the underlying structures and patterns (the "skeleton") of which the native, ensconced "in it, cannot be aware" (*Argonauts*, 83). In a position echoed by Weaver's Melville (and Sapir's anthropologist and grammarian, and Cather's Tom Outland), the Ethnographer must be both inside and outside, participant and observer, creator and recorder.

Malinowski himself suggests that if the ethnographer's knowledge is derived in part through "magic," it is properly represented aesthetically, and its aesthetic superiority in turn guarantees its authority for representing the "real." Weaver contrasts the "truth" of Melville's imaginative narratives to the "'scientific' historian, proudly unreadable [who] has no style"; similarly, Malinowski imagines the ethnographer conveying a "plasticity and ... vividness" unavailable to "the purely scientific accounts." Malinowski's explicitly literary ambitions for his ethnography are captured in the now-famous phrase he wrote to his colleague B. Z. Seligman, "[W. H. R.] Rivers is the Rider Haggard of Anthropology: I shall be the Conrad!"[34]

Critics like Stocking have glossed this comment as Malinowski's ambition to portray the natives' deep psychological complexity; however, it underscores Malinowski's thinking of his ethnography in literary terms. If Malinowski conceives culture as a person, he also conceives it as a literary character: much like Weaver proclaiming Melville the "literary discoverer of the South Seas," Malinowski writes, "It is I who describe them or create them [the Trobriands].... This island, though not 'discovered' by me, is for the first time experienced artistically and mastered intellectually."[35] Malinowski was deeply concerned not just with collecting accurate data, but also with representation and how to "bring [his experience] home to his readers in a clear, convincing manner" (*Argonauts*, 21). As Stocking has shown, beyond gestures toward his own experience, Malinowski turned to several rhetorical and literary techniques to accomplish this: the "scene/act ratio" that puts the reader within a vividly described environment ("When, on a hot day, we enter the deep shadow of fruit trees and palms, we find ourselves ... " [35]); the "author/reader equation" ("Imagine yourself suddenly set down ... alone on a tropical beach close to a native village" [4]); and the narrative structure of the ethnography itself, taking the reader step by step on the long voyage of the Kula circuit, and in a way that strongly suggests that Malinowski himself made the journey (when in fact he did not, and much of his account is reconstructed from interviews with informants). Malinowski's "tale" (as he called it in the initial title, "Kula: A Tale of Native Enterprise and Adventure in Eastern New Guinea") consciously presents itself as both objective and aesthetic, science and "magic."[36] It is in this tension between "describing" and "creating," "experiencing artistically" and "mastering intellectually," that I locate both Malinowski's ethnographic method and Weaver's South Sea Melville; this tension, I argue, characterizes the problematic of culture in both its anthropological and its literary expressions.

Composing Culture, Making Myth

For both Weaver and Malinowski, this combination of the experience and imagination is closely related to "myth." Myths, of course, are one of the overt subjects of Malinowski's ethnography; throughout his work, he relates Trobriand myths about the Kula, the complex inter-island circuit of ritual and economic exchange around which the narrative is organized. More important for my purposes here, however, are the mythic resonances that Malinowski gives the narrative. As the Homeric title of the ethnography suggests, Malinowski clearly wants to endow the Trobriands and especially the Kula with a mythic aura. He refers to the natives as "Homeric heroes" (*Argonauts*, 295), and in tracing the circular pattern of the Kula ring, the narrative enacts the classic myth of the voyage quest and return. Moreover, as several critics have pointed out, the real hero of the myth embodied by *Argonauts* is "the Ethnographer," whose own trials and tribulations are described in a narrative parallel to the narrative of the Kula. As Clifford puts it, "*Argonauts* is a complex narrative simultaneously of Trobriand life and ethnographic fieldwork," which describes Malinowski's own experience in the field, and thereby prescribes the archetypal narrative of the fieldworker's experience as such.[37] Creating what Stocking calls "a kind of euhemerist myth—divinizing ... not its ostensible Trobriand heroes, but the European Jason who brings back the Golden Fleece of ethnographic knowledge," Malinowski establishes the anthropologist as the hero of culture.[38]

Weaver's account of Melville similarly establishes Melville as a hero of mythic proportions, repeatedly describing Melville as a "Ulysses" whose entire career formed a "tragic Odyssey away from home, out in search of the 'the unpeopled world behind the sun'" (*Mariner*, 15, 19). And just as Malinowski's account of the Trobriands mythologizes the ethnographer as the true hero, so too does Weaver's interpretation of Melville's novels add up, not to an assessment of their qualities as individual works of literature, but to the greatness of their author. "Indeed," writes Weaver, "Melville's complete works, in their final analysis, are a long effort toward the creation of one of the most complex, and massive and original characters in literature: the character known in life as Herman Melville" (*Mariner*, 29). For both Weaver and Malinowski, myth marks the attempt to fuse the imaginative and the real, the material and the ideal. Malinowski defines myth in *Argonauts* as having both a prescriptive and a legitimating function, describing ideal forms of behavior and anchoring them in a distant but living past. Acting as a "cultural force" legitimating and giving value to certain norms and institutions, myth, Malinowski elaborates in *Myth in Primitive Psychology* (1926), "functions especially where there is a sociological strain," bridging the gap between past tradition and present, perhaps very different, conditions.[39] Similarly, for both Malinowski in his own ethnography and Weaver in his account of Melville, myth marks the attempt to bridge the epistemological gap between the materialist knowledge of science and imagination, intuition, and art.

Thus, Weaver's presentation of Melville at the start of the Melville revival, and Malinowski's groundbreaking work in the methods and theory of anthropology must be seen as participating in similar projects. Both texts construct an epistemology and aesthetic based on the fusion of experience and imagination, the material and the ideal, that is intended to serve as an alternative to the partial knowledge of either scientific abstraction or practical utility. For both, the South Seas provide a realm in which such Brooksian experience is available. For Weaver, Melville's combination of experience and imagination allows him access to the native's point of view, expressed in *Typee*; for Malinowski, the ethnographer achieves a similar glimpse at the native's view of "his world," through the combination of scientific observation and empathetic identification that is participant observation. Melville emerges from Weaver's description as the heroic author who can represent this experience in art; for Malinowski, the ethnographer is the hero who is able to comprehend the native's way of life, and to capture it forever in the form of the ethnography even as that way of life is disintegrating through contact with modernity.

Thus, Weaver's account of Melville and Malinowski's ethnography rest on two versions of culture in complex tension. For Weaver, Melville represents the romantic genius whose art is beyond the understanding of a Philistine public, both in his own time and in Weaver's. Melville's unique knowledge and its representation are "art" and take their place in a hierarchy of "Culture" that is more like Arnold's definition than Brooks's organic culture. At the same time, Melville's art is generated in the fruitful tension between observation and imagination, or in genuine experience produced by the interaction of both.

This same problematic structures the tension in Malinowski's theory of ethnography, but in reverse. Malinowski's methodology of participant-observer is intimately linked to, and indeed made necessary by, his version of culture as a complex, meaningful whole. The ethnographer cannot master just one or another aspect of tribal life but must comprehend "the whole area of tribal culture" in order to uncover "the consistency, the law and order which obtain within each aspect [and join] them into one coherent whole" (*Argonauts*, 11). Forming a functional whole, self-contained and self-defining, the "law and order" governing it can be understood only from the inside, from a position that allows the ethnographer to see each utterance and practice as connected to and given meaning by its place within that complex whole. Thus, as Malinowski points out, one cannot understand the significance of even a single object without the intimate knowledge that comes from living among the natives. He uses the Trobriand canoe as an example:

> a canoe is an item of material culture, and as such it can be described, photographed and even bodily transported into a museum. But . . . the ethnographic reality of the canoe would not be brought much nearer to a student at home, even by placing a perfect specimen right before him.
>
> The canoe is made for a certain use, and with a definite purpose. . . . Further sociological data, referring to its ownership, accounts of who sails in it, and how it is done; information regarding the ceremonies and customs of its construction, a sort of typical life history of a native craft—all this brings us nearer still to the understanding of what his canoe truly means to the native. (*Argonauts*, 105)

Thus, knowledge of any one aspect of a culture necessarily leads to every other. At the same time, the ethnographer must also be the outsider, able to discern the structure that remains invisible to the native within the encompassing horizon of the cultural whole. Thus, the ethnographer marks the limit of the "whole" native culture; he himself however is not part of an organic culture of his own, as proven by his own mobility. Weaver's Melville is thus in some respects a hero of Culture; Malinowski's ethnographer is the hero of cultures; and both Weaver and Malinowski engage in a common conversation through the problematic of culture.

Van Wyck Brooks: *Moby-Dick* as Melville's Wine

I have argued that Raymond Weaver's biography of Herman Melville takes as its point of departure a fundamental split between the artistic genius and a Philistine public that echoes Van Wyck Brooks's diagnosis of a divided America. It is Brooks himself who takes the next step, imagining Melville's art as healing that split, becoming the textual embodiment of the kind of organic culture that Brooks envisioned in his earlier writings. Brooks's comments on Melville, in a series of articles in his "Reviewer's Notebook" in the radical journal *The Freeman* between October 1921 and May 1923, are important in the history of the Melville revival both because of Brooks's status as one of the preeminent American critics of the period and because Brooks simultaneously shifts Melville criticism, and the debate over culture implicit in that criticism, as the revival moves through the 1920s. Brooks's shifting assessment of Melville—moving from calling him "a garrulous old man" whose flights into "theory" crippled his writing to proclaiming the supreme "craftsmanship" in *Moby-Dick*—marks not only the increased critical attention on *Moby-Dick* at the expense of *Typee*, but also a corresponding relocation of the signs of culture from Melville himself to the formal feature of the texts. Where Weaver makes Melville himself a hero of Culture or values *Typee* as *describing* an alternative to modern civilization, Brooks locates Melville's embodiment of culture within the "craftsmanship" of the text of *Moby-Dick*, which embodies the fusion of highbrow and lowbrow that Brooks envisions in *America's Coming-of-Age*.

Brook's Melville, Part 1: The "Isolation of Spirit"

When Van Wyck Brooks wrote the first of several articles on Melville in "A Reviewer's Notebook," the Melville revival was just picking up speed. The centenary of Melville's birth had passed, eliciting a flurry of articles like Weaver's and Mather's lamenting the author's neglect; this rise in interest was further stimulated by the publishing of several new editions of *Typee, Oomo, White-Jacket,* and *Moby-Dick* in both the United States and England between 1919 and 1921.[40] It was in anticipation of Weaver's biography that Brooks wrote his first column on Melville, and despite his own call for a reevaluation of Melville in "On Creating a Usable Past" (1918), Brooks was not optimistic about the permanence of the revival. Repeating the pessimistic assessment of the American public's receptivity to art that was central to *America's Coming-of-Age* and his *Seven Arts* essays, Brooks says that "only in England [has Melville] been justly appreciated," and that the current flurry of interest is due only to "our indefatigable national appetite for investigation and research." This appetite is superficial, however, and "next year Melville will have been forgotten again. The 'hatred of literature,' as Flaubert called it, which prevents our literary authorities from recognizing a genius prevents them also from retaining the memory of one."[41] More importantly, he seems uncertain of that "genius." Dismissing the popularity of *Oomo* and *Typee* as part of "the vogue of the South Seas," Brooks argues that only in *Moby-Dick* does Melville "rise to his real height and [reveal] himself not as a chronicler but a creator" ("Notebook," 26 October 1921). But even with respect to *Moby-Dick*, Brooks applies to Melville the argument he utilizes in his recently published biography of Mark Twain: the division between highbrow and lowbrow in American civilization fundamentally prevents even a "genius" from developing his or her talent fully.[42] Unlike Twain, who Brooks argues succumbed to the pressures of lowbrow commercial success, Melville falls victim to the highbrow preoccupation with theory. "Theory got the best of him," he argues in another column, "the grey theory that Goethe contrasted with the green of life's golden tree." Losing himself in metaphysical speculation, suffering from the "isolation of spirit" resulting from the absence of organic culture, "he found himself . . . looking forward into utter night; . . . he became, like Ambrose Bierce, like Mark Twain, like so many of the men of his generation . . . the blackest of pessimists" ("Notebook," 21 December 1921).

This "arrested development" is revealed in the form of Melville's writing. Even in *Moby-Dick*, which Brooks acknowledges is a "masterpiece," Melville "was devoid of the sentiment of form"; his many philosophical speculations and cetological digressions make him "like a garrulous old man, who cannot recall, at the conclusion of a discourse, the idea with which he began" ("Notebook," 26 October 1921). In contrast to Melville's lack of form, Brooks cites the example of Coleridge: "If Coleridge had permitted the ancient mariner to tell his story in his own language, we should have had no doubt a thousand pages of entrancing talk. . . . Something was gained, however, by Coleridge's taking the words out of his mariner's mouth and shaping them with the last severity . . . What a place *Moby-Dick* would have had among the great stories of the world if its author, having seized upon that thread, had held it firmly in his hand and followed it, with a single eye!" ("Notebook," 16 October 1921). The turn to Coleridge here is crucial, for it is Coleridge who articulates for Brooks the connection between a theory of organic culture and one of artistic form. In *America's Coming-of-Age*, Brooks draws on Coleridge's theory of the "focal center" as the unifying element that defines both "a national culture" and the harmonious work of art (*Coming-of-Age*, 119). Thus, the work of art serves as a synecdoche for the organic culture in which it is produced: the harmony of the work of art indexes the organic wholeness of the culture in which it is produced, and the organic culture itself becomes an artistic "composition." In contrasting Coleridge's "shaping" of language to Melville's "garrulousness," Brooks is simultaneously criticizing the formlessness of American society, which is precisely not "a culture." Thus, unlike Weaver, who locates his argument about Culture in the character of Melville, Brooks transposes his argument about culture—or the lack thereof—into an argument about form: in the formal shortcomings of *Moby-Dick*, Brooks finds the reflections of the cultural shortcomings of Melville's America.

Brooks's Melville, Part 2: "Our Sole American Epic"

By the time Brooks wrote his next several articles on Melville and *Moby-Dick*, the terms of his argument about art and culture remained the same, but his evaluation of Melville had shifted. Whereas Melville's excessive theorizing in 1921 appeared to Brooks as a symptom of the fragmented society of which Melville was a product, by 1923 Melville emerged as the "craftsman" whose "deliberate art" unified the material and the ideal. Reviewing the first twelve-volume edition of *The Works of Herman Melville*, Brooks "wonder[s] if all [*Moby-Dick*'s] felicities have dawned even yet on people's minds." After reading the novel a third time, he argues, "It seems to me now less chaotic, better shaped, than it seemed at first: nothing has surprised me more than to discover how conscious Melville was of what he was doing" ("Notebook," 16 May 1923). Whereas Brooks had previously seen Melville's metaphysical and scientific explorations as unnecessary digressions, he begins to see them, in their relationship to the tale of Ahab's hunt for the White Whale, as exemplifying the fusion of lowbrow and highbrow, concrete and metaphysical, that Brooks envisioned as genuine culture in his earlier essays: "If 'Moby-Dick' is his supreme achievement, it is because here, and here alone, the subjective and objective elements in his mind achieved some sort of equilibrium" ("Notebook," 9 May 1923). In achieving this equilibrium, *Moby-Dick* represents "our sole American epic," and reconciles Brooks to what he earlier called Melville's "garrulousness." "An epic," he concludes, "requires ballast. Think of the catalogue of ships in Homer, the mass of purely historical information in the 'Aeneid,' the long descriptions in 'Paradise Lost': how immensely these elements add to the density and the volume of the total impression . . . ! This freight of inanimate or partially inanimate material gives 'Moby-Dick' its bottom, its body, in the vintner's phrase" ("Notebook," 16 May 1923).

In referring to "body, in the vintner's phrase," Brooks harkens back to his earliest writings, *Wine of the Puritans*, where wine served as a metaphor for the division that characterized American civilization. Anticipating the dualism of the highbrow and the lowbrow that he will elaborate in *America's Coming-of-Age*, he argues that the Puritan settlers in America arrived with a fully formed European culture that was ultimately incompatible with the new environment. The result was like putting "old wine into new bottles[;] . . . when the explosion results, one may say, the aroma passes into the air and the wine spills on the floor. The aroma, or the ideal, turns into transcendentalism, and the wine, or the real, becomes commercialism."[43] Melville, in contrast, reunites the ideal and the real into a full-bodied wine.

In having "body," Melville is further linked to Whitman, Brooks's "precipitant" of American culture who also achieves fusion of the material and the ideal. As he says in another column, Melville "suggests Whitman also in the profundity of his appetites, in the ruddy glow of his physical nature, in that somnolence of a mind that had lived in close communion with the elements of sea and earth. As with Whitman, the images that float in his imagination are often images derived from the rustic life. . . . To such facts as this, I wonder, or rather to what they symbolize, how much do we owe the solidity, the depth, the breadth and height of 'Moby-Dick' and 'Leaves of Grass'?" ("Notebook," 16 May 1923).

For Brooks, the culture embodied in this fusion of ideal and real is specifically a national culture; that is, the unit of culture is the nation, as opposed to a cosmopolitan, global culture or a regional one. Thus, in naming the novel an "epic" and likening him to Virgil and Whitman, Brooks's Melville becomes "a poet in . . . the most radical and primitive sense of the word, a man . . . who first gives to a nation a certain focal centre in the consciousness of its own character" ("Notebook," 12 April 1922).

While this passage refers to Melville himself, Brooks's suggestion of Melville as a potential focal center of culture translates into an argument about the text itself. Giving a reading of Father Mapple's sermon, Brooks demonstrates "the skill with which Melville excluded from our minds every irrelevant detail [and] by a process of simplification . . . heightens their effect without removing them from reality." The book is thus the result of "deliberate art" and "cunning . . . craftsmanship"—a term that, given Brooks's admiration of Morris and his arts-and-crafts ideal, makes Melville the equivalent of the medieval artisan, the model of organic culture for Brooks and Morris.

Here Brooks's privileging of "simplification" as the mark of "craftsmanship" is similar to Cather's argument in "On the Art of Fiction"

(1920). Like his contemporaries from Henry Adams, to T. S. Eliot, to Allen Tate and Lewis Mumford, Brooks often looked toward the medieval town, and particularly the artisan guilds, as models of communal, organic art both functional and aesthetic—which in turn produced a politics of culture often in conflict with Brooks's progressive socialism. In his essay "Amor Fati," for example, Brooks argues that literature flourishes only when there is an "indifference to forms of life that are beyond one's power of realization"; that is, a caste system, where the artist is tempted to think only of his or her own art, not about materially improving that life.[44] It is "the guild-spirit, the pride of the métier, out of which the art and literature of the past have come; but how far has not that pride been a consequence of the stratification of life in societies in which the individual has had virtually no chance of 'rising in the world'? That heights can exist, as it were, at every social level is a notion that seems to lodge only in minds that accept their level as predetermined" (163). Thus, "for this reason, the closing of the American frontier may fairly be taken to portend a certain intensification in our literary life.... [We] may say that the star of hope rose over our literature on the day when the last barefoot boy in Missouri ceased to dream of inhabiting the White House." The current "American Renaissance," he concludes, "will not get very far unless it develops the guild-spirit in place of the spirit of log-rolling" (163, 166). Labeling Melville a "craftsman," then, Brooks makes him a model for the hoped-for American Renaissance of Brooks's own decade and indexes the argument about organic culture in the 1850s that will operate both in Mumford's *The Golden Day* and in Matthiessen's later *American Renaissance*.

Thus, whereas Weaver makes the combination of experience and imagination the defining characteristic of Melville's mode of perception—an epistemology, I have argued, that is also the model for the anthropologist as participant-observer—and erects Melville as a hero of Culture, Brooks sees this fusion of the material and the ideal as a characteristic of *Moby-Dick* and in turn makes this fusion a mark of a potential organic culture. I say "potential" because Brooks remains in the end unable to decide if the artist-as-focal-center, like Whitman or Melville, can arise only in what is *already* an organic culture, or if he or she can transform a fragmented culture into an organic one in the image of his or her art. In either case, Brooks argues that Melville, like Whitman, ultimately fails: after declaring the organic craftsmanship of *Moby-Dick*, Brooks goes on to argue that Melville falls victim, after *Moby-Dick*, to "an arrested development" caused by an excess of "emotional mysticism" and "isolation" from an unsympathetic public, the "suffocation of a mighty genius in a social vacuum" ("Notebook," 23 May 1923). "As the strongest peasant disintegrates in urban surroundings," the primitive wholeness that Melville possessed fractures in the face of modern American civilization. It remained for Mumford, in his biography of Melville, to complete the "synthesis" of Melville, organic culture, and the organic work of art, and in doing so to mark an important link among American literary history, anthropology, and what would become the New Criticism.

Lewis Mumford, *Moby-Dick*, and Regional Culture

While Raymond Weaver's *Herman Melville: Mariner and Mystic* decisively launched the Melville revival in 1921, Lewis Mumford's *Herman Melville* (1929) could be said to have solidified Melville's place in the literary canon, with *Moby-Dick* as his masterpiece. When he began writing his Melville biography, Mumford was already an important young critic, enmeshed in the intellectual circuits of American modernism. As a young man growing up in New York City, he had been inspired by the radical social and aesthetic criticism of the *Seven Arts* group of Van Wyck Brooks and Randolph Bourne; by the early 1920s, he had become a regular contributor to a number of journals crucial to the formation of American modernism, including *The Dial*, *The Freeman*, *The Nation*, and *The American Mercury*.[45] A generalist whose interests and writings spanned sociology, philosophy, architecture, and literature, by 1929 he had already published his *Story of Utopias* (1922) and the first full treatment of American architecture, *Sticks and Stones* (1924), and served as an editor at both *The Dial* and *The New Republic*, during which time he published, often in the same issues as his own articles, pieces by a range of intellectuals including such anthropologists as Franz Boas and his student Edward Sapir, as well as the rising critic Allen Tate. Most important for his work on Melville, Mumford had just completed his critically praised assessment of American literature and thought in the mid–nineteenth century, *The Golden Day* (1926), which promoted Emerson, Thoreau, Hawthorne, Whitman, and Melville as the key figures in American literary history.[46] That the Doubleday publisher George Doran approached Mumford for its series of literary biographies indicates both Melville's and Mumford's rising stock in the years since Weaver's book. When Mumford's book became too big for the series, Harcourt, Brace and Company took it up, and then Carl Van Doren's prestigious Literary Guild adopted it, further establishing Melville as a canonical author.

In his biography, Mumford draws on many of the same materials as Weaver, but he changes Weaver's reading in two important ways. First, as opposed to Weaver, who saw Melville descend into "silence" after the public rejection of *Moby-Dick* and *Pierre*, Mumford analyzes Melville's later poetry and prose to suggest Melville's "acceptance" of the dark aspects of the universe, an acceptance that culminates in "Billy Budd." Whereas Weaver spends more than 100 pages on Melville's South Seas experience, and only 50 for the last forty years of his life, Mumford compresses Melville's sea adventures to about 25 pages and spends about 140 pages on the material after *Moby-Dick*. The departure from Weaver that perhaps has the most significant impact on the course of Melville studies is Mumfords devotion of the central chapter of the book to an extensive analysis of the form and content of *Moby-Dick* as a literary composition rather than, like Weaver, subsuming it into Melville's biography. In the context of the debates over culture and form that I been tracing, Mumford's reimaging of the relation between Melville and the world he inhabits is even more important. Weaver reads Melville as an isolated genius neglected by a Philistine public; Mumford, on the other hand, views Melville, and *Moby-Dick* in particular, as arising *out of* a specific way of life—one that was reaching its highest moment of fulfillment, and that was also about to dissolve. Whereas Weaver makes Melville a hero of Culture, Mumford makes him the hero of "a culture," more specifically, of what he elsewhere calls a "genuine" culture destroyed by the industrial civilization that both precipitates and is embodied in the Civil War.

In this section, then, I argue that Mumford's argument about Melville is an argument about culture itself. Specifically, in answer to Van Wyck Brooks's diagnosis of a divided America, Mumford imagines Melville as the embodiment of Edward Sapir's "genuine culture," the "Golden Day" of New England defined by the "synthesis" of an entire way of life—the economic, the spiritual, the intellectual, the artistic—into a meaningful whole. For Mumford, as for Cather and Sapir, a whole culture has an aesthetic: in the genuine culture, daily practices and institutions, everyday objects as well as architecture and literature, are all characterized by "form," both reflecting and producing the wholeness of that culture. Thus, Mumford argues that the form of *Moby-Dick* is a synecdoche for the genuine culture of which it is a part. Mumford yokes the aesthetic theories of Joel Spingarn's Crocean "new criticism" and the spatial structuralism of Sapir's genuine culture to argue that *Moby-Dick* constitutes a formal whole. Just as any one element of a culture can be understood only in its relation to the whole system of meaning of which it is a part, similarly, the individual elements in the novel—the generic mix of realism, adventure story, cetology, philosophy, whaling history—can be understood only in the context of that artistic whole. Finally, for Mumford, as for Sapir, the unit of culture is the region, and *Moby-Dick* emerges in Mumford's reading as a regional novel, which is also, by virtue of its regionalism, a universal masterpiece. This combination of a theory of regional culture and aesthetic form complicates critical interpretations of Mumford's "cultural nationalism" and the canonization of *Moby-Dick* as the "American" novel and points to significant affinities to the New Criticism of Ransom and Tate.

Mumford, Melville, and the "Esthetic Filaments" of Culture

Mumford's biography constructs Melville and the period of which he was a part as the antidote to Brooks's divided culture. Mumford's Melville embodies the "synthesis" of the practical and the ideal, the scientific and the artistic, in his life as a sailor: "During the years of his early manhood, as he wandered about the world and contemplated existence under the stars and bore a hand in working the ship, his environment, his experience, and his vital relationships were an integer.... There was astronomy and natural history and art and religion within the bulky hold of a whaler, as well as technics and business and the daily logbook."[47] Melville, Mumford argues, like his fellow representatives in *The Golden Day*, "did not disdain practical life... but instead... saw that what was called business was only a small part of the totality of living" (*Melville*, 366).

Central to the synthesis represented by Melville is the integration of science and imagination. While Mumford sees the "abstractions" of science as both a cause and a symptom of the dissociation of modern civilization, in Melville's mid-nineteenth century, he argues, science and imagination achieved a new synthesis. "Science," he argues, "did not, as has been foolishly believed, destroy the myth-making power of man.... this has been the accidental, temporary effect of a one-sided science, serving... a limited number of practical activities." Instead, poets "like Shelley, Wordsworth, Whitman, Melville, did not feel themselves robbed of their specific powers, but rather found them enlarged and refreshed" (*Melville*, 191). This fusion of science and imagination indeed is characteristic of the figures of Mumford's Golden Day: "None of the fine minds of the Golden Day was afraid to welcome the new forces that were at large in the world. Need I recall that Whitman wrote an apostrophe to the locomotive, that Emerson said a steamship sailing promptly between America and Europe might be as beautiful as a star, and that Thoreau, who loved to hear the wind in the pine needles, listened with equal pleasure to the music of the telegraph wires?"[48] For Melville and his contemporaries, science or the material "was for the first time completely wedded to the imagination.... [The nineteenth century] no longer deified the empirical and the practical at the expense of the ideal and the aesthetic; on the contrary, these qualities are now completely fused together, as an expression of life's integrated totality" (*Melville*, 192).[49]

The prime example of Melville's synthesis is, of course, *Moby-Dick*, in which Melville draws on science, experience, and art in an attempt to know the "whole" whale. Combining different perspectives and genres throughout the novel, Melville demonstrates the limits of any one system of knowledge, and the synthesis required to apprehend the whole: "The whale is a symbol in the heart of man," Mumford argues, "but the whale is also a creature in natural history, and its shape, its bulk, its anatomical characteristics, family relations, its place in politics, economics, history, and human adventure, is a further part of that natural history." Seeing the whale as part of an extended web of significance (much like Malinowski's canoe), Mumford concludes that "the whale that science investigates ... is not, however thoroughly it may be dissected and articulated and labeled, the whole whale," and thus "Melville gives a completer account of the whale than the anatomists: he approaches it with a harpoon as well as the dissecting-knife" (*Melville*, 162, 163, 164). In integrating science and imagination, anatomical analysis with living experience, *Moby-Dick* "brings together the two dissevered halves of the modern world and the modern self—its positive, practical, scientific, externalized self, bent on conquest and knowledge, and its imaginative, ideal half, bent on the transposition of conflict into art, and power into humanity" (193).

Melville, then, becomes in Mumford's argument the "focal center" that Brooks argues Whitman might have been in *America's Coming-of-Age*. But where Brooks sees Whitman as an isolated genius, arising miraculously out of a divided society, Mumford sees Melville as symptomatic of an emergent, whole way of life, "the product of two hundred and fifty years of settled life in America" that "produced Walden, Leaves of Grass, Emerson's Notebooks, and Moby-Dick" (*Melville*, 364). As he puts it, "One cannot separate a man from his social environment.... Melville's triumph, like that of his contemporaries in the Golden Day, was the last expression of a provincial society, and the first prophetic achievement in a newer and deeper *culture*" (346, emphasis added). Mumford sees Melville's individual achievement—his "cultivation"—as inseparable from the "newer and deeper culture" of which he was the first result. That "deeper culture," Mumford suggests, is defined precisely by the "integration of man and nature and society shadowed forth" in the writing of Emerson, Thoreau, Whitman, and Melville—a promise cut short by the Civil War and industrial age that would follow (364).

Thus, for Mumford's argument about Melville—and indeed throughout Mumford's writings on architecture, sociology, literature, and regional planning—"culture" emerges as a central conceptual term. For Mumford, culture is, by definition, the integration of elements to create a "whole"; that whole, moreover, is constituted from "meaningful" "forms" or "patterns." As he elaborates in *The Golden Day*, "confronted by the raw materials of existence, a culture works them over into new patterns" (279):

> [Just as] eating... is not a mere hacking and gnawing at flesh and bones, but an occasion for sociability and civil ceremonies[,] ... so every act tends to be done, not just for its own sake, but for the social values that accompany it: the taste, the conversation, the wit, the sociability are *esthetic filaments* that bind men together and make life more pleasing. To the extent that these *shared meanings* come into existence and spread over all the details of the day's activities, a community is cultured; to the extent that they disappear, or have no place, it is barbarous. (253, emphasis added)

Culture, then, "works over raw facts" to produce "esthetic" forms that constitute "shared meanings": as Mumford puts it in *Herman Melville*, the "effort of culture" is "the effort to make Life *significant* and durable" (364, emphasis added).

Mumford, Sapir, and "Genuine Culture"

In constituting culture as an integrated whole, in which the material and the spiritual, the economic and the artistic, form a "whole tissue of meaning" (*Golden*, 13), and reconstructing Melville as the exemplar of that culture, Mumford reveals how the problematic of culture was central to the emergence of the Americanist literary canon and literary criticism as well. Specifically, Mumford's construction of culture has much in common with Sapir's conceptualization, in "Culture, Genuine and

Spurious," of culture as spatial form, a semiotic system where meaning arises out of the structural relation of parts. For Sapir, "genuine culture" is "inherently harmonious" and "unified," in which "nothing is spiritually meaningless," but in which "the significance of any one element of civilization" can be understood only "in its relation to all others" ("Genuine," 314–15). In contrast to the "spurious culture" of modern industrial society, with its emphasis on "technical routine that ... answers to no spiritual needs" (316), genuine culture is characterized by "the firmness with which every part of that life—economic, social, religious, and aesthetic—is bound together into a significant whole" (318). In this conception, culture is thus an aesthetic object, spatially conceived.

Thus, in Mumford's construction, Melville and *Moby-Dick* become examples of Sapir's genuine culture. Sapir's argument contrasts culture to what he sees as the "spiritual hybrid of contradictory patches, of water-tight compartments of consciousness" that divide American civilization ("Genuine," 315), separating economic, practical activity from spiritual and aesthetic value. Mumford likewise contrasts his vision of the "integrated totality" embodied by Melville and his Golden Day to the "narrow, mechanistic, money-bent society" that followed the Civil War. Mumford's Melville embodies, like Sapir's Indian, the binding together of "every part of that life—economic, social, religious, and aesthetic" into a "significant whole." For both Sapir and Mumford, the whole of culture is constituted specifically through the creation of "shared meanings," arising from the "esthetic filaments that bind men together." Thus, for Mumford, the synthesis represented by Melville and his art is—using a term repeated in both *The Golden Day* and *Herman Melville*—the "beginnings of a *genuine culture*" in very much the Sapirian sense ("Golden," 12, emphasis added).

As with Cather, I have not found any direct evidence or statements by Mumford pointing to Sapir's direct influence on him. However, there are strong reasons to believe that Mumford was familiar with Sapir's writing. Mumford clearly moved in the modernist circles where anthropologists, artists, and critics intersected: Mumford, for example, was one of the members of Harold Stearns's symposium that included Elsie Clews Parson and Robert Lowie (Mumford contributed a chapter, "The City," to Stearns's *Civilization in the United States*). As noted in chapter 1, Sapir frequently contributed throughout the 1920s to important journals of art, politics, and society, in which Mumford also frequently appeared. Most significantly, the first version of "Culture, Genuine and Spurious" appeared in *The Dial* under the title "Civilization and Culture" in

September 1919—precisely in the middle of Mumford's ten-month tenure as an assistant editor for that publication. Mumford himself contributed an article to that issue entitled "The Place of Community in the School."

Mumford went on to edit *The New Republic* for several years in the 1920s, when several articles by Sapir appeared—including one issue in which articles by Sapir, Mumford, and Allen Tate appeared side by side, each addressing issues crucial to the debate over culture: Sapir's review of a treatise on Navajo pottery design, Mumford's review of Alfred North Whitehead's *Process and Reality*, and Tate's review of I. A. Richards's *Practical Criticism*. Again, as with Cather, Mumford was linked through a dense web of intellectual and professional connections to anthropology and linguistics. Rather than reflecting a general attitude or Zeitgeist, both, I argue, were *actively producing* this approach to culture, engaging in a specific, interdisciplinary conversation involving anthropologists, artists, social scientists, and literary critics. These new conceptions of culture reshaped the way anthropologists like Sapir understood the elements of "a culture," *and* the way such literary critics as Mumford would read a text like *Moby-Dick* and understand its relation to American literary history.

While Mumford, then, parallels Sapir's formulation of culture as a set of practices and ideas that constitutes a whole system of meaning, like Cather, Mumford makes explicit Sapir's formalist aesthetics of culture. As quoted earlier, culture for Mumford is that which infuses "existence with meaning, and facts with forms"; "form," in turn, becomes the mark of culture as such (*Melville*, 363). While critics like Brooks also make the connection between culture and form, Brooks's metaphors for cultural form are most often organic—say, in the image of the Sargasso Sea and its marine life or of the tended garden in *America's Coming-of-Age*. Although Mumford's theory of culture is likewise sometime expressed in organic metaphors, he most often uses metaphors of handicraft to describe a culture's integrity: culture "works over" experience, weaving a "pattern" of meaning, "smelting," "refining," and "stamping" empirical facts into aesthetic form. The integrity of Melville's provincial culture is in turn marked by the aesthetic quality of its functional tools: Melville's fellow whalers carved various tools "with a more sure aesthetic touch than any of the contemporary arts could show in America, [and] these whaling implements . . . are worthy to have a place . . . in a museum of American folk-arts" (*Melville*, 45). The whaling ship—the space within which this "whole" life was carried out—was, according to Mumford, itself "the supreme esthetic achievement of the day and land, better by far than current architecture or painting.... On board and in port, the beauty and brutality of the life mingled[;] ... the fierce press of work in a storm contrasted with ... the immensity of quiet nights under the stars" (*Golden*, 143–44). The aesthetic quality of the object reflects, and constitutes, the integrated (and thus cultured) life lived through it.

Moby-Dick and the Composition of Genuine Culture

Mumford's supreme example of aesthetic form, however, is *Moby-Dick* itself: uniting science and experience and imagination, "the book itself has a hundred sides.... Moby-Dick is an imaginative synthesis; and every aspect of reality belongs to it, one plane modifying the other and creating the *modelled whole*" (*Melville*, 171, emphasis added). Just as a culture is constituted through the interweaving of fact and idea into formal patterns, so too do the multiple genres that constitute the novel—adventure tale, drama, philosophy, history, science, cetology, mythology, and so on—form a pattern within the work: "These passages about the whale and the methods of whaling, about its dignity and adventure, these comments upon the science of cetology—all these things are not uncouth interruptions of the narrative: they are profoundly part of it.... The universal, symbolic aspect of the story, and its direct, scientific, practical aspect move in and out like the threads of a complicated *pattern*" (164, emphasis added). The patterns formed by these disparate discourses constitute the meaning of the work itself, and this meaning in turn is inseparable from "his manner of projecting it" (181). "The conception of Moby-Dick," he writes, "organically demands the expressive interrelation, for a single total effect, of a hundred different pieces" (182).

Mumford, then, reads *Moby-Dick* as an aesthetic object whose meaning arises, not out of its accurate depiction of whaling, nor out of its philosophical ideas, but from the interplay between content and form, which creates a "modelled whole." The meaning of *Moby-Dick*, to borrow Sapir's terms, is not in "what" it says but in "how" the different elements in the text are "significant" in "relation to all others." Conceiving of a text in this way, Mumford's reading of *Moby-Dick* marks the intersection of anthropological debates over culture and debates within literary criticism over aesthetics and meaning. To put it another way, the problematic of culture structures both the debates within anthropology over how to conceive of and interpret a culture and debates within literary criticism over how to conceive of and interpret a literary text.

Mumford's aesthetic and Sapir's theories of language and culture specifically intersect with the ideas of Italian philosopher and historian Benedetto Croce. In *Herman Melville*, Mumford credits his attention to form to Croce, who "has correctly taught us that every work of art is... uniquely what it is, and cannot be understood except in terms of its own purpose" (178). Sapir also cites Croce in the preface to his textbook *Language*, as "one of the very few who have gained an understanding of the fundamental significance of language" and "its close relation to the problem of art."[50] And it may have been the relationship between Croce's aesthetic theories and Sapir's conception of language and culture that led Mumford to recommend Sapir's *Language* to the readers of *The Freeman* in a 1922 book review.[51]

Mumford had been introduced to Croce's aesthetic theories through his friend Joel Spingarn, the former Columbia University literature professor and publisher whom Mumford had met while participating in Stearns's symposium on "American civilization" in 1921. Spingarn became Mumford's adviser, friend, and sometime patron through the 1920s. His new publishing house, Harcourt, Brace and Company, published Sapir's *Language*, Mumford's *Herman Melville*, and Stearns's *Civilization in the United States*.[52]

Spingarn most famously articulated his version of Crocean aesthetics in his 1911 lecture "The New Criticism." Spingarn argued—in many ways anticipating the arguments of the *new* "New Critics" in the 1930s and 1940s—that art is an "organic expression," the aesthetic value of which lies in its unique interrelation of parts. The poem is its own "reality," and therefore the critic, Spingarn claims, should ask not if the work conforms to standards of historical accuracy or moral value but instead if it is "true to the laws of its own being." The formal properties of a poem are inseparable from the content—the poet "has expressed his thought in its completeness, and there is no equivalent for his expression except itself"—and therefore any alterations of its language, through paraphrase or through translation, create a different object.[53]

Drawing on Spingarn's Crocean aesthetic, Mumford reads the features of *Moby-Dick* that had puzzled even admiring critics—its mixture of science and romance, the improbability of its characters as "real" sailors, its variety of tone and language—as inseparable elements of its modeled whole. Thus, in answer to critics who ask if Ahab is a "realistic" figure, Mumford asserts, "Ahab and Stubb and Starbuck and Tashtego live within the sphere where we find them.... Ahab is a reality in relation to *Moby-Dick*; and when Melville projects him, he ceases to be incredible, because he is alive" (*Melville*, 180). A self-contained aesthetic object, "Moby-Dick stands by itself as complete as the Divine Comedy or the Odyssey stand by itself" (178), and its poetic language achieves unity of form and content such that "it is absurd and ineffectual to give a summary of Moby-Dick, or to quote, dismembered, some of its great passages.... Like the paintings in the Ajanta caves, the beauty of Moby-Dick can be known only to those who will make a pilgrimage to it, and stay within its dark confines until what is darkness has become light, and one can make out, with the help of an occasional torch, its grand design, its complicated arabesque, the minute significance of its parts" (176–77). In the inseparability of the "minute significance of... parts" in its "grand design," *Moby-Dick* formally embodies the whole culture of which it, and Herman Melville, are synecdochic parts.

What is interesting here is the way Mumford's theory of culture and his society-bracketing Crocean aesthetics mirror each other, as a whole culture is constituted through the fusion of fact and idea, and the whole poem through the fusion of meaning and form; these theories of culture and poetic form, in turn, converge on *Moby-Dick*. Mumford's aesthetic of culture is doubled in his aesthetic of poetry, and in a way that, like Cather, highlights the convergence between modernist anthropology—here, Sapir's structuralist definition of culture and meaning—and modernist aesthetics and criticism, as represented by Croce's and Spingarn's literary criticism. This connection is made explicit, of course, in Sapir's own linguistic anthropology, as he approvingly cites Croce's (and Spingarn's) theory of a poem's linguistic relativity, and the idea that the "innate formal limitations [and] possibilities" of each language mean that "a work of literary art can never be translated."[54]

Malinowski similarly emphasizes the difficulty of translating native languages because "the whole manner in which a native language is used is different from our own"; thus, the meaning of a single word cannot be understood "without constant reference to these broader contexts of verbal utterance." This broader context, in turn, ultimately leads into "wide fields of custom, of social psychology and of tribal organization which correspond to one term or another"—in other words, the whole culture.[55] In each case, the primary object of analysis—language, a literary work, a culture—is newly viewed as a relative, internally coherent system of meaning. Mumford's claim that "Moby-Dick has a meaning which cannot be derived or dissociated from the work itself" (194) is a statement of Crocean aesthetics (via Spingarn) that later New Critics would call the "fallacy of paraphrase"; it is, to put it another way, a statement of literary pluralism. Conversely, Sapir's admiration for the "firmness with which every part of [American Indian] life ... bound together into a significant whole" is a statement of both cultural pluralism and Crocean structuralist aesthetics.

Similarly, Spingarn's aesthetic is deeply intertwined with the anthropological innovations of Boasians like Sapir. Spingarn's is essentially a pluralist aesthetic, with the standards for value arising from within each (different) work of art, and he deploys the idea that an art object is separate from historical and biographical context in opposition to ideas of "the 'evolution' of literature."[56] His synchronic, structural approach to form reflects, at another level of analysis, the synchronic, antievolutionary approach to culture implied in Sapir's "unified" whole, "the significance of any one element" of which is seen "in relation to all others." Spingarn's "art," in short, sounds a lot like "culture," as in this statement in which Spingarn asserts the relativism of his approach to "primitive art": "Art has no origin separate from man's life.... Though [in ancient times] she wore savage raiment, she was no less the Muse. Art is simple at times, complex at others, but it is always art. The simple art of early times may be studied with profit; but the researches of anthropology have no vital significance for Criticism, unless the anthropologist studies the simplest forms of art in the same spirit as its highest; that is, unless the anthropologist is an esthetic critic."[57] Just such an anthropologist, I would suggest, is Sapir in his theory of cultural wholes, and just such a critic, with his doubling of a theory of culture with a theory of aesthetics, is Mumford in *Herman Melville*.

Thus, while critics—including contemporaries of Mumford—have seen Crocean formalism (as applied by Spingarn), as well as the related formalism of New Critics like John Crowe Ransom and Allen Tate, as separating art from social context, Mumford's work reveals instead the intimate connection between some versions of modernist formalism and modernist theories of culture. For Mumford, the connection between society and art is not one of *content*—how accurately, say, the work reflects the conditions of the working class or teaches morals (to use examples valued by some progressives and scorned by New Critics in Mumford's own period)—but of *form*, in which the formal wholeness of the art object both reflects and constitutes the formal wholeness of a culture. When Mumford writes, then, that Melville "wrought ideality and actuality into the same figure" in *Moby-Dick*, he is indexing this connection, both pointing back to the arts-and-crafts ideal and forward to Cleanth Brooks's *The Well Wrought Urn* (*Melville*, 182). And in his assertion that Melville's poetic form constitutes a "reality" superior to the abstractions of science or its literary counterpart "realism," allowing "the whale [to emerge] as a complete body" (170), he anticipates in many ways, as I examine in chapter 4, John Crowe Ransom's argument that science robs the "body and solid substance of the world," while poetic knowledge wants "to realize the world, to see it better."[58] In each case, the key term—for Sapir, "genuine culture"; for Mumford, *Moby-Dick*; for Ransom, the poem—is deployed against the abstraction and fragmentation of modern industrial civilization. This similarity is deeply significant, for, despite the apparent opposition of Mumford's and Sapir's progressive liberalism to Ransom's agrarian reactionary politics, a common conception of culture and its embodiment in poetry undergirds their approaches.

Regional Culture, the Nation-State, and Literary Form

Moreover, for Sapir and Mumford (as for Ransom), the spatial form of both a culture and a text finds its analogue in the geographic region as the unit of culture. In this way the argument *for* culture is also an argument *against* the modern industrial state. As Sapir writes, the "geography of culture" is regional, reaching "its greatest heights in comparatively small, autonomous groups [but] rarely remain[ing] healthy and subtle when spread thin over an interminable area" like the nation-state. Thus, while "the national-political unit tends to arrogate culture to itself," it succeeds "only at the price of serious cultural impoverishment of vast portions of its terrain" ("Genuine," 328–29). Sapir argues, in effect, that the idea of an American culture itself is an oxymoron: "In the New World, the unsatisfactory nature of a geographically widespread culture . . . is manifest. To find substantially the same cultural manifestations . . . often indeed to the minutest details, in New York and Chicago and San Francisco is saddening" ("Genuine," 330).

Likewise, for Mumford the unit of culture is the region, in contrast to the industrial state. Mumford, of course, was deeply involved in regional planning through the 1920s and 1930s, and it is for this groundbreaking work, along with his architectural and urban criticism, that he is perhaps best remembered today—a reputation enhanced with the recent rise of environmental studies and the "new urbanism." Mumford's interest in regional planning began early in his career, as he read the works of and corresponded with the Scottish biologist, sociologist, and regional planner Patrick Geddes, and that interest intensified through the 1920s. In

1923 Mumford joined architects and landscape planners Clarence Stein and Henry Wright and environmentalist Benton MacKaye to found the Regional Planning Association of America (RPAA), which worked to alleviate the unrestrained growth of urban "megalopolises" through planned regional "garden cities" such as Sunnyside Gardens in Queens, New York (where Mumford and his wife lived during the time he wrote *The Golden Day*), and Radburn, New Jersey. The group most famously was also behind the establishment of the Appalachian Trail.[59] Mumford articulated the RPAA's philosophy in numerous essays written in the mid- and late 1920s, including in the group's manifesto, published in what became known as the "regional number" of the journal *Survey Graphic* in 1925.[60]

For Mumford, a region is "any geographic area that possesses a *certain unity* of climate, soil, vegetation, industry and culture," made up of both the "physical facts" of geography and also "social heritage, laws, customs, morals, and ... history." "A region" is by definition inseparable from "culture": "We think of the region as a whole," he argues, in which "industry, education, housing, culture, recreation, *are not separable activities*; they exist within a regional complex."[61] In this theory, the spatially conceived structure of meaning that makes up culture and the physical space of the geographical region quite literally map onto one another; the region "considered as a social heritage" and "the region considered as a body in space ... interfuse" to produce a genuine culture.[62]

This formulation of regional culture crucially links Mumford's work in regional planning to his work on the Melville revival. Throughout *The Golden Day* and *Herman Melville*, Mumford emphasizes the "thriving regional culture" of which Melville was a part (*Golden*, 158). In the first paragraph of the biography, he announces that "the society into which Herman Melville was born was in the fullest sense of the word a provincial one ..., which finds its sources and motives within its own region, and that achieves a certain balance and continuity by a restricted development" (*Melville*, 9). The "certain unity" of this "whole" culture—which now is revealed to be a specifically *regional* culture—produced, and was reflected in, the formal integrity of its artifacts, first and foremost in *Moby-Dick*. As significant, the *passing* of this ordered way of life—swept away, according to Mumford, by the Civil War and the subsequent triumph of the industrial state—resulted in the *loss* of form:

> The disruption symbolized by the Civil War was expressed in a hundred ways; and when one examines these manifestations

> carefully they can all be characterized by a single figure: the failure to achieve form. One sees the difference between provincial and industrial America in the political definition of their units: New England, for example, is a natural region ... with a mode of thought and an institutional form based upon certain common geographic features and cultural history; the new states and territories that were founded beyond the Alleghenies had no form other than that expressed by the arbitrary lines drawn by the surveyor: their content was simply so many blank square miles. (*Melville*, 292–93)

Here, in a figure that Mumford would repeat in several of his essays on regionalism, the formal contours of the New England states contrast with the abstract formlessness of boundaries (formless *because* abstract) drawn without regard for natural geographic features, signaling the industrial imperialism of westward expansion. This political formlessness is mirrored for Mumford in Melville's relative inability to achieve form in his later writing.

As the quoted passage indicates, Mumford—in *Herman Melville* as well as his work on regional planning as a whole—joins Sapir in deploying a theory of "genuine" regional culture in contrast to the industrial, bureaucratic state, which represents exactly the kind of abstraction that culture and form resist. Early in his writing career, Mumford joined colleague Randolph Bourne as one of the Young Americans' most consistent and outspoken critics of state power. The state by definition, Mumford argues, is a coercive institution that arises "out of military conquest" to promote the interests of a small group; even in the absence of external threats, the state seeks to organize and control all aspects within its borders, striving for "mechanical unanimity of purpose."[63] This "mechanical unanimity" is in part achieved by the establishment of a spurious "national culture," uniformly promoting one standard way of life within the arbitrary political borders of the state. The idea of a "national culture" is a "stupendous sleight-of-hand, [which] make[s] an institution [i.e., the state] whose capital functions are odious seem the repository of all the community's hopes, aspirations and virtues.... By propaganda, by education, and at times even by law and military coercion, the capital city inflicts its local culturalism upon the other regions that make up the country."[64] Thus, "the culture of the capital succeeded in passing itself off on the provinces as the one authentic and indisputable 'national' culture."[65] The "*formless* unity" of national culture is therefore "a highly artificial condition, ... run[ning] against the natural grain of local interests and local activities" (emphasis added).[66] For Mumford, then, efforts to identify an "American" national culture are by definition imperialist, attempting to create a "spurious uniformity."[67]

At the same time, neither Sapir's nor Mumford's regionalism is simply nostalgic localism, withdrawing from broader transnational concerns. As I argued in chapter 1, for Sapir the answer to the problem of national culture comes in part through new modes of economic and political internationalism, which weaken the primary role of the nation-state, thereby freeing up regional cultures. Similarly, Mumford's regional cultures are part of transnational circuits, made possible through the dissolving of artificial state boundaries. When, Mumford argues, people are seen as "individuals and as members of groups," as opposed to citizens of a political state, their interests "polarize naturally about particular concrete, locally-embodied institutions—the school, the synagogue, the market, the business corporation, the trade union, the city, and in the absence of national boundaries these institutions tend to flow naturally across frontiers and to link up, one with another, in an increasingly complex pattern."[68] Indeed, echoing Cather's account of the movement of goods through Jewett's New England noted in the previous chapter, this mobility is part of Mumford's construction of Melville's regionalism, in whose work "one sees ... the local influence of the brisk cosmopolitan port of New York, adventuring out to other parts of the world, or on shore, welcoming each new cargo of men and goods."[69] Mumford's point here is to argue that Melville identifies himself first and foremost with the region, and only secondarily with the "United States." The "thriving regional culture" of New England's past, as Mumford would have it, matches Sapir's vision of the ideal cultural future, where, between the "integration of economic and political forces" and the "small units whose life is truly virile and individual," the "fetich [sic] of the present state" fades to insignificance. Thus, for both Mumford and Sapir, regional cultures are connected to, and made possible by, transnational connections.[70]

This argument in turn has implications for the idea of "American" culture and "American literature." For Mumford, efforts to identify an "American" national culture are in effect imperialist, attempting to find (or create) a false unity where there is none. The result, echoing Sapir's terms, is "spurious" culture: if, Mumford argues, "America is not a 'land of bewildering variety and richness of life,'" it is because "we have persistently sought to make a *spurious* uniformity prevail" (emphasis added).[71]

This "spurious unity" is evident even in attempts to define American literature. For example, while Mumford in several instances mentions Mary Austin's tales of the desert Southwest as one of the signs of growing regional cultures in America, his review of Austin's *The American Rhythm* (1923) criticizes the author for not being regional *enough*. Austin's argument about American Indian song, rooted in "primitive organic experiences," as forming the basis for "American" poetry, Mumford claims, is hampered by her "interest in an Americanization program." She is not interested in "the influence of rustic occupations and experiences on poetry, but the influences of *American* occupations on *American* poetry" (emphasis in original):

> It is one thing to go back to the soil in Rhode Island, with old, cultivated farms and a steady rough of life and a landscape that at times recalls Kent or Sussex; and it is another to go back to it in the midst of the corn carpeted prairie. If Mrs. Austin's essential theory is worth anything, a quite different rhythm will arise in poetry and music out of these two different backgrounds; and to call both of these American, or to attempt to identify them with the art of the aborigine, is to relate them to a political unit and to a past which, from the standpoint of our present culture, can scarcely be said to exist.[72]

Mumford's logic of regional culture, literary form, and the state in turn shape the terms by which Mumford canonizes *Moby-Dick* as a regional, not a national, novel. Mumford emphasizes from the outset Melville's "provincial" society, characterized by "balance and continuity"; this regional culture is opposed explicitly to "the United States, [which,] as an abstract political entity, scarcely existed"—that is, the political and economic ties between individual regions were not yet matched by the sense of "a mystic relation with other parts" that would characterize later claims of national culture (*Melville*, 9). This "certain unity" of regional culture, in turn, governs Mumford's reading of the *formal* unity of *Moby-Dick*, as he repeatedly emphasizes the impossibility of separating different aspects of the novel, or reducing it to a particular allegorical message. It is precisely in its "whole unity," whose meaning resists paraphrase, that the novel displays its regionalism: whole aesthetic structures synecdochically embody whole cultures; whole cultures are by definition regional; therefore, whole aesthetic objects (like *Moby-Dick*) are whole precisely because they are products of genuine regional cultures.

Correspondingly, Mumford does *not* characterize the novel as "American," nor does he—as will become common in Americanist criticism from the 1940s onward—read Ahab (or Ishmael) as allegories for particular American values or ideologies, positive or negative.[73] Rather than "American," Melville repeatedly figures in Mumford's work as "modern": Melville's concerns are "distinctly modern," and "*Moby-Dick* . . . is one of the first great mythologies to be created in the modern world" (*Melville*, 361, 193). It is "modern," Mumford claims, because it is created "out of the stuff of that world, its science, its exploration, its terrestrial daring, its concentration upon power and dominion over nature, and not out of ancient symbols" (193). Thus, Mumford characterizes *Moby-Dick* as uniting the "dissevered halves" of the "*modern* world and the *modern* self" (193, emphasis added). Thus, just as Sapir and Mumford posit the units of culture to be both regional *and* cosmopolitan, skipping over the spurious culture of the nation-state, Mumford reads *Moby-Dick* as reflecting these two scales of culture: the "certain unity" of the region, which synthesizes and puts into particular form the otherwise "dissevered" parts of a more universal, cosmopolitan "modern" (or at least "Western") life.[74]

In contrast to much later Americanist criticism that focuses on Ahab in relation to "America," for better or worse, Mumford in his emphasis on the formal whole produces in turn a reading in which Ahab is relatively *decentered* (occupying only about four pages of text in a chapter of forty pages), only one element in a whole system of meaning. When Mumford does suggest what Ahab "means," he represents the work of meaning and culture as such, the heroic effort to make meaning from an otherwise purely material existence—albeit, in Ahab's case, tragic and misapplied because worked out in force and violence. Ahab is, for Mumford, still a monomaniac—but there is nothing particularly "American" in his monomania, and that monomania also arises from the heroic desire to make meaning, or culture. But this work of culture, Mumford goes on to state, is embodied by all of the crew: Melville, he argues, "summons into the whaler the several races of the world" to express "the universal nature of that effort which caps nature with culture, existence with meaning, and facts with forms" (*Melville*, 363). Thus, if culture is the creation of "meaning" and "forms," then that effort is both "universal" *and* "regional"—a universal concept (all groups make culture) that finds its fulfillment in specific regional settings (genuine culture is regional and plural).

Indeed, Mumford argues that the novel's regionalism is precisely what makes it universal. Writing elsewhere in response to critiques of the "weakness for what passes as regional literature," Mumford admits that as long as regions are not considered "economic and social units"—that is, as cultures—literature will "succumb to the tourist's silly desire for local colour and 'quaintness,'" only the "patina" of local experience: "What we need for a good universal literature [instead] is a little *more* regionalism, and a little less of the universalism symbolized by national advertising, Ford cars, and Child's restaurants."[75] Replacing metaphors of surface (regional difference as "patina") with depth (regional difference as a "economic and social unit," or, in Sapir's words, a "unified and consistent" culture), Mumford argues that through this specificity, a universal "art" will emerge: "He who writes for the pleasure of his neighbors . . . may presently find himself speaking to the world."[76] The true hero of Mumford's reading is, of course, Melville himself, who succeeds in creating, in *Moby-Dick*, a meaningful whole that embodies both regional and universal—but not national—culture.

Culture, Aesthetics, and the Origins of American Studies

Thus, for both Mumford and Sapir, a genuine regional culture is opposed to a "spurious" national culture. Where, for Sapir, the Indian exemplifies genuine culture in contrast to modern American civilization, for Mumford, it is Melville and *Moby-Dick*, the formal wholeness of which attests to the formal unity of the genuine regional culture from which it emerges. Seeing Mumford's contribution to the Melville revival—and by extension his contribution to the restructuring of the Americanist literary canon as it emerged within American Studies through the next two decades—in this light makes visible the terms of that revival in new ways. Critics examining the Melville revival have frequently argued that it represented a conservative reaction against the threats of immigration and class struggle by asserting an essential American, Anglo-Saxon set of values. Lauter, for example, contends that critics involved in the revival were "looking back into the nation's history for a new champion [to] uphold against British condescension American claims to an equality in culture which would be consonant with America's established title to military and diplomatic [power, in order to] sustain certain established American values now at contest."[77] Spanos similarly asserts that Mumford and others were uniformly invested in seeing *Moby-Dick*, "not simply as Melville's 'masterpiece,' but as an American 'masterpiece.'"[78] These arguments in turn are mirrored in accounts of the rise of American Studies and the institutionalization of American literature in the twentieth century, of which the Melville revival formed a crucial part. As Donald Pease and Robyn Wiegman have put it, American Studies enforced an "imaginary homogeneity out of discrepant life worlds [to create an] isomorphism of the sovereign people, U.S. territory, and national culture."[79]

But Mumford's reading of *Moby-Dick* as the embodiment of regional culture was mobilized precisely *against* the problem of "American" "military and diplomatic" power, and the establishment of an "imaginary homogeneity" of "American values." For Mumford, as well as for anthropologists like Sapir, culture—and thus Mumford's Melville as culture's avatar—was antithetical to the idea of homogeneous "American values." And instead of marking, as Lauter puts it, "the way in which 1920s critics used Melville to mark American 'civilization' off from 'savagery,'" or to resist what Spanos calls "the threat of barbarism posed by the enfranchisement of the hitherto quiescent immigrant masses and . . . the emergent 'Red Scare,'" Mumford and Sapir used culture precisely to undo, in the name of pluralism, the normative opposition between civilization and savagery (even as they established another normative model of wholeness).[80] This pluralism in turn was deployed by Sapir and his fellow Boasians, as well as Mumford, Kallen, Bourne, and others to recognize the immigrant as a member of "a culture" in a "transnational America," and to *oppose* the state that would enforce a "national" cultural homogeneity in the name of the "Red Scare." And rather than serving a "unifying function" to create this isomorphism of people, culture, and political boundaries, as Pease and Wiegman would have it, the specifically interdisciplinary study of culture, as enacted by Mumford and Sapir, was meant precisely to *disrupt* this isomorphism and establish multiple unities that formed a counter-narrative to the centralized state.

At the same time, recognizing the definition of regional culture that Mumford (and Sapir) deploy and the model of textual aesthetics and interpretation that follows complicates other versions of the rise of American literature and American Studies. Critics have often told the story of American literature and American Studies as that of a discipline rooted in the positivist epistemology of philology and literary history, rising in political and aesthetic opposition to the textual, hermeneutic epistemology of the New Criticism.[81] Mumford's contribution to the Melville revival, however, reveals a common conversation about culture and aesthetics that connects the revision of the Americanist canon in the 1920s and the rise of the New Criticism, even before the well-known fusion of the two in Matthiessen's *American Renaissance*.[82]

My point here is neither to rescue Mumford and the Melville revival from charges of conservatism nor to equate Mumford and Sapir with the New Critics. Of course, as Walter Benn Michaels has shown, the idea of cultural pluralism in the 1920s could be deployed for both progressive *and* nativist positions, as the logic of "difference" could be used to validate multiple "ways of life" within a symphonic America (as it is for such figures as Mumford, Sapir, and Horace Kallen) *or* to justify exclusion (in the hands of such nativists as Lothrop Stoddard or Madison Grant, who would argue that immigrant groups would always be "different" and, therefore, never "American," whatever their citizenship).[83] But to overlook the multiple ways new conceptions of culture could be used is to miss the complexity of the debate over culture—and its corollary debates over aesthetics and literary canons—and the variety of political and aesthetic positions it made available in the period.

It is also to miss the ways in which these early debates over culture, canon, and politics continue to shape our current discussions about the history and future of American Studies and American literature as a discipline. As a recent anthology has narrated it, in the wake of "anticolonial independence projects of the immediate postwar period, the new social and political movements of the 1960s, [the emergence of a] global economy [and] extensive migration of peoples from place to place," New Americanists have challenged the white, male, heteronormative, nationalist "assumption of American exceptionalism" that had dominated American Studies through mid-century with a "multiculturalism" that has unearthed the "counter-narratives" of women, ethnic and racial minorities, and the working class.[84] But as the examples of Mumford and Sapir make clear, the deployment of culture in the 1920s—a deployment that included Mumford's contribution to the Melville revival—was for these critics precisely "anticolonial" in its opposition to the homogenizing power of the nation-state in favor of regional diversity, and it was connected to the "global economy" and the "migration of peoples from place to place" that was already evident in their period. Moreover, the *model* of culture currently deployed to counter the "imagined homogeneity" of American Studies and to undergird multiculturalism and the establishment of the counter-narratives organized around ethic, gender, class, or sexual identities is in many ways the same model of culture established by such critics as Sapir and Mumford in the 1920s. As John Guillory has suggested, "The construction of alternative canons . . . is very much concerned to reassert the culture *unity* of subcultures or countercultures[, and] the present very anxious fixation on the canon . . . can be read as symptomatic of a certain anxiety associated with the perceived disunity . . . of the culture as a whole, as a *fragmented* whole, by constituting new cultural unities at the level of gender, race, or more recently ethnic subcultures, or gay and lesbian subcultures."[85]

Mumford's and Sapir's deployment of culture as a concept that moves both below and above the nation-state thus anticipates, in interesting ways, current work among scholars of American Studies that challenges the model of national sovereignty upon which their discipline (according to one narrative) has been based and moves toward a model that is both more local and more transnational. Both Russ Castronovo and Wai Chee Dimock, tellingly, turn to the "aesthetic" as a concept that might bypass the nation: as Dimock puts it, the aesthetic "is both local and global," a way for a global community "to individuate each of its members even as it affirms its integrative common ground." In the process, the aesthetic "invokes a map that predates the nation-state, one that allows for multilateral ties, more complex and far-flung than those dictated by territorial jurisdictions."[86] Both Dimock and Castronovo note that the universalism of the aesthetic has, in recent critical theory, been seen as opposed to the pluralism of the "cultural" in cultural studies. Mumford's and Sapir's aesthetic conception of culture reveals how culture and the aesthetic have always been intertwined; their deployment of this concept in opposition to the state both complicates New Americanist accounts of their own disciplinary history and provides a potential "usable past" for the current transnational turn in the field. Attentiveness to the complexity of the debate over culture and canon formation in the 1920s and the varieties of political and aesthetic positions it made available, in other words, illuminates the ways in which these complexities continue—in much the same terms—in contemporary debates over American Studies, the Americanist canon, and the interdisciplinary approaches of cultural studies.

To sum up, then, the Melville revival must be seen in the context of the broader interdisciplinary problematic of culture. The problem of culture arises, as Raymond Williams has put it, when "the change in the whole form of our common life produce[s], as a necessary reaction, an emphasis on attention to this whole form[;] . . . the working-out of the idea of culture is a slow reach again for control."[87] In response to the perceived social, political, and technological shifts of modernity, anthropologists, social and literary critics, and artists attempted to "reach again for control" by thinking about new ways to conceptualize (and construct) this "whole form of life," and called it "culture." These multiple, overlapping, and competing conceptualizations of culture, each with its own political, epistemological, and aesthetic ramifications, in turn structure the debates in several disciplinary arenas, from anthropology to literary criticism, as new ways to conceive of and interpret ways of life become new ways to think about and read literature.

In this way, key texts of the Melville revival become reflections of, and participants in, the debate over culture. For Raymond Weaver, deploying culture in something like the nineteenth-century Arnoldian sense of the term, Melville becomes the romantic hero of high Culture, above the Philistine public that failed to appreciate him. At the same time, Weaver's Melville deploys an epistemology of "experience," played out in the romantic arena of the South Seas, that echoes many of the epistemological and methodological innovations being produced in precisely the same moment by Bronislaw Malinowski, whose *Argonauts of the Western Pacific* would establish the model of participant-observation through fieldwork as the proper anthropological method.

Van Wyck Brooks's criticism on Melville further shifts the terms of the debate over Melville in the direction of Malinowski's model of culture, and that being developed in the U.S. context by Franz Boas and his students. Brooks shifts from seeing Melville as a symptom of the fragmentation that characterizes American life, to seeing Melville as representing the kind of Coleridgian "focal center" around which he might organize a usable past. That shift is reflected in Brooks's changing evaluation of the form of Melville's writing, from seeing his work as "garrulous" and fragmented to achieving a controlled "equilibrium." This shift in evaluating Melville—and, more important, the criteria by which a literary text should be read and valued—is most fully articulated by Lewis Mumford. Deploying a conception of culture that echoes the structural model articulated within anthropology by Edward Sapir, Mumford argues that Melville embodies the "whole" culture, rooted in the geographic region, of nineteenth-century New England and New York; moreover, that spatial conception of culture as a whole system of meaning in turn becomes a method for reading the text, and *Moby-Dick* emerges as a model of the unified literary object. Mumford's model of regional culture, deployed against the imperial state, and his elevation of *Moby-Dick* as a unified, regional novel, complicates nationalist accounts of the reconstruction of the Americanist canon and American Studies. It also reveals the way in which new definitions of cultures and texts—with both being defined as bounded, internally unified and constructed through the meaningful interrelationship of parts, in contrast to the superficial abstractions of the industrial America—are deployed in the period by groups that are often seen as politically and methodologically opposite, linking liberal and progressive critics like Mumford and Sapir on the one hand and reactionary critics like Allen Tate and John Crowe Ransom on the other. It is to the deployment of culture by these New Critics, to construct their own version of regional culture and poetic structure, that I turn in the next chapter.

4 / Recovering the Whole: Culture, Region, and Poetry in the Literary Criticism of John Crowe Ransom and Allen Tate

In his essay "Literature as Knowledge" (1941), Allen Tate tellingly begins his survey of recent semiotic and psychological theories of language not with a discussion of semiotics or psychology, but with a discussion of "culture"—specifically, the "Culture" of Matthew Arnold. Faced with "the accumulating body of the inert, descriptive facts of science," Arnold, Tate argues, decided "something had to be done about it"; he proposed Culture as that thing.[1] Arnold's "program," according to Tate, was "culture added to science, and perhaps correcting it" ("Knowledge," 72). This formula, he concludes, "has not worked," in part because of the very relationship it imagines between culture and science, and the corresponding ideas of poetry it produces: regarding culture as something that could be "added to" the concrete "facts" of science, Tate suggests, renders the poet as "merely the scientist who achieves completeness"; poetry becomes "descriptive science ... touched with emotion" (73, 74). As a decorative add-on to the subject matter of science, "the language of poetry is of secondary importance" (76).

This "neoclassical" distinction between poetic language and its "prose subject," Tate goes on to argue, also characterizes recent scientific philosophies of language proposed by the early work of I. A. Richards and others: all of these theories find the "meaning" of poetic language in the pragmatic measure of "how ... we behave when we read it: what, in a word, does it lead to" (91). Tate's goal in the essay, of course, is to challenge this pragmatic version of poetic language, in a way that would become central to the New Criticism he would come to represent in the next decades. Asking "Is it possible to distinguish the language from the subject? Are not the subject and language one?" (76), Tate answers "no" to the first and "yes" to the second: poetry finally stands as a "unique" experience in offering the reader "complete knowledge," the completeness of which lies precisely in the fusion of language and subject (104–5).

If, in Tate's argument, Arnold's conception of Culture gives rise to his (flawed) conception of poetic language, then in this chapter I will suggest that Tate's critique of Arnold's theory of poetry is in turn a critique of the version of culture that produces it. In its stead, Tate, along with his colleague and fellow New Critic John Crowe Ransom, proposes a new conception of poetic language that itself rests on a new conception of culture.

In the preceding chapters, I argued that in response to a perceived state of fragmentation and "dissociation" brought on by modern industrial society, critics and intellectuals from across a wide variety of disciplines through the 1920s and 1930s attempted to imagine "whole" and "meaningful" units, be they linguistic structures, works of art, or entire ways of life. This problematic is worked out within anthropology in debates over new ways to conceive of culture as the discipline's central concern, as anthropologists such as Edward Sapir and Bronislaw Malinowksi attempt to construct culture as a relative, whole system of meaning, the importance of any one element of which can be understood only within the context of that whole. This "anthropological" debate is inseparable from debates over literary form and value—debates that emerge in situations as diverse as Willa Cather's fascination with literary composition and the composition of Cliff Dweller culture, and in the new ways of reading and valuing literature that lay behind the revival of Herman Melville and the canonization of *Moby-Dick* at the heart of a restructured version of American literary history. New conceptions of culture as spatial form, in particular, work themselves out in questions of the boundedness of regional or national culture, and the boundedness of the text and the construction of canons of national literature.

The intertwining poetic and cultural theories of John Crowe Ransom and Allen Tate bring together several of the lines of thought traced in the preceding chapters. Tate and Ransom, like the other figures I have been tracking, participate in constructing new models of culture as a "whole way of life" in explicit contrast to the abstractions of science and industrialism and conceive of this cultural "whole" as itself a spatialized, aesthetic object. This spatialized culture is in turn, like for Mumford and Sapir, grounded in the physical region and represents the fusion of art and economy. As with Sapir and Malinowski, Tate's and Ransom's works link a concern for culture with a concern with language and meaning: composing culture as a whole, relative way of life, formed by the fusion of art and economy into a meaningful, organic system, Tate and Ransom in turn construct a corresponding argument about the "meaning" and ontology of the poem as a "whole" object formed by the fusion of poetic form and prose meaning. The structure of regional culture as a self-sufficient, patterned whole, in short, finds its embodiment for Tate and Ransom in the New Critical structure of the poem as a unified aesthetic object.

Grounding the New Criticism in the debates over culture is important in several ways. First, it challenges the accounts of the New Criticism that have framed the rise of poststructuralism and cultural studies in the past decades. For critics writing "after the New Criticism" (to quote the title of one of the more influential works inaugurating this phase in literary studies), the New Criticism is notorious for its supposed insistence on the separation of poetry from culture and historical context. Imagining the poem as a self-contained form of knowledge, and demanding a critical focus on the language of the text as opposed to the historical context or moral content, the New Criticism inaugurated by Ransom and Tate has been critiqued for ripping the poem "free of the wreckage of history and hoisting it into a sublime space above it."[2] In contrast, poststructuralist theory and cultural studies claim to counter the New Critical emphasis on the stability and universalism of poetry with an analysis of the instability of poetic language, an emphasis on cultural pluralism, and attention to the ways in which literature must be seen as part of a broader cultural context—where "culture" refers to the broader systems of meaning and power within which literature is situated.

In recent years, several critics have responded to these poststructuralist charges of the New Critics' "ahistoricism" by grounding New Critical theory in its own social and historical context, tracing a connection between the early writings of the Southern Agrarians such as Tate and Ransom and the later New Critical theories. These critics have generally focused on the ways in which the New Critical emphasis on the poem as a special form of knowledge counters the pragmatic knowledge of science, in the same way that Tate's and Ransom's agrarian politics of the early 1930s opposed a regional, agrarian life to the "cash-nexus" of industrialism. Mark Jancovich, for example, argues that the poetic theories of Ransom, Tate, and other New Critics like Warren and Brooks do not represent (as some critics would have it) a retreat from the agrarian social and political commitments of their earlier writings, but a "tactical" shift that extended these commitments.³ More recently, critics such as Edward Pickering have pushed this argument a step further by arguing that the politics and philosophy of the Southern Agrarians—opposing the "organic" agrarian community to scientific, utilitarian industrialism—became the New Critical emphasis on the "organic" poem whose language provides an alternative to the practical knowledge of science.⁴

Although this antimodern stance is part of my concern here, I argue that the relationship between Tate's and Ransom's agrarianism and New Criticism goes even deeper, to the very way they construct both "culture" and "the poem" as such. If, as Pickering points out, there is a common language of organicism connecting Ransom and Tate's Southern Agrarian rhetoric to their New Criticism, it is not because, as he puts it, "a culture of the soil valued the organic over the artificial and the mechanical"—that is, because it values a different relation to *nature*—but because they participate in the construction of a new definition of *culture*. The spatial terms by which this agrarian "way of life" is imagined in turn describe the structure of a good poem. I argue, in other words, that the New Critical conception of the poem as a "sublime space," self-referential and internally meaningful, is *itself* a theory of culture. Tate's and Ransom's versions of how a poem "means" is in fact rooted in and routed through the shifting conceptions of culture that I have been tracing through this project.

Grounding Tate's and Ransom's theories of poetry in the problematic of culture itself troubles what have come to be accepted sets of oppositions governing the narratives of literary critical history, then and now. Proponents of cultural studies have cast the New Criticism, in their supposed bracketing of culture and history from issues of poetic form, as the reactionary past against which they pose the progressive alternative through their attention to culture. This narrative is doubled by histories of literary criticism in the 1920s and 1930s, which set liberal or progressive critics interested in being, as Alan Trachtenberg put it, "critics of culture"—the list usually includes Randolph Bourne, Van Wyck Brooks, Lewis Mumford, Waldo Frank, and, going further, Franz Boas and his students—against reactionary critics like Ransom, Tate, Eliot, and others, who isolate culture from aesthetics. Grounding Tate's and Ransom's theories—both of regional agrarianism and of aesthetics—in debates over culture as such in these decades reveals the ways in which a common conception of culture undergirds *both* progressive and reactionary positions. For both progressives like Sapir and Mumford and reactionaries like Tate and Ransom, culture is a "whole" internally coherent system of meaning grounded in a regional geography, and as such, the concept of culture is itself an aesthetic concept, not its opposite. Where contemporary critics set their own emphasis on postmodern and multicultural "difference" against Tate's and Ransom's supposed commitment to a hierarchical "universalism," grounding the New Criticism in emergent theories of cultures as meaningful wholes reveals, I would suggest, the ways that Tate and Ransom themselves enact a version of cultural and poetic "pluralism." What is crucial in this version is not a universal standard of values upon which an artifact can be judged "higher" or "lower," but "difference"—between regional cultures, distinct from a homogenized imagined national culture, and between the concrete, infinitely particular poetic experience and the universalization of that experience that is the goal of science. Attention to the idea of culture and the idea of aesthetics in the 1920s and 1930s cannot be seen as separate or opposite, but as different disciplinary forms of an interconnected, interdisciplinary conversation or problematic—an idea that might cause us to reexamine the relationship between cultural studies and its bête noir, the New Criticism, as well as shed light on the more recent "aesthetic turn" in literary studies.

I begin by examining John Crowe Ransom's interventions, through his essays in *The World's Body* (1938) and *The New Criticism* (1941), in the debates that raged throughout the 1920s and 1930s over the "meaning" of language, debates whose principles included psychologists and anthropologists such as I. A. Richards and Bronislaw Malinowski. Despite their apparently opposite vocabulary—Malinowski articulates his theories of language in the name of science, whereas Ransom opposes poetry to science—I argue that Malinowski's and Ransom's theories of the way language creates meaning must be seen as part of a common problematic of culture, engaged in trying to recover a "whole"—the whole meaning of a word, a whole way of life—that is obscured by a pragmatic, interested knowledge. In both cases, I argue, a theory of the meaning of language is inseparably connected to a theory of culture. Malinowski's theory of the meaning of "primitive languages" (and, indeed, any language) is inseparable from his construction of culture as a relative, organic whole. By working backward from Ransom's poetic theories, most clearly articulated in his essays in the late 1930s, to his agrarian writings of the early 1930s, I argue that Ransom's version of poetic meaning is also rooted in a theory of cultural wholes similar to Malinowski's, a theory that produces what Ransom calls a "regional aesthetic." For Ransom, as for Edward

Sapir and Lewis Mumford, "culture" is by definition a "whole" way of life, whose various integrated activities and traditions are "meaningful" insofar as they relate to one another, and to the physical environment from which they arise; the unit of culture is therefore the region. The key terms of this regional culture system—meaning through interrelation of part, wholeness, stability—in turn become key terms in the New Critical conception of the poem. Poetry, then, becomes a synecdoche for culture.

Turning to Allen Tate, I argue that Tate similarly links the form of culture to the form of poetry. In particular, I want to show the way in which, for Tate, the argument about culture (and politics) becomes the argument about literary form, and in ways that shape critical tastes and canons of modernist poetry for decades to come. Focusing on Tate's response to Hart Crane's *The Bridge*, I suggest that Tate's negative response to the poem as not "unified" is predicated on Tate's theory of cultural "unity" as by definition regional, as opposed to national. Crane's poem—the project of which is explicitly "national," to encompass all of American history and geography—is not unified, in Tate's eyes, because its subject does not exist as a unit of culture. In the process, I argue that Tate's definition of poetic unity is founded on a version of cultural pluralism—where the unit of culture is explicitly the region—that differentiates his definition of culture and tradition from both Crane's vision of national culture on the one hand, and the universalism of critics like T. S. Eliot on the other. Finally, I argue that this common conception of culture as an integrated "whole," and the corollary conception of the aesthetic object it produces, in turn creates a common model of authority that becomes central to both anthropology and literary criticism—namely, the model of the anthropologist who is the participant-observer of the "whole" culture and the poet-critic who likewise interprets the whole poem.

John Crowe Ransom: Literary Anthropologist and Anthropological Critic

In his essay "The Idea of a Literary Anthropologist" (1959), John Crowe Ransom advances a complex theory of science, poetic meaning, and cultural pluralism. Ransom imagines the possible advantages a "literary anthropologist"—"a professional anthropologist who is at the same time deeply accomplished in the understanding of literature"—might have in understanding Milton's *Paradise Lost*, and specifically Milton's treatment of Adam and Eve's expulsion from the Garden. Ransom frames his argument in favor of what he calls "anthropologism" as a response to

Roy Harvey Pearce's plea for "historicism." In answering the question of how a modern reader should properly relate to poetry produced in a different historical era, Pearce suggests that historicism will allow the critic to place himself or herself within that remote historical context and ultimately "consent" to, or see as reasonable, the action described there. By granting that consent, the reader "feels we have discovered an evidence of the continuity of our culture, and indeed of our human nature."[5]

To the humanism and universalism of Pearce's literary historian, Ransom opposes the literary anthropologist, who, he argues, is "more radically a scientist than our historian is expected to be. He will be a good naturalist, or economist, and his understanding of literature,... as of the culture of a society generally, must have to do with its adaptation to the natural economy" ("Literary Anthropologist," 331). Ransom reiterates this formulation of scientific knowledge when he turns to his reading of Milton's poem itself. In Ransom's account of (Milton's account of) the Fall, he argues that the knowledge acquired by Adam and Eve upon eating the apple was specifically the "knowledge of science," which is "knowledge which bears directly upon the economy" (331). More specifically, Ransom's literary anthropologist understands "literature... [and]... culture in general" to be formed through "*adaptation to the natural economy.*" With this knowledge of the relation between art and economy, the literary anthropologist, Ransom suggests, is thus uniquely able to comprehend a central tension in Milton's account of the Fall—the tension between the orthodox Milton who condemns Adam and Eve as sinners and the progressive Milton who knows that Adam and Eve "must have science," or the knowledge that produces the "series of economic stages out of which will come eventually the human society as we know it and as the anthropologists have taught us to figure it" (335, 332). Thus, the literary anthropologist is able to find the whole meaning of the poem—in this case in the tension surrounding the loss of prelapsarian wholeness that makes scientific knowledge possible.

Moreover, the literary anthropologist can recognize both Milton's theology and the economic conditions to which he was reacting as precisely *different* from his own: he practices what Ransom calls a "comparative theology," with his observations of "the widest range [of] patterns of behavior which become organized in collective cultures" (334). Thus, the tension that the literary anthropologist is able to uncover between elements within the poem is mirrored in his ability to properly see the tension between his own culture and that in which the poem is produced. Pearce's literary historian, he suggests, would "enter the mind of his author, acquiring of course the language and the style, and assimilating just as faithfully the moral and theological ideas," and in the process the "self-effacing scholar is so identified with his author" that he relinquishes his own values "assent[ing] to facts of life other than [his] own" (326). As opposed to Pearce's universalist assimilation, Ransom's literary anthropologist is a poetic and cultural pluralist: recognizing not the "continuity of our culture" but the difference between cultures, he is likewise committed to that culture that is "his" (324).

Although I return later to the categories of science, economy, and cultural pluralism mobilized in Ransom's essay, for now I would like to pursue the idea of the literary anthropologist or, more specifically, the connection between Ransom's theories of poetry and modernist anthropological theories of culture and language. Specifically, I will relate Bronislaw Malinowski's essay "The Problem of Meaning in Primitive Language," published as a supplement to Richard and Ogden's *The Meaning of Meaning* (1923), and Ransom's theories of poetic language articulated in *The World's Body* (1938) and *The New Criticism* (1941), particularly in his essays "The Tense of Poetry," "The Mimetic Principle," and "Wanted: An Ontological Critic." I argue that Malinowski's theories of the functioning of language within culture and Ransom's theory of the ontology of the poem engage the same problematic: each opposes theories that abstract "part" of a word's meaning by arguing that meaning can be derived only from an analysis of the "whole." In Malinowski's case, this "whole" is literally the whole culture in which the word is spoken; in Ransom's case, it is the "whole" poem. Furthermore, if Malinowski's argument about how language means is linked to a theory of culture, then so, too, is Ransom's: where anthropologists of language like Malinowski and Sapir formulate a new version of cultures as self-referential, meaningful wholes, for Ransom the poem emerges as the embodiment of "a culture," whose stable structure, formed by the interaction of art and economy and spatially grounded in the region, finds its analogue in the stable tension between meter and prose in the poem, conceived as an object in space.

Ransom and Malinowski: Culture and Meaning in Primitive and Poetic Language

The pairing of Malinowksi and Ransom is significant because of the central place both figures occupy within the "modernisms" of the disciplines with which they are identified— modernist anthropology, and the

New Criticism—and relatedly within modernist debates over the nature of language. Although I am not arguing that Ransom and Malinowski were in direct contact with each other or directly responded to or were influenced by each other, both figures occupy key and related positions in the "matrix of modernism."[6] In that key year of 1922, which for many marked the beginning of literary modernism with the publication of Eliot's *The Waste Land*, Malinowski published his *Argonauts of the Western Pacific*, which is often cited as the founding text of modernist anthropology. In this same year, Ransom, along with Allen Tate, Donald Davidson, and several other of Ransom's students at Vanderbilt, began publishing *The Fugitive*, in whose pages both Tate and Ransom would begin working out their theories of poetry, both in the poetry they published and in essays.

More importantly, as historians, anthropologists, and literary critics have all pointed out, the 1920s and 1930s were characterized by an intense interest in the "meaning" of language, with scientists and philosophers from a wide variety of perspectives bringing new scientific, psychological, and linguistic techniques to bear on the problem.[7] Malinowski and Ransom, each from his own particular disciplinary perspective, were engaged in this common problem and were linked through key figures in this debate. One of the most prominent of these was the British psychologist and literary critic I. A. Richards, who, in such works as *The Meaning of Meaning* (1923), *Principles of Literary Criticism* (1924), *Science and Poetry* (1926), and *Practical Criticism* (1929), attempted to ascertain the "meaning of meaning" through the careful analysis of reader's psychological responses to poetry. Richards became a particular target for Ransom's and Tate's critique: they regarded his pragmatic approach to language function as typifying the abstraction of the scientific worldview.[8] Although Ransom does not, as far as I have been able to find, refer to Malinowski himself, Malinowski's argument about language is closely linked to Richards's, both in theory and in practice. Malinowski published his essay "Meaning in Primitive Language" as a supplement to Richards and C. K. Ogden's *The Meaning of Meaning*; throughout that essay, Malinowski repeatedly asserts the similarity between his work and Richards's, especially between Richards's "sign situation" and his own "context of situation," and to their common argument that meaning is pragmatic, or resides in action as opposed to cognition. For my purposes, what is more crucial than this transitive connection through Richards, however, is what Malinowski adds to the discussion: precisely the theory of culture that Ransom will find so valuable in his "literary anthropologist." Malinowski and Ransom, I argue, both produce theories of language that are also theories of culture.

At first glance, Malinowski's approach to language would seem diametrically opposed to Ransom's: Malinowski elaborates his theory of primitive language under the aegis of "science," whereas Ransom articulates his ideas about poetic language in explicit *opposition* to the prose language of "science" and "positivism." This opposition between Malinowski's "science" and Ransom's "poetry," however, is at least in part dissolved when one more closely examines what each means by "science." For both critics, the favored term (for Malinowski "science," for Ransom "poetry") designates a mode of knowledge that is able to apprehend a more complete reality, rather than a partial one. For Malinowski, the scientific study of language is opposed to "practical" knowledge: a "practical" approach to understanding primitive language wants to put its knowledge to "use," but science aims simply for knowledge for its own sake and is thus able to apprehend its object of study in its entirety.

Malinowski begins his essay with a discussion of the difficulties involved in accurately translating particular words and phrases of the Trobriand Islanders into English. Consulting extant dictionaries and grammars of Oceanic languages during his own field work, Malinowski discovers that "the authors, . . . mainly missionaries who wrote for the practical purpose of facilitating the task of their successors," were satisfied with "the next best approximation in English to a native word."[9] This "equivalence," he argues, "is only approximate, suitable for some practical purposes, such as trading with the natives, missionary preaching and translation of Christian literature into native languages." Against this "approximate," practical translation, Malinowski opposes the accuracy of "scientific translation": "the object of a scientific translation of a word," he states, "is not to give its rough equivalent, sufficient for practical purposes, but to state exactly whether a native word corresponds to an idea at least partially existing for English speakers, or whether it covers an entirely foreign conception" ("Meaning," 299).

This theory of language is based on a version of cultural pluralism. Rather than placing cultures on a universal, evolutionary scale, Malinowski stresses relative difference: beyond individual words or phrases, "the *whole manner* in which a native language is used is different from our own" (300, emphasis added). To understand the "meaning" of a single word, Malinowski suggests, one must analyze the "whole" language, which means ultimately the "whole" culture: "language," he argues, "is essentially rooted in the reality of the culture, the tribal life and customs of the people, and . . . it cannot be explained without constant reference to these broader contexts of verbal utterance," or what he calls the "context of situation" (305). This "context," it turns out, is an ever-widening circle of inquiry, through which one is drawn into "a long and not altogether simple process of describing wide fields of custom, of social psychology and of tribal organization which correspond to one term or another." Moving from part to whole, Malinowski suggests that "linguistic analysis inevitably leads us into the study of all the subjects covered by Ethnographic field work"—that is, all of (a) culture (302).

Thus, Malinowski's argument about the function of language is an inseparable part of his theory of culture as plural, relative "wholes"— the "modern anthropological" culture for which Malinowski is in part credited by some historians of anthropology. As discussed in the previous chapters, in the standard disciplinary histories of anthropology, the publication of Malinowski's *Argonauts of the Western Pacific* in 1922 marks a moment at which the very definition of the anthropologists' object of study—"culture"—shifted, and along with it, the methods with which the anthropologist was expected to conduct his or her research. As Marc Manganaro has put it, the "dramatic appearance of Malinowski's monograph sounded a death knell for Frazer's comparativist form of anthropological discourse."[10] Frazerian anthropology, operating under the same evolutionary, comparative model of culture as Tylor's and Morgan's model as described in chapter 2, collected and compared individual myths and rituals across time and across a wide variety of societies, to construct a universal scale of cultural "progress." In this sense there were no "cultures" as such, but "Culture," a continuum upon which individual traits could be compared and judged.

In contrast, Malinowski's ethnographic method marks a conceptual shift from a universal version of culture to a relativist, pluralist version of "cultures." Rather than seeking similar traits across various societies, or comparing societies as "more" or "less" evolved, this new version of cultural wholes stressed "difference": individual traits were essentially incomparable, because they could be fully understood only in the context of the whole culture. Thus, just as the meaning of an artifact like a canoe—to use Malinowski's example cited in chapter 3—can be understood only in the full context of its place within its cultural system (an understanding available only to the ethnographer as participant-observer), so too can the meaning of an individual word or phrase be given only within the context of the whole culture.

Although not identical to the versions of culture articulated by Boas and his students such as Sapir who have been the main focus of this study, this version of culture is similar in its emphasis on culture as an integrated whole, where meaning is produced through the interrelationship of parts. The similarities between the Boasian/Sapirian model of culture and the Malinowskian model of culture, which I argue becomes a forceful intertext in understanding the rise of the New Criticism, speak to the international "matrix of modernism," connecting conversations between figures in the United States, England, and Europe that cross the conventional national disciplinary narratives that are often produced. The Anglo-American anthropological conversations about culture and the Anglo-American conversations about the meaning of language and literature intertwine in their common concern to counter what they argue was the "partial" or abstract knowledge of scientific discourse that was being deployed in each field.

If Malinowski, then, opposes the partial understanding of language generated for practical purposes to the whole apprehension of a culture in order to attain pure knowledge called "science," then Ransom too argues for a form of whole knowledge versus partial, practical knowledge. For Ransom, however, partial knowledge is represented precisely by the term "science," and whole knowledge of the natural world is contained in "the poem." Ransom articulates this definition of science and poetry in the preface to *The World's Body*. Science, he argues, gives only partial knowledge of any particular event or object: representing "only the cognitive department of our animal life" through which we know the world "only as a scheme of abstract conveniences," science robs the "body and solid substance of the world." In contrast, he continues, "The true poetry only wants to realize the world, to see it better" (*Body*, x). Ransom elaborates this argument in "The Mimetic Principle": "Science" he argues, "is a work of classification in terms of universals"; "by its graphs or formulas, [it] record[s] the universal relations" of nature (*Body*, 199, 208). Art, in contrast, strives to capture an "infinite degree of particularity"; wanting "full representations of nature," poetry is interested "entirely in individuals" (208, 199, 205, 206). Precisely because it is interested in the individual and particular and not the universal or general, "we cannot possibly use it" (208). Scientific statements, then, are different from poetic statements precisely because scientific statements are not accurate *enough*: generated for its use-value, prose language captures only the utilitarian side of a situation or experience, whereas poetic language embodies a complete knowledge that is precisely without practical application. The "fulness of poetry," he claims, is "counterpart to the world's fulness"; in recovering "whole and indefeasible objects," poetry helps us "atone for having to be hard practical men and hard theoretical scientists" (x–xi).

Ransom and Malinowski, then, use a vocabulary that seems to put them at odds—Malinowski pursuing a "scientific" study of language, with Ransom opposing poetry to "science." What is crucial here is that this apparent opposition must be viewed within the context of the problematic of culture, and the critique of science and industrialism it involves. Malinowski posits his methodology of participant-observation in *Argonauts* as "the objective, scientific view of things," as opposed to the "interested" knowledge of the trader and missionary (*Argonauts*, 6). Furthermore, Malinowski's ethnographic method, with its emphasis on "experience," is intended precisely to overcome the abstraction of theoretical science to which Ransom opposes poetry in the previous quote. The merely observing scientist, Malinowski argues, can distill the "abstract, general rules" of native society and custom, the knowledge of which is necessary, but not sufficient: its "very precision is foreign to real life, which never adheres rigidly to any rules" (17). It is only through participant-observation that these "imponderabilia of actual life" can be discovered, putting, as Malinowski phrases it, the "flesh and blood" of real life on the "excellent skeleton" of general rules to form the living body of culture (18, 17). Similarly, Ransom contrasts the abstractions of interested knowledge—which for him define conventional science, with its interest in prediction and repetition—with the attempt to "confront reality *disinterestedly*," accepting "the bundle of complementary qualities and inexhaustible particulars" of the real.[11] As in Malinowski, this "bundling" does not so much reject as (literally) incorporate the "concepts" of science, along with conceptless "images," into the aesthetic object, to construct a "mixed world composed of both images and concepts or a sort of practicable reconciliation of the two worlds." Echoing Malinowski's "imponderabilia," Ransom goes on to say, "We are not really opposed to science, except as it monopolises. . . . We require merely the fulness of life."[12] Both Malinowski and Ransom want to apprehend the world's—or a culture's—body.

In the same way that Malinowski, writing in 1923, argues that the meaning of any given utterance must be understood as inseparably part of the complex whole of a culture, Ransom, writing in 1941 in the collection of essays that would give its name to the critical movement he helped create, argues for the irreducibility of the whole poem. In "Wanted: An Ontological Critic" (to which I return later), Ransom suggests that a poem is constructed by the inseparable interaction between the idea represented by the words in a poem and meter, or the physical sound of the words themselves. "The meter-and-meaning process is the organic act of poetry," he argues, and thus cannot be separated without destroying the poem's particularity, or, to put it another way, its identity.[13] To abstract simply its prose sense would be to disrupt this stability and is the heresy of paraphrase. In this way, Ransom's theory of poetic structure echoes the structure of Malinowski's culture: just as Malinowski suggests that to translate a Trobriand phrase into English without accounting for whole culture behind it would be to distort its meaning, Ransom argues the poem ontologically "goes beyond its paraphrase into the realm of the natural objects or situation themselves," and to translate a line of poetry, from one language to another or from poetry to prose, is to commit "ontological annihilation" (*New Criticism*, 293, 329). A poem, like a culture, is its own reality.

In articulating their versions of culture and language, on the one hand, and poetry, on the other, Malinowski and Ransom have the same goal: overcoming the dualism of thought-action and subject-object that characterizes the language theories in their respective fields. Again, the terminology by which both Malinowski and Ransom describe their projects often seems opposite: Malinowski argues that language in its "primitive function and original form has an essentially pragmatic character"; Ransom, in his essays on I. A. Richards in both *The World's Body* and *The New Criticism*, critiques Richards's "pragmatic" theory of poetry as limiting the meaning of words to their practical effect. However, as in the analysis of the category "science" given earlier, one must consider to what the term "pragmatic" is opposed in each case. Malinowski's theory of speech-acts—that language is a "mode of action"—is explicitly opposed to theories that see words either as objects containing their own meaning or, relatedly, as "countersign to thought," whose meanings come from thought abstracted from external reality. Such theories Malinowski associates both with primitive magic and Platonic idealism: the "attitude in which the word is regarded as a real entity, containing its meaning as a Soul-box contains the spiritual part of a person or thing, is . . . derived from the primitive, magical uses of language." In the second theory, the meaning exists only "in Plato's realm of Ideas" ("Meaning," 308). By arguing that the meaning of a word arises out of "practical and active acquaintance with relevant situations," Malinowski reconnects mind to world to overcome, as he says, the distinction between the "verbal" and the "real."

Ransom similarly seeks to reconnect the real and the ideal. Ransom, however, wants to overturn an argument that begins at the other end of the opposition: arguing against a pragmatic semiotics that defines meaning purely in terms of practical effect—another abstraction of science—Ransom seeks to use poetic language to reattach meaning to the knowing mind that apprehends external effect. Richards's pragmatism, he argues, limits the meaning of poetic language to the emotional and ultimately physiological effects the words have on the brain; because its only "meaning" resides in the reader's physiological responses, poetry does not, for Richards, qualify as "knowledge," a term reserved only for science's ability to describe the world separate from the mind. As described earlier, Ransom turns Richards's opposition of poetry and science on its head: the kind of knowledge embodied in poetry is, Ransom argues, ontologically distinct from the *abstract* knowledge of science, which for Ransom is precisely a kind of idealism. For Ransom, as for Malinowski, Plato embodies this idealism: Plato "was an aggressive idealist with a head full of Big Ideas," and with a "passionate preference for universals over particulars" (*Body*, 200). If, for Malinowski, Plato is the heir of the primitive magician, for Ransom, he is the forerunner of the modern theoretical scientist. All three—Plato, the primitive magician, and the theoretical scientist—engage in an idealism that identifies the meaning of language in only one aspect of the totality in which any utterance is embedded. To the idealist/magician/scientist, Malinowski opposes the whole knowledge of the anthropologist; Ransom opposes the literary critic.

Southern Agrarian to New Critic: Regional Culture and/as Poetic Form

As I have suggested, Malinowski's theory of language is part and parcel of his theory of culture as an organic whole. Ransom's theory of poetry, I argue, not only parallels Malinowski's attempt to define the meaning of language as part of a whole, but also emerges from a conception of culture as a *structure*, spatially conceived, in which meaning arises from the internal dynamic of parts forming an integral whole—a conception of culture that echoes Sapir's theory of culture as itself an aesthetic object. This structural conception of culture is ultimately what connects Ransom's Southern Agrarian writings to his New Criticism. Working back from Ransom's New Critical descriptions of the ontology of the poem in the late 1930s to his Southern Agrarian writings of the early 1930s, it becomes clear that for Ransom, the stable tension between form and content, meter and prose, that constitutes the whole poem, conceived of as an object in space, is the equivalent in language of "a culture," constituted by the dynamic interaction of art and economic activity, grounded in a geographic space, to produce a whole way of life that is "stable," "realistic," and aesthetically beautiful.

An essay that forms a key pivot between Ransom's theories of poetic structure and the structure of culture is "The Tense of Poetry" in *The World's Body*. For Ransom, poetry is a kind of knowledge that reunites the knowing mind to the "world's body" and rescues the particularity of the world from the partial, abstract prose representations of science. As in "The Idea of a Literary Anthropologist," in "The Tense of Poetry," Ransom turns to the story of the Fall to illustrate this theory. In the prelapsarian Garden of Eden, he suggest, "prose and poetry were one" (*Body*, 237). The Fall is the fall into the dualism of poetry and prose: "The tree of knowledge from which man abstained originally . . . was the tree of prose; that is of knowledge as technique and knowledge as power, of all those hard calculations by which he could have set in to act more effectively upon nature" (238). It is also, as Ransom indicates in his interpretation of Milton with which I began, the fall into science and economy. Poetry is therefore a way of attempting to recover the completeness of this prelapsarian condition: by "exhibiting actions in complete settings rather than pure or efficient actions, [poems] furnish our perfect experiences"; experiencing poetry, we "expel the taint of original sin and restore to our minds freedom and integrity" (251).

This is not to say that Ransom argues that poetry *achieves* this prelapsarian, undifferentiated unity—indeed, the point of the essay is that this is impossible, as the existence of poetry relies on, and indeed is in part constituted by, prose. The titular "tense" of poetry points in two directions. First, it is the "past tense" of all poetry, referring nostalgically back to an imagined prior condition of wholeness, "expelling the taint of original sin." Second, it is the tension *within* the poem, which is constituted precisely through the struggle between poetic and prose effects: as Ransom describes, "The brilliant effect we admire in a poem is the result of compounding many prose effects, and technical or specific ones. The business of poetry, in fact, is to take the technical prose effect, which is hard, and soften or dissolve it in a *total experience*" (*Body*, 241, emphasis added). The "totality" of the poem results from the interaction of difference, rather than homogeneity. Ransom restates this in "Wanted: An Ontological Critic" when, shifting his terms from prose and poetry to the "semantic" and the "phonetic," he argues that "the law of [a poem's] corporate existence [is that] the two properties shall not be identical, or like, or homogeneous, they shall be other, unlike, and heterogeneous" (*New Criticism*, 327). Thus the "combination of the semantic property and the phonetic property"—or prose sense and meter—that constitutes the "fine poetic phrase" becomes possible only through the dissolution of the very unity to which the "fine poetic phrase" nostalgically refers. This combination, Ransom indicates, results in the poem's "enduring stability."

The dissociation precipitated by the now fortunate Fall not only enables poetry itself; it also allows for its recognition as an aesthetic experience. "Adam," argues Ransom, "in the absence of technical thought-process, was incapable of a distinguished aesthetic experience. No percept without a concept, sharp percepts mean sharp concepts, rich percepts mean a multiplicity of concepts.... His integral or unitary experience could not have been like the thing exhibited in the work of art, but must have resembled the life of the uninformed child" (*Body*, 241). Art itself, then— or at least the recognition of art *as* art—was not possible without the Fall, where here the Fall is precisely into "technique" and "knowledge."

Ransom's interpretation of the Fall as the necessary condition of both poetry and prose, then, brings us back to the literary anthropologist and his interpretation of Milton with which I started. The complex understanding that the literary anthropologist employs—transferring his understanding of the relationship between art and economy to an understanding of the function of the poem—reappears on "The Tense of Poetry," only in reverse: beginning with a critical analysis of the workings of poetry, Ransom becomes an anthropologist speculating on Southern culture. The prelapsarian Adam, he suggests, lacking either economy or aesthetics (because one enables the other), "could not have been anything so admirable as an ante-bellum Louisiana planter. He could not have smoked cigars, nor trimmed his beard, nor had money and accounts, nor, in the modern sense, traveled, nor sat on the piazza reading the newspaper, nor savored in one intelligent breath the magnolias on the lawn and the odor from his kitchen, nor comforted himself with allegiance to any cause or principle, church or state, nor raised cotton or know the uses of it, nor enjoyed any one of those pointed interests whose sum is what we generally mean by civilization" (*Body*, 243). The "Louisiana planter" is, it seems, more "admirable"—and one might say, more poetic—for his ability to operate in both the realm of economy and science on the one hand and of aesthetics on the other. Just as the tension between prose and meter, idea and physical reality, constitutes a poem, the tension between art and economy, as represented in Ransom's list of the Louisiana planter's interests, *constitutes* for Ransom "what we generally mean by civilization," or, as he will consistently call it elsewhere, "culture." Ransom's theory of poetry, then, is also a theory of culture.

Ransom's anthropology of the South as expressed in "The Tense of Poetry," then, provides a turning point connecting Ransom's theory of poetry to his theory of culture. This idea of culture is most clearly articulated in his essays as a Southern Agrarian in the early 1930s, particularly in *I'll Take My Stand* (1930), the Agrarian manifesto Ransom compiled with his fellow Fugitives, among them Allen Tate and Donald Davidson. In the collective introduction to that volume, written primarily by Ransom himself, the varied aesthetic and practical activities enjoyed by Ransom's Louisiana planter are designated as precisely "a culture." Echoing the Sapirian opposition between "genuine culture" and modern industrialism discussed throughout the previous chapters, Ransom counters the "abstraction" of scientific industrialism, represented by the North, to the Southern "humanism," which is in his words "a culture, the *whole* way in which we live, act, think, and feel. It is a kind of imaginatively balanced life lived out in a definite social tradition . . . in its tables, chairs, portraits, festivals, laws, marriage customs."[14] Thus, like Sapir, Ransom is not just arguing for a *particular* way of life, but the *form* of that way of life—"imaginatively balanced" and "lived out" in every aspect of that life from its furniture to its festivals. This form, moreover, is by definition "a culture." And, as with anthropologists like Sapir, literary critics like Mumford, and artists like Cather, this formal "whole way of life," or "a culture," is invoked in contrast to the fragmentation and "abstraction" of industrial modernism. Ransom's Southern Agrarianism, in other words, is rooted in the problematic of culture that occupies the interdisciplinary debate traced in the previous chapters.

The terms by which Ransom argues this culture is generated in turn anticipate the key terms of his theory of poetic structure. The "whole" way of life described in the introduction to *I'll Take My Stand* is specifically generated through the dynamic interaction between human activity and the physical environment. In Ransom's contribution to the manifesto, "Reconstructed But Unregenerate," he argues that Southern culture was characterized by a "stable economic system" in which "human life . . . came to terms with nature, fixed its roots somewhere in the spaces between the rocks and in the shade of the trees, founded its comfortable institutions, secured its modest prosperity—and then willed the whole into perpetuity."[15] In all "provincial" societies, including the South, Ransom argues, man "adapted himself to environment, [and] conclud[ing] a truce with nature . . . his loving arts, religions and philosophies come spontaneously into being" ("Reconstructed," 7). This language is echoed in Ransom's essays on poetry such as "Wanted: An Ontological Critic." In that essay Ransom describes how the heterogeneous "combination of the semantic property and the phonetic property into a fine poetic phrase"—akin to "human life [coming] to terms with nature" in the agrarian culture—results in what he calls the "wonderful 'fitness,' harmony[,]. . . even an enduring stability" of the poem (*New Criticism*, 327). Thus, just as a whole *poem* is constructed in the "stable" tension or accommodation between prose and meter, idea and sound, in an impossible effort to return to the prelapsarian condition where poetry and prose were one, the whole *culture* is constituted by the "stable" tension between aesthetics and enjoyment on the one hand, and the necessity of economy brought on by the Fall into scientific knowledge on the other.

The parallel terms Ransom applies to both culture and poetry are crucial. Insofar as it is "successfully adapted to its natural environment," Ransom designates the "provincial life" embodied in the old South as "realistic" and "stable" ("Reconstructed," 5). Similarly, the myriad effects produced by the interaction of meter and prose sense in the "fine poetic phrase" results both in the "fullness of content" that is characteristic of the "world of actual object" (and in this sense realistic) and in an "enduring stability" (*New Criticism*, 293, 327). The relationship between economy and art that produces a whole culture is for Ransom, of course, linked to an agrarian way of life, in which culture is produced from literal cultivation. In his account, the tiller's relationship to the soil mirrors the critic's relationship to the poem: just as the poem emerges in the critic's analysis as the site of infinite particularity and contingency, the farmer "identifies himself with a spot of ground, and this ground carries a good deal of meaning. . . . He would till it not too hurriedly and not too mechanically to observe in it the contingency and the infinitude of nature" ("Reconstructed," 19).

Finally, Ransom's theory of culture is pluralist. Arising from the "contingency and infinitude" of a particular "spot of ground," culture for Ransom is bounded and self-referential—"self-sufficient, backward-looking, intensely provincial, . . . local and peculiar"—where its status as "a culture" is determined not by reference to a universal standard of value, but by the internal "stability" of the system of meaning and practice by which it is constituted. Ransom thus links regionalism and pluralism, and the abstraction and universalism represented by Northern industrialism becomes a "foreign invasion of Southern soil," to be resisted by the "natives" ("Reconstructed," 23). Given the number of times Ransom turns to Civil War metaphors in his criticism—Sherman's march is particularly prevalent—one might argue that for Ransom the triumph of North over South is the triumph of prose over poetry, of abstraction over "fullness," and of universalism over pluralism. This opposition to universalism as a kind of assimilation is mirrored in Ransom's version of reading a poem: as opposed to the universalism of Pearce's historicism with which Ransom begins "The Idea of a Literary Anthropologist"—whose "consent" is "evidence of the continuity of our culture"—the literary anthropologist's technique refuses such "assimilation," instead recognizing the culture of the author, like the quality of the poem, as above all particular and resistant to the attempt to universalize experience.

Thus, far from being merely an aesthetic theory that brackets questions of culture and history beyond the poem's borders, as some critics have charged, Ransom's New Critical theories of poetry must be seen as part of a very specific theory of culture itself. Moreover, beyond these poetic theories being merely a continuation of the general antimodern and anti-industrial politics of Ransom's Agrarian phase in a different arena, as other critics have contended, Ransom's agrarian theory of culture and his New Critical theory of poetry must be seen as more intimately related at the level of structure. The structure of Ransom's regional culture finds its specific analogue in language in the structure of a poem: just as the intimate interaction between tiller and infinitely particular soil produces a way of life that is "stable" and "self-sufficient" in contrast to the abstract universalism of industrial society, the interplay of prose sense and poetic meter construct the "stable" poem whose infinite particularity reflects the fullness of the "world's body," in contrast to the abstract transcript of experience captured in scientific language. In chapter 2, I argued that Cather constructs an aesthetics of culture that imagined culture as an object in space, and that this spatialization of culture represented a transition from Sapir's and Malinowski's construction of cultural wholes to the modernist conception of the poem as a spatial object. In the movement from Ransom's theory of culture to the New Criticism, this transition is completed. Connecting culture directly to the "spot of ground" tilled by the farmer-poet—indeed, the physical soil "carries" the "meaning" of culture itself—Ransom makes culture coterminous with a physical space; similarly, in drawing on physical, almost architectural metaphors of interacting forces—"tension," "stability," "unity"—Ransom likewise formulates the poem as an object in space, the literal embodiment of a genuine culture. If Malinowski and Sapir represent within anthropology a shift from universal "Culture" to plural "cultures," a shift that in turn produces new theories of meaning in language in which the meaning of any utterance can be understood only within the context of the whole culture, then Ransom's poetics must be seen as part of this same development, participating in and drawing from the romantic antimodernism and anti-industrialism that characterize the development of the culture concept in this period.

Ransom explicitly connects the form of regional culture and aesthetic form in his essay "The Aesthetic of Regionalism." In a manner that echoes Cather's use of the Indian in *The Professor's House*, and Sapir's turn to the Indian as the exemplar of culture in "Culture, Genuine and Spurious," Ransom uses the Pueblo Indian "culture" as a model for both a way of life that is itself specifically aesthetic and the structure of which replicates—or more accurately, is replicated in—the structure of the fine poem. Ransom, riding the "eastbound train out of Albuquerque," observes the threshing rituals of a Pueblo village from the window:

> On the floors Indians were beating out the grain; on some the work was nearly done, the grain had been separated from the chaff and lay in a golden pile. The threshers were old and young, of both sexes, and beautifully arrayed. They laughed and must have felt pleased with their duties, because the harvest was a success, and bread was assured them for the winter.
>
> So this was regionalism; flourishing on the meanest capital, surviving stubbornly, and brilliant. In the face of the efforts of the insidious white missions and the aggressive government schools to "enlighten" these Indian people, their culture persists . . . and they live as they always have lived. It may be supposed that they find their way of living satisfactory. . . . They prefer it above others, receiving from it the two benefits which culture can afford. First, the economic benefit. . . . And second, a subtler but scarcely less important benefit in that their way of living is pleasant; it feels right, it has aesthetic quality.[16]

Committed cultural pluralists—recognizing other modes of life, they "prefer" their own "above others"—these people receive the "two benefits which a culture can afford": first, the "economic benefit" of being self-sufficient and independent of the "universal market," second, like

Ransom's Louisiana planter, "their way of living is pleasant; it 'feels' right, it has aesthetic quality."

Moreover, the "aesthetic" quality of Indian life emerges from a dialectic between the geographic region and human needs. Just as Ransom describes the aesthetic object as capturing the fullness of the world precisely by incorporating within its structure the "concepts" of science or prose, in a passage that bears strong similarities to Mumford's regionalism as discussed in the previous chapter, Ransom describes how, "as the community slowly adapts its life to the geography of the region, a thing happens which is almost miraculous...an event of momentous consequence to what we call the genius of human 'culture.' As the economic patterns become perfected and easy, they cease to be merely economic and become gradually aesthetic.... It is as if man and nature had declared a truce and written a peace;... the fine arts arise, superficially pure or non-useful, yet faithful to the regional nature and to the economic and moral patterns to which the community is committed" ("Aesthetics," 49). As in Sapir's formalist version of genuine culture—"inherently harmonious, balanced, self-satisfactory, ... richly varied and yet somehow unified and consistent"[17]—Ransom defines culture as a "pattern[ed]" whole ("Aesthetics," 47). That whole is spatially constructed (here, literally contained in the physical landscape of the geographic region) and internally referential, where economic activity, as Sapir put it, "works in naturally with all the rest of the Indian's activities" ("Genuine," 316) to create "aesthetic quality" ("Aesthetics," 46). The division between the economic and the artistic dissolves and—in a manner echoing an arts-and-crafts aesthetic of Carlyle and Morris that we have traced through Cather, Van Wyck Brooks, and Mumford—their economic actions become also their arts ("Aesthetics," 49).

It is this kind of regionalism, and its aesthetic, that Ransom desires for his "New South": Ransom ends the essay with a view of the Louisiana State Capitol Building, lamenting its "shameless eclecticism [of] New York artists, French and Italian marble, African mahogany [and] Vesuvian lava for the paving" ("Aesthetics," 57). In this critique the Indian emerges as a kind of aristocrat, resistant to the movement of history represented by Ransom's moving train and the "eclecticism" that such movement brings with it.

"The Aesthetic of Regionalism" is revealing both for the connections between Ransom's theory of culture, region, and aesthetic and for the way it highlights the complexity of the rise of the modernist theory of culture in this period, specifically the ways in which new conceptions of culture could be deployed in similar ways by critics of very different politics. The idea of cultural wholes as articulated by Boas and Sapir—and, to a lesser extent, Malinowski—was deployed explicitly in a progressive gesture against the racism and racialism of the period: disentangling race from culture, Boas and Sapir were intent on arguing both that one's race does not determine one's personality and practices (thus behavior could be altered through proper education and training) and that there existed alternative ways of life to American "civilization" that were equally—or even more—coherent and meaningful. With this cultural pluralism, Boas and Sapir rejected the universalism that underpinned arguments that ranked the practices of groups such as Native Americans as "inferior" and posited American or European practices as higher on a progressive scale of "Culture." For Sapir, and for Mumford, this cultural pluralism further was deployed against a homogenizing idea of "American" culture and the industrial state, as they locate the unit of culture in the region. Mumford's articulation of this regionalism, with its emphasis, as we have seen, on the balanced interaction between the physical environment and human activity, has earned him in the eyes of some critics a prominent place in the history of American environmentalism.

In his articulation of culture and aesthetics in "The Aesthetics of Regionalism," as well as in his other writings considered here, Ransom's positions echo these concerns. In his emphasis on the "stable" accommodation between man and nature, and what he takes to be industrialism's domination and exploitation of nature, Ransom echoes the environmentalism of Mumford—Mumford's "liberalism" is mirrored in Ransom's "conservatism." Just as Sapir, Mumford, and critics such as Randolph Bourne used the culture concept to counter the strident nationalism that characterized much of the postwar political discourse, Ransom's and Tate's regionalism is also deployed against what is taken to be the essentially imperial state, resisting the very idea of American "nationalism" itself: here, the Indian—like the Southerner—is resisting the "aggressive government" of the United States to change Native American lifeways. Turning to the Indian as an example of a particular way of life—unique, self-sufficient, irreducibly "different" rather than "higher" or "lower"— Ransom enacts a cultural pluralism similar to that of the Boasian anthropologist. Pluralism in fact emerges throughout Ransom's writings as a key concept, poetically and socially: Ransom describes modernist poets like Eliot and Tate as "pluralists, relativists, and irrational," recognizing that "the law of [a poem's] corporate existence" is that its elements will be "heterogeneous," not "homogeneous," as opposed to the "eleaticism [of] the everyday world of business, science and positivism [that] conceives that... properties must unite by virtue of their sameness" (*New Criticism*, 335, 327). Thus, rather than the totalitarian vision some critics have associated with "organic" social and poetic theories, Ransom imagines that "a poem is a democratic state.... It restrains itself faithfully from a really imperious degree of organization [and] wants its citizens to retain their personalities and enjoy their natural interests" (43–44).

At the same time, that pluralism also has a cost: using the Indian as the embodiment of genuine regional culture, Ransom imprisons the Indian both temporally and geographically. The Indians "live as they always have lived," and this temporal stasis is doubled by their physical immobility: frozen in time and space, they are the object of observation by a narrator whose own location—on a moving train—signifies his ability (however much he might regret it) to move across space and with history. This, of course, is precisely the postmodern critique of bounded cultures that anthropologists themselves have made.[18] Finally, of course, Ransom's pluralism recognizes cultures, but this does not preclude a value judgment of a different kind: rather than choosing a particular trait or action because it is "better" or "worse," Ransom chooses it because it is "his"—and indeed the logic of pluralism, positing the absolute difference between cultures, requires such a choice. And what he seeks to exclude from his fantasy of a whole Southern regional culture are the bloody histories of violence inflicted on African slaves that undergirded that "way of life" in the antebellum period, and the continued discrimination and violence against the African American and immigrant populations represented by the "New York artists," "Italian marble," and "African mahogany" that Ransom disdains.

My point here is that the emergent definitions of cultural pluralism—redefining culture as plural, relative wholes—in this period makes available positions both progressive and reactionary, liberal and conservative. The same logic of culture undergirds positions on opposite sides of the political spectrum, and often in the same critic. Recognizing the pluralist logic of culture and regionalism that produces similar positions on aesthetics and identity in figures commonly regarded as being on the left or right politically complicates the dichotomies into which the literary and intellectual history of this period has been divided—for example, seeing reactionary New Critics committed to a hierarchical, elitist Culture on one side, and progressive Young Americans like Mumford, along with socially progressive anthropologists like Sapir, Boas, Mead, and Benedict, committed to democracy and pluralism on the other; and cosmopolitan, modernist New Critics on one side, "cultural nationalists" promoting American literature on the other. The complication that arises in these categories—cultural pluralism, universalism, cultural nationalism—becomes particularly clear when we turn to Ransom's one-time student and fellow Fugitive, Agrarian, and New Critic, Allen Tate, and his construction of culture and poetry in relation to the parallel modernisms of T. S. Eliot and Hart Crane.

"Several Different Americas": The Cultures of Allen Tate, Hart Crane, and T. S. Eliot

In chapter 3 I argued that the modernist problematic of culture shaped the ways in which critics both conceived of and "read" "culture" on the one hand, and conceived of and "read" literary texts on the other hand. This problematic in turn structured the ways in which individual texts such as *Moby-Dick* were organized into canons that reflected the relationship between bounded cultures and bounded texts, in the question of national or regional cultures and canons. In this section I extend this argument to New Critical conceptions of poetic form and aesthetics, to show how one New Critic, Allen Tate, deployed these ideas of the culture-unit/the poetic unit to construct the poetic canon of high modernism.

In 1930 Tate reviewed *The Bridge*, the new epic poem written by Hart Crane, whom Tate had known since the early 1920s, and with whom he had maintained a close, if rocky, friendship. In his notoriously scathing review, Tate judged the work a grand failure. In language that anticipated the importance of formal "unity" in the New Criticism that he would help institutionalize in American universities by the 1940s, Tate pronounces that though Crane was a poet "endowed with gifts of the highest order," the poem, taken as a whole, suffered "from a lack of a coherent plot, whether symbolic or narrative"; it was "arbitrary and broken," "unfused," each section "a new start, and but for the broken chronology the poem constantly begins over again." Taken "as an historical epic," *The Bridge* represented a "breakdown."[19] After this condemnation on the basis of a lack of formal "unity," however, Tate goes on in a very non–New Critical way to address issues beyond the bounds of the poem—namely, the state of culture in America. "If anthropology has destroyed the credibility of myths," he states, "it has shown us how they rise: their growth is mysterious from the people as a whole; and it is probable that no one man ever put myth into history. . . . Mr. Crane is a myth maker, an in an age favorable to myths he could have written a mythical poem in the act of writing an historical one" ("Hart Crane," 102.)

Tate's review of Crane is important in the way it has shaped both subsequent assessments of Crane's poetry by those critics who have followed on Tate's New Critical heels, and critical analyses of the cultural politics of the New Criticism itself. As Langdon Hammer has observed, "The simple permanence of [Tate's] judgement, ... which R. P. Blackmur, Yvor Winters and other critics upheld, and which Crane's suicide could be seen to strangely confirm, give it the intractable feeling of fact."[20] Critics who have come after Tate have felt the need to negotiate this "fact" when analyzing Crane's work, either to uphold it or to refute it. What is even more striking is the manner in which critics on both sides of the debate over *The Bridge*'s "success" or "failure" largely maintain the initial oppositions of "unity" versus "fracture" that Tate initially invokes against the poem. Those who, following Tate, deem the work a kind of "noble failure" inevitably find some version of discontinuity in its poetic structure.[21] Those seeking to extricate Crane from Tate's grasp have merely reversed the terms and argue that the work does indeed represent a deeper structural or symbolic unity. As Lee Edelman has put it, critics seeking to reevaluate Crane have had to prove that "the poetry was *not* incoherent, was *not* confused, was *not* seriously obscure" (*Janus*, 36, emphasis in original).

The New Critical principle of poetic "unity" that Tate and subsequent critics have applied to Crane's poetry is in turn intimately related to the versions of "tradition" or "culture" that Tate has commonly been read to represent. He has been widely interpreted as representing a version of European "Tradition" similar to the tradition represented by T. S. Eliot. Accordingly, those critics (primarily of the mid-century) who took Eliot's—and, in turn, Tate's and the New Critics'—modernism as the heroic defense of a high art Tradition against the corrosive influence of mass culture cast Crane as a poet whose "incoherence" was symptomatic of the breakup of that Tradition. For those critics, however, who in the past decades have recast Eliot's and the New Critics' modernism as an elitist, white male defense against the literary encroachments of women, minorities, and the working class, the terms are reversed: Crane, particularly in his role as a homosexual poet, becomes the prophet of a unity that is specifically inclusive and democratic, whereas Tate, as Eliot's proxy, is recast as the defender of a "tradition" that is inherently exclusionary. Hammer points to this subtext in the Crane debates when he observes that "the fairly recent rise of Crane's reputation is coordinated with the equally recent *devaluation* of Eliot's" (*Janus*, 36, emphasis in original). He further notes that "this systematic alteration of critical taste is consistent with the tendency of poststructuralist interpreters to sustain, even as they revalue, conceptual oppositions central to the New Criticism: symbol and allegory, speech and writing, unity and difference" (36). The persistence of these dichotomies, however, is evidenced in Hammer's own use of them in his study of the ideological, literary, and personal relationship between Tate and Crane: despite his claim that he avoids the temptation of seeing "one poet as the bearer of modernism's liberating promise, another as the agent of its discipline," he nonetheless ultimately characterizes the "special promise of American modernity in Crane's work [as the] forging of a nonhierarchical, fully democratic community," prefigured in his poetic scenes of "intimate communication between male peers" (xi). Tate, on the other hand, "identified himself with [Eliot's] 'tradition' [and] spoke for a developing intellectual consensus, a fashionable 'pessimism' associated with *The Waste Land*, from which Crane"—and other minorities—"felt personally and programmatically excluded" (xii–xiii). Thus, "unity" becomes a highly charged ideological term in debates about Tate, Crane, and Eliot, whose valence and relation to "tradition" or "culture" change according to which party the critic is valorizing.

In examining more closely this concept of "unity" of tradition or culture that has been kept in play around Tate, Crane, and Eliot, I argue that these polarities of "unity" versus "division"—Tate as defender of high Culture versus Crane's fractured modernism; Crane as representative of an inclusive, democratic unity versus the divisive elitism of Tate's Eliotic Tradition—are part of the problematic of culture I have been tracing in this book, and in particular the complex ways in which ideas of poetic "unity" intersect with theories of "culture" *as* a unit, and where that unit is located. What kind of unity does culture embody? What, more succinctly, is the unit of culture, and, by extension, of poetry?

It is the link between the New Critical unity of poetic form and the composition of cultures, or what anthropology had "shown" Allen Tate, that I address in this section. By focusing upon Tate's initial critique of *The Bridge* and working outward to other essays written by Tate between 1927 and 1930, I suggest that Tate's judgments on *The Bridge* are based precisely upon a version of unity and tradition that differs both from Crane's *and* from T. S. Eliot's. Specifically, Tate's conception of culture, like Ransom's, is a pluralist conception of cultural wholes, imagined as spatial structures. Unlike Crane, however, who tries to locate a "national" cultural unity, Tate locates unified traditions "sectionally," with the unit of culture as the region. It is this aversion to a national identity in favor of a regional one that informs from the outset Tate's charges of discontinuity in *The Bridge*: embodying the proper unit of culture—in Tate's case, the region—translates into poetic unity, whereas attempting to capture a false unit of culture—as Tate reads Crane's ambition to create a "myth of America"—inevitably produces a fragmented poem. At the same time, this sectional pluralism also differentiates Tate from Eliot: although the two use similar language, Eliot's Tradition is a universal Tradition composed of "all the poetry that has ever been written," and not grounded in any one particular region or country. Finally, I will focus on Tate's version of "wholes," cultural and aesthetic, to suggest that for both the anthropological and the literary versions of the problematic, the idea of wholes—cultures as structured wholes, and poems as formal units—serves a similar professional function for the anthropologist and the poet-critic, establishing each as the expert participant-observer authorized to preserve a vanishing unity in a fragmented world.

Returning to Tate's review of *The Bridge*, at first Tate seems to be most concerned with the poem's internal workings, utilizing a language and criteria for evaluation that anticipate the tenets of the New Criticism. Anticipating what would become the "heresy of paraphrase," for example, Tate states that "the poem as a whole says vastly more than any literal paraphrase of it could possibly convey, if such a paraphrase could be written" ("Hart Crane," 99). Focusing on the poem's internal logical and stylistic continuity, on the positive side he claims that "Mr. Crane has perfect mastery over the quality of his style," and taken as "a collection of lyrics ... the best ... are not surpassed by anything in American literature" (102). Taken as one poem, generically an epic or myth, however, Tate decides that the "fifteen poems, taken as one poem, suffer from the lack of a coherent plot, whether symbolic or narrative." Thus the unity that Tate seems to be searching for is a particularly poetic unity, seemingly unconcerned with issues beyond the borders of the poem: on the surface, it is not truth value of the ideas themselves, but the fact that the poem "lacks an objective pattern of ideas elaborate enough to carry it through an epic or heroic work" that keeps it from achieving poetic unity (100).

Upon closer examination, however, it is clear that what seems to be a formal evaluation is inextricably linked to Tate's particular view of culture and tradition beyond the boundaries of the poem. Echoing Crane's own pronouncements that *The Bridge* was meant to create a "myth" or "epic of America," Tate suggests early in the essay that the "emotional intention" of the poem is something like "the grandeur of America."[22] This "idea" of "American" cultural identity that Crane seeks to construct is not merely executed poorly; the formal flaws Tate sees are a direct result of the fact that, for Tate, the very idea of a unified American culture is an impossibility. Pointing decidedly beyond the borders of the poem, Tate reveals that "the impulse in *The Bridge* is religious, but the soundness of an impulse is no warrant that it will create a sound art form, *which depends on too many factors beyond the control of the poet*" ("Hart Crane," 102, emphasis added). "The historical plot of the poem" is for Tate "arbitrary and broken" precisely because America itself is "broken": "For American history being vast and disordered, and as various as American citizens[,] . . . there was no settled version for the poet to draw upon and intensify" (102). Asking rhetorically "does American culture afford such a subject" upon which to forge a national unity, he concludes that "it probably does not" (101). Thus, Tate's critique of the formal failure of *The Bridge* is ultimately grounded, not in the internal properties of the poem, but in Tate's rejection of Crane's idea of an American culture itself.[23]

In many ways, Tate's judgment of *The Bridge* as a failure, and the argument about culture and nation upon which it is founded, was anticipated in Tate's more favorable review of Crane's *White Buildings* in 1926. In similar language, Tate calls Crane's poetry "ambitious," with each poem being "facets of a single vision; they refer to a central imagination, a single evaluating power, which is at once the motive of the poetry and the form of its realization."[24] This attempt at forging a poetic unity based upon imagination, Tate claims, is one attempt to solve the "leading contemporary problem of . . . art," namely, the "dissociation of the modern consciousness," the fact that "the poet no longer apprehends his world as a Whole" (*White Buildings*, xi). Turning to T. S. Eliot, as he frequently did in other essays dealing with tradition, Tate asserts that *The Waste Land* similarly grapples with the breakdown of a unified tradition: instead of Crane's romantic "central imagination" as the organizing principle, however, Eliot "displays vision and subject once more in traditional schemes, [but the] vision for some reason is dissipated, and the subject dead. For while Mr. Eliot might have written a more ambitiously unified poem, the unity would have been false; tradition as unity is not contemporary" (xi). With this absence of a unified tradition, the "ready-made themes" that control and guide poetic "vision," the poet's vision and his subject are fatally separated. This, according to Tate, accounts for the "difficulty" of modern poetry like Crane's: "Until vision and subject completely fuse, the poems will be difficult. The comprehensiveness and lucidity of any poetry, the capacity for poetry being assumed as proved, are in direct proportion to the availability of a comprehensive and perfectly articulated given theme"(xii).

Thus for Tate, the form of poetry is inextricably linked to the state of tradition or, as he puts it elsewhere, "culture." "I am convinced," he writes in a letter to Donald Davidson, "that Milton himself could not write a *Paradise Lost* now. Minds are less important for literature than cultures; our minds are as good as they ever were, but our culture is dissolving."[25] Without this "available . . . comprehensive and perfectly articulated" set of ideas—what Brooks called the "fabric of ideas and assumptions,"[26] and Sapir called the "richly varied but somehow unified and consistent attitude toward life" ("Genuine," 233)—the epic, as the embodiment of "a culture," is impossible. This dissolution of cultures dictates Tate's preference for the lyric over the epic: the occasion of Tate's letter is to dissuade Davidson from writing a planned epic of the South (one that would seek to do for Tennessee what Crane in that moment was seeking to do for America in *The Bridge*), and he concludes that "Eliot is about right in saying there are no important themes for modern poets. Hence we all write lyrics." As with Ransom, Tate's New Critical emphasis on unified form arises directly from a desire for cultural wholeness—or more accurately, a definition of culture and poetry as wholeness—and the formal properties of a poem are a product of the state of the culture in which the poet lives. As he puts it in a later essay, the formal "tension, . . . the unity of all the meanings from the furthest extremes of intension and extension" that characterizes the good poem is a reflection of the unified culture that "illuminate[s] from a fixed position all its experience . . . [and brings] to full realization the high forms as well as the contradiction and miseries inherent in human society."[27] Lacking this Coleridgian "fixed position," the poet like Crane or Davidson trying to write epic poetry, a genre spanning both time and space to embody the history of a whole people or nation, can muster poetic unity only at the level of the lyric. Thus, *The Bridge*, argues Tate, "is a collection of lyrics, the best of which are not surpassed by anything in American literature." Out of the dissolution of an overarching culture that would sustain the temporal expansiveness of the epic precipitates the lyric, representing only—as Tate describes the successive sections of Crane's poem—a "moment," each of which has a "complete form" but "stands alone" ("Hart Crane," 102–3).

Critics like Hammer have noted both Tate's turn to culture in these passages and his turn to Eliot. As Hammer rightly notes, "Tate's term culture should . . . be distinguished from [Arnold's] 'the best that has been thought and said.' Instead, Tate means the aggregate of myth and custom that the anthropologist studies, and he understands the making of a given culture not as the conscious project of specific persons and groups . . . but rather as the occult emanation of a homogeneous 'people'" (*Janus*, 37). In pointing to the distinction between Tate's and Arnold's versions of culture, Hammer makes a point similar to my own. What Hammer neglects, however, is that the very idea of what constitutes the "culture" that "the anthropologist studies" is *itself* undergoing reconstruction at the moment that Tate writes his review of Crane—and that moreover literary critics like Tate are *participating* in that reconstruction alongside other literary critics, linguists, anthropologists, and artists, rather than simply drawing upon a definition produced from within that other discipline.

Further, although critics like Hammer read Tate's references to Eliot in these moments as revealing Tate's allegiance to Eliot's version of Tradition and its modern breakdown, it is precisely this transition in "what the anthropologist studies" that separates Tate from Eliot in this historical moment. I would argue, however, that the introduction to *White Buildings* and his letter to Davidson illuminate Tate's argument about culture and *The Bridge* not in its description of the impossibility of poetic unity in the face of the collapse of an Eliotic Tradition, but by connecting this "dissociation" precisely with "America" as a "nation," and in turn attempting to relocate the unit of culture in the region. At the outset of the essay, Tate specifically identifies Crane's poetry as "an American poetry." What makes it "American," he reveals, is that it embodies "the complex urban civilization of his age: precision, abstraction, power"—in other words, precisely the forces of modernity that are breaking down tradition. In connecting America with the collapse of tradition, Tate is pointing the way toward a unified tradition that is regional as opposed to national. In making the unit of culture the region—whose relation to the state bears the same relation as the lyric to the epic—Tate articulates a version of cultural pluralism that echoes that of Edward Sapir or Lewis Mumford, as opposed to the universal, Frazerian version of culture articulate by Eliot. This cultural pluralism in turn, I would suggest, paradoxically brings Tate's version of tradition closer to Crane's nationalism, and further away from Eliot's universalism.

Tate's pluralist version of culture or tradition—and the grounds by which he will reject Crane's poem in a few short months—is articulated in Tate's "American Poetry since 1920" (1929). In this article, Tate evaluates the attempts by American poets to depict a national culture or tradition and judges their attempts to be failures. What is crucial, however, is that their failure is not due to a general fragmentation of the "modern world," but because Tate relocates the site of tradition from the national to the regional. By rejecting national unity, he is not left with "fracture," but instead a different level of unity, a regional unity. The poets who attempted to forge an "American" identity, he proclaims, "exhibited, in spite of their local differences, a singleness of outlook that seemed to prove that we had, after all, a national spirit and that our period of servitude to foreign models had ended."[28] There was, however, "something misleading in the unified Americanism of their attitude: it was not all that it seemed to be" ("American Poetry," 79). In fact, for Tate, this "unified Americanism" is an impossibility, because there is no such thing as an "American" tradition. These would-be national poets failed because of the "failure of their predecessors to leave them firm ground to stand upon. The sociological excitement of the preceding generation was not disciplined; it yielded no permanent values.... [It] was not strong enough to make a tradition" (82). Thus, the "experiment that tried to find values for the whole of the American scene succeeded [only in] erecting a set of fictions which collapsed" into apparent chaos: "In this chaos there are several different Americas, none of which contains all the values of the whole and which, with respect to the whole, represents disorder" (82).

What is crucial for understanding Tate's idea of tradition is to see that the alternative to a national tradition is not pure "disorder," but a different unit upon which the unity of a tradition is to be measured. The "disorder" is only disorder when taken "with respect to the whole" nation. Precipitating out of this national disorder, however, are the multiple unities of "several *different* Americas" (emphasis added). These "several different Americas," Tate makes clear, are defined by region, each having a particular "spirit" and tradition. Thus, "in the South there is the attempt to define the past in terms of an unsympathetic reaction to the industrial era, ... [whereas] ... the New England mind is ... still ... a single mind" (83). In fact, the very impulse to create a national identity is the function, according to Tate, of the "spirit" of a particular region: the "leading figures [of the nativist movement] came from the Middle West. The spirit of the region was boomed much as its land had been two generations before.... [They] tracked down the local character of their section, and, once found, it easily fitted, under the pressure of frontier optimism, into the framework of national types and heroes who seemed to speak for the whole country" (79). Instead of a "Tradition," there are many "tradition*s*," each belonging to the inhabitants of that region. Tate thus can speak of the poets of the South being "conservative with respect to *their own* traditions," as opposed to a common American tradition ("American Poetry," 83, emphasis added).

Further, the success of an artist's work can be judged by the degree of adherence to the local spirit that is "his" or "hers": "The personal resources of the poet are capable of further intensification if they can be brought back to contact with the local cultures from which, in each instance, they originally sprang. Only a return to the provinces, to the small, self-contained centres of life, will put the all-destroying abstraction, America, safely to rest" (88). In contrasting "small, self-contained centres" with the "abstraction" of America, Tate reveals his engagement with the same problematic that occupied Brooks, Sapir, Mumford, Malinowski, and Ransom, each of whom, as we have seen, articulates his own version of this opposition.

The relative unity of sectional tradition and culture is in turn reflected in the greater formal unity or success (in Tate's estimation) of contemporary sectional poets, who "have achieved a triumph over a limited material . . . greater than that achieved by the preceding generation envisaging a more comprehensive surface" (82). When a poet like Crane, with avowedly national aspirations for his poetry, "envisages a more comprehensive surface" in creating a mythic "American" history, Tate insists on a pluralism in which one must ask "which American history?" ("Hart Crane," 101). *The Bridge* itself formally reflects, in Tate's language, the collapse of the false unity of "American" identity into the "truer" unities of "several different Americas." Like America, "each *section* [of the poem] is a new start, and but for the broken chronology the poem constantly begins over and over again" (102, emphasis added). Tate's emphasis of the lyric over the epic, then, can be seen as a reflection of location of unified tradition in the local or sectional. What emerges out of the "disorder" of America as a "whole" is not "chaos," but a different level of wholeness grounded in the "local culture*s*" or "small, self-contained centres of life." In this move from American culture to sectional cultures, then, Tate replicates the move to distinct cultural wholes rooted in the region that I have argued characterizes the theories of Mumford and Sapir.

Tate's idea of multiple "traditions" in turn distinguishes him from T. S. Eliot's Tradition as articulated in his early writings. In "Tradition and the Individual Talent," Eliot argues that the individual work of art or artist can have value only in the context of the "tradition," that "ideal order" that stretches across time and space, made up of "the existing monuments [of] the dead poets, his ancestors."[29] Although Eliot's construction of the reciprocal relationship between the individual and tradition is complex and subtle, what is crucial to my argument is that Eliot's Tradition is a universal one. In the terms of Eliot's essay, there is no sense of different traditions from which one can choose, or of some artists "belonging" to one tradition over another. There is only *the* Tradition, the alternative to which is not a *different* tradition, but *no* tradition. This universal Tradition encompasses works of art of all national origins and historical periods, including simultaneously "Shakespeare,... Homer, [and] the rock drawings of the Magdalenian draughtsmen," and there is ultimately no distinction between "the mind of Europe" and "the mind of [the artist's] own country" ("Tradition," 6). The literature of the artist's country is in fact a subset of the literature of Europe: the traditional writer writes "not merely with his own generation in his bones, but with a feeling that the whole of the literature of Europe from Homer and *within it* the whole of the literature of his own country has a simultaneous existence and composes a simultaneous order" (4, emphasis added). Thus, in this structure of set and subset, there is no point at which the "national" is distinct from the "European" and constitutes a separate, distinct tradition or culture.

This stance is expanded in the essay "The Function of Criticism," in which Eliot, in discussing the differences between French Classicism and English Romanticism, claims that "the question is ... *not* what comes natural or what comes *easy* to us, but what is right?"[30] By appealing to "what is right," Eliot posits a common, universal basis or scale for comparison, as opposed to Tate's sectionalism, in which there is no "right" or "wrong," but "different." In contrast, for example, Brooks's nationalist pluralism leads him to ask (along with Sainte-Beuve) not "what is right," but "what is important *for us*?"[31] For Eliot, both the English and the French are aspects of a single unified European Tradition. Indeed, at moments in the essay, Eliot's universalism extends to include not just Europe, but the world: poetry is, he claims, "a living whole of all the poetry that has ever been written" ("Tradition," 7). Eliot, like Cather's Thea in *The Song of the Lark*, sees "all poetry [as a] long chain of human endeavor."[32] Culture here is a "living whole," as in Tate, but it is a "living whole" that encompasses all literature across time and space. Eliot, as he puts it, thinks "of literature of the world, of the literature of Europe, of the literature of a single country ... as 'organic wholes,' as systems in relation to which... individual works of literary art... have their significance" ("Function," 68). Although Eliot invokes the figure of "organic wholes," these wholes are each part of, or subsets of, a larger whole, and from which they are ultimately not distinct. The "literature of the world" is here placed in the same relation to "the literature of Europe" as the "literature of Europe" is placed in relation to the "literature of a single country"—although not identical, they are of the same order, and thus fundamentally comparable. There is no distinction between "his" culture or tradition and one that is not "his"; it is for this reason that Eliot is authorized, for example, to draw upon Buddha's Fire Sermon and the Indian Upanishads in works such as *The Waste Land*—as "fragments" to "shore against my ruins," alongside elements of Greek and Egyptian mythology and classics in European literature. All are part of "*the* Tradition" and thus are all equally "his."

It is in this drawing in of elements from around the world and across history as "his" Tradition that Eliot reproduces the logic of culture of Frazer's *The Golden Bough*. As many critics have pointed out, Frazer's work—a multivolume compendium of myths and practices from around the world and across history—represents a universalist version of culture, whose comparativist accumulation of data from a multitude of sources attests finally to the common basis of comparison for all. This universal, comparativist model is much the same as the model deployed by Tylor and Morgan, as discussed in chapters 1 and 2. As Marc Manganaro has shown, Frazer's comparative juxtaposition of various periods and cultural practices—and the authoritative stance of the ethnologist/author coordinating and comparing them—significantly influenced the early Eliot of *The Waste Land*: as Manganaro puts it, *The Waste Land* enacts "a comparativist profusion of voice and sources" that replicates the transnational and transhistorical range of Frazer's examples in *The Golden Bough*.[33] But as Manganaro goes on to point out, the rhetorical model of Frazer's comparative text deployed a paradigm of culture that was about to be eclipsed with the publication of Malinowski's *Argonauts of the Western Pacific* in the same year, and Sapir's "Culture, Genuine and Spurious" two years later.[34] The emergence of this new paradigm, the shift from Frazer to Sapir and Malinowksi, I am arguing, is doubled in the shift from Eliot's Tradition to Tate's (and Crane's) regional or national traditions.

Tate's sectional brand of pluralism, and its contrast to Eliot's universalist Tradition, is developed further in "Remarks on the Southern Religion," Tate's contribution to *I'll Take My Stand*, which as a whole served as a manifesto for the kind of sectionalism that Tate discusses in "American Poetry since 1920." The intent of the collection was, as the introduction put it, to "support a Southern way of life against what may be called the American or prevailing way."[35] In his essay Tate elaborates on the threats of scientific rationalism to the unity of Tradition in the modern world. As opposed to true religion, embodying a totality of experience and belief, "American religion" is according to Tate "preeminently a religion of how things work, [the] religion of the half-horse" that recognizes only abstract utility.[36] In analyzing the threat to "Tradition" posed by such abstract scientism, Tate seeks to answer the question "How may the Southerner take hold of his Tradition?" ("Remarks," 174).

Throughout the essay, Tate describes the "Southern" tradition as essentially the "European" tradition: as he says, "The South ... was Europe" ("Remarks," 171). This idea that the South is, in a sense, the repository of the "European Tradition" echoes similar statements in other works in which Tate explores Southern identity and history. In his biography of Jefferson Davis, for example, he sees the antebellum South as "the last stronghold of European civilization in the Western hemisphere."[37] In a letter to Donald Davidson, referring to the upcoming essay collection, Tate admonishes that "we must be the last Europeans—there being no Europeans in Europe at present."[38] This identification with European Tradition, combined with further references to T. S. Eliot and *The Waste Land* in the essay, has reinforced the critical tendency to read "Remarks on Southern Religion" as committed more to an Eliotic version of Tradition, rather than to a separate Southern identity. This impression is reinforced by Tate's objection to the title of the collection, claiming that "it is a special plea" that would alienate the "foreign" reader.[39] Thus, critics such as Hammer conclude that "his emphasis was on ... the cosmopolitan, not the local."

As in "American Poetry since 1920," however, what separates Tate from Eliot is his pluralist conception of tradition, a pluralism that leads him through the course of the essay from asking "How can Tradition ... be defended?" to "How can an *American* take hold of Tradition?" to, finally, "How may the *Southerner* take hold of *his* Tradition?" ("Remarks," 166, 174, emphasis added). Tate argues that the threat to tradition is precisely that there are many traditions to choose from, but only one to which one truly "belongs."

In a passage that seems a direct allusion to the Frazerian method, Tate argues, for example, why "we" should prefer Christ to Adonis, even though both are "vegetation myths." The "whole Christ and the whole

Adonis are sufficiently differentiated in their respective qualities," he argues, "that our tradition compels us to choose more than that half of Christ which is Adonis and to take the whole, separate, and unique Christ" ("Remarks," 162). Tate's critique of what he calls "the Long View" of history—the view that abstracts temporal separation into a logical series proceeding in a scientifically definable way—rests on the fact that such an abstraction collapses difference, making it impossible to differentiate *between* traditions to determine which one is "ours." Drawing a distinction between Greek and Roman culture, he claims that "it is apparent that a solvent which reduces the Greek and the Roman cultures to identity takes from us the privilege of choosing between them; or assuming that we are the offshoot of one of them there is no reason why we cannot take up the other. The Long View is, in brief, the cosmopolitan destroyer of Tradition" (162–63). In contrast to Eliot, who, for example, sees the French and the English Tradition as manifestations of one cosmopolitan "mind of Europe," there are different traditions even within the European context: here, Tate is arguing for a fundamental difference between Greek and Roman cultures. The South's mistake in the Civil War was, according to Tate, precisely that it did not remain true to its own tradition: "The South ... did not realize its genius in time, but continued to defend itself on the political terms of the North" (168).

Tate's critique of the "Long View" of tradition on nativist grounds is extended in his essay "The Fallacy of Humanism," which appeared in a collection of essays entitled *The Critique of Humanism*, published the same year as *I'll Take My Stand*.[40] In criticizing the Humanists' recourse to "the wisdom of the ancients" for the authority of the values they espouse, Tate claims that "[the Humanist's] idea of the 'past'—of tradition—is infinite regression ... [He] convinces himself that his logical series is a temporal past, and as such affords him a stopping place—some fixed doctrine or some self-contained wisdom of the ages" ("Fallacy," 125). This is a mistake, however, because abstract "naturalistic science is timeless, [and] a doctrine based upon it ... can have no past, no idea of tradition, no fixed center of life. ... To de-temporize the past is to reduce it to an abstract lump" in which every tradition is equal (126). The values derived from such a process are precisely not Tate's idea of tradition because they do not "work from the inside"; rather, "'decorum' must be 'imposed' from above" (126–27).

The adoption of values imposed from above rather than born from within is ultimately akin to miscegenation. Tate uses the term "assimilation" to describe a tradition he considers intact: "The belief held at various times since the Renaissance that the ancients are models of attitude and value is innocent enough; and it was useful so long as the classics could be *assimilated* to a living center of judgment and feeling" (124, emphasis added). This "assimilation" is acceptable for Tate precisely because, in the terms of his argument, it is *not* "assimilation"—that is, the adoption of a way of being that comes from without or, to use his words, "imposed from above"—but the manifestation of a tradition that is already at "work from the inside." If here assimilation is the incorporation of that which, by the very fact that it can be assimilated, is ultimately revealed as essentially the same, the "eclecticism" of Humanists like Professor Babbitt is a kind of miscegenation, in which "the mind [combines] mechanically upon a tabula rasa a variety of unlike elements into a unity." Unity achieved through the combination of "unlike elements," however, is a false unity: "We know that mechanical interaction, were it possible, could not yield a whole, but an aggregate" (124–25). This "aggregate" is of course precisely what poetry like *The Bridge*, in its attempt to create a national identity, becomes: an "aggregate" of fine lyrics, but a fragmented epic (that is to say, not an epic at all).

Again, with his emphasis on "traditional values" as coming from within, Tate reveals another crucial difference between his "tradition" and T. S. Eliot's. Turning back to the quote from "The Function of Criticism" given earlier—that "the question is ... *not* what comes natural or what comes *easy* to us, but what is right?"—Eliot explicitly denies that tradition "works from inside." Although he admits that the terms "inside" and "outside" are problematic when discussing tradition, he ultimately accepts that Tradition is found "outside" the individual: as he says, "Men cannot get on without giving allegiance to something outside themselves" ("Function," 70). Values derived from "within" he associates with the Romantic or Humanistic "inner voice." Ventriloquizing the relativism that, in his view, this produces, he mockingly asks, "Why have principles, when one has the inner voice?" Those who follow this "inner voice," he claims, are "not interested in the attempt to find any common principles for the pursuit of criticism" (72). This necessity to give oneself over to a Tradition outside oneself is also taken up in "Tradition and the Individual Talent," in which Eliot claims that "tradition cannot be inherited and if you want it you must obtain it with great labour" ("Tradition," 4). Laboring toward that Tradition, in turn, defines what is most essential in an individual; indeed, it is what seems to constitute his or her individuality. Rather than "dwell[ing] with satisfaction upon a poet's difference from his predecessors," the "most individual parts of his work may be those in which the dead poets, his ancestors, assert their immortality most vigorously" (4). Thus, working toward a Tradition outside him- or herself, the poet finds what is most essential, or individual, within him or her.

In insisting that tradition comes from within, as he does in "The Fallacy of Humanism," Tate reverses the poles of Eliot's argument. "What comes easily for us," or most naturally, is what for him defines Tradition. In a sense, Tate suggests that rather than surrendering oneself to Tradition to find one's individuality, it is when one expresses one's individuality and does not think about tradition that one's authentic tradition emerges. Thus, in "American Poetry since 1920," Tate sees the Fugitive poets as "quite unconsciously . . . fostering a sectional spirit." They were, he claims, "all private persons trying to solve the aesthetic problem each in his own way. They were willing to draw upon all the resources of poetry that they knew, for it was obvious that their sectionalism, if it existed . . . *would take care of themselves*. Fugitive poetry turned out to be profoundly sectional in that it was supported by the prejudices, feelings, values, *into which the poets were born*" ("American," 81, emphasis added). Whereas Eliot sees Tradition as "not inherited," and which one must "labour" to attain, Tate's Fugitives are born into their Southern tradition, which "takes care of itself" most in the moment when they are conscious of it least.[41]

Thus, for Tate, culture is a pluralist concept, with each section or region having its own tradition or culture; furthermore, the wholeness of culture ultimately enables the structurally whole poem. If the proper unit of culture is the region, then poetry that seeks to locate culture at the level of the nation—like Crane's epic *The Bridge*—founds itself on a "false" unity, and therefore itself must fail to achieve a unified poetic form. This pluralist regionalism is in turn opposed to what I have called Eliot's "universalism": for Eliot, there is only one Tradition, an ordered system stretching across time and space, located outside any one individual and knowable only through "great labour." The shift from Eliot's universal Tradition to Tate's sectional traditions parallels the conceptual shift in the meaning of "culture" in anthropology from the Frazerian comparative, evolutionary method, to Sapir's and Malinowski's versions of discrete cultural wholes, the elements of which are understandable only with respect to that whole.

Recognizing the pluralism of Tate's version of culture in turn complicates the political valences erected around Tate, Eliot, and Crane by critics like Hammer. If, for example, "universalism" implies a common standard, thus allowing judgments of "better" or "worse," then calling Eliot's idea of unity "hierarchical" (as does Hammer) acknowledges its universalism, rather than opposing it to universalism. Eliot's hierarchy and Hammer's "totality" (that he reads into Crane) are based on the same system, with merely a different ranking, perhaps, of the system's elements. By the same token, if, as Hammer suggests, poststructuralists favor "difference" over New Critical "unity," that emphasis on "difference" rests on an idea of culture that, at bottom, is the same as that which undergirds Tate's sectionalism and Crane's nativism. All three take a definition of "culture" as plural and bounded, with no basis of comparison between elements—no "better" or "worse," only "different." Again, the difference between them is revealed to be one of affect toward the constituent elements of the system (more or less "tolerant" of difference, for example), not a different system. Thus, the pluralism that these critics favor does not automatically mean "democracy," and there remains a tension in works like Hammer's in the attempt to simply contrast Crane's "universalism" to Eliot's and Tate's "hierarchy."

Professing Wholeness: The Poet-Critic and the Anthropologist

Seeing Tate's and Ransom's construction of culture and the New Critical theories of the structure of poetry as different aspects of the same problematic, and further that this problematic of culture also structures the debates within anthropology and the restructuring of the Americanist canon undertaken by figures such as Brooks and Mumford, suggests ways in which the "hero of culture" in each of these disciplines—the anthropologist, the literary critic, and the literary historian—is likewise structured by the problematic of culture. At the most basic level, I have been arguing, modernist anthropology and modernist literary criticism both come to conceive their object of study *as* "objects," as structured, spatially conceived "wholes," individual elements of which—be they a religious rite or a metaphor—cannot be understood without the surrounding structure within which they occur and derive their meaning. Neither a poem nor a culture can thus be "paraphrased." Both disciplines, with their emphasis on wholeness, present their object of study as in crucial ways "spatialized," removed from temporality, in much the same way I have argued in chapter 2 that Cather spatializes culture. As I suggest in that chapter, Joseph Frank argues that modernist poetry frustrates "the reader's normal expectation of a sequence and [force] him to perceive the elements of the poem as juxtaposed in space rather than unrolling in time."[42] In similar terms, James Clifford has discussed the modern anthropologist's "'allochronic' representations," in which the ethnographer—partially because of the constraints of short-term fieldwork—does not historicize the culture under study, but portrays a culture in a perpetual "ethnographic present," a "synchronic suspension [that] effectively textualizes the other, and gives the sense of a reality not in temporal flux."[43]

The parallels between literary modernism's "poetic unity" and modernist anthropology's "cultural wholes" in turn construct similar authoritative positions for the "professional" within each field: the "poet-critic"(later, the "literary critic") and the ethnographer. As Clifford has noted, one of the key elements of the "ethnographic authority" asserted by the Malinowskian monograph is the ethnographer's status as participant-observer: combining the personas of the heroic explorer and the scientific observer, the participant-observer could be seen "continuously tacking between the 'inside' and 'outside' of events," on the one hand, "grasping the sense of specific occurrences and gestures empathetically," and on the other, armed with scientific theory and training, "stepping back to situate these meanings in wider contexts."[44] Thus, the ethnographer becomes the authoritative "expert" who can mediate between the radically different perspectives of his or her audience and the culture under study. The participant-observer in modernist literature is the poet-critic, typified by men such as Eliot, Tate, and the other Southern Agrarians-turned-New-Critics. Already in "The Function of Criticism," Eliot sets forth the ideal of the poet-critic, stipulating that "criticism" was crucial for poetic "creation." Adopting the same heroic posture we find in the fieldworker, Eliot claims the "larger part of the labour of an author in composing his work is critical labour; the labour of sifting, combining, constructing, expunging, correcting, testing: this frightful toil is as much critical as creative" ("Function," 73). As Hammer puts it, Tate and John Crowe Ransom saw themselves as "poet-tillers," practitioners of a "traditional craft" constituted by technique "not only of prosody, but a formal apprehension of structures, linguistic and narrative, that could only come from long and intensive study of tradition" (*Janus*, 27). They were poets who not only could write poetry, but could also reflect on them, write about them, and teach them. They were in a sense "scientists," armed with their knowledge of "The Tradition" (in Eliot's case) or "his tradition" (in Tate's case), but scientists with "experience." To put it in Cather's terms, they were, like Tom Outland, able to "select" and "compose," as much as discover, their objects of analysis. In chapters 1 and 3, I argued for the importance of "experience" in the theory of culture of critics like Van Wyck Brooks, in the program of "participant observation" developed by anthropologists like Malinowski, and in the construction of Herman Melville in the Melville revival. A similar impulse is evident in the position of the poet-critic: as bearers of "objective" knowledge and training as well as "experience," the ethnographer and the poet-critic establish their authority.

The authority of the ethnographer is also enhanced through the persistent trope of "salvage" in modernist monographs, in which ethnographers repeatedly portray the cultural formations they are describing as "dying out" or in the process of "dissolving," even as they are being recorded. Looking toward "primitive" societies for a wholeness the ethnographer desires, this wholeness is inevitably in the process of passing away, to be "rescued" only in the ethnographer's text.[45] Thus Malinowski complains that "ethnology is in the sadly ... tragic position, that at the very moment when it begins ... the material of its study melts away with hopeless rapidity, [as] within a generation or two ... their culture will have practically disappeared" (*Argonauts*, xv). They will, as Sapir laments, "slip out of the warm embrace of a culture into the cold air of fragmentary existence" in the face of European contact ("Genuine," 318). This same position characterize Mumford's version of Melville: part of *Moby-Dick*'s "romantic allure," he suggests, is that it portrays whalers and whaling "at the moment when they were about to pass out of existence, or rather, were being transformed from a brutal but glorious battle into a methodical, slightly banal industry."[46] The most important way of life on which Mumford's Melville pronounced "valedictory" was, of course, the "thriving regional culture" of New York and New England, of which *Moby-Dick* is the monument.

If the ethnographer "rescues" a passing cultural whole in his or her monograph, Tate's poet-critic seeks to uncover the organic unity of the poetic text in a modern world where culture was no longer whole. In his function as a critic, commenting on, evaluating, correcting poetry, he "rescues," reconstitutes, and perpetuates the threatened Tradition or culture for which he stands. Similarly, the critic like Mumford, in his or her position as the rediscoverer of this "usable past," literally salvages the literary object that had nearly been lost, and which now, through his efforts, is being reconstituted and reinterpreted for the first time *as* a "whole." Tate's and Ransom's constructions of the literary critic, Mumford's project in reviving Melville, and more broadly the project of restructuring the Americanist literary tradition could be seen as a kind of "salvage ethnography."

Both of these last points—the participant-observer status of both the ethnographer and the poet-critic and the allegory of "cultural rescue" they seem to enact—feed directly into the professionalization and institutionalization in the academy of both literary criticism and anthropology that occurred in this period. As discussed earlier, both disciplines legitimized themselves through their respective narratives of "cultural decline." For the literary critic, it was the decline of modern society from the unified Tradition of the past. For the anthropologist, the "culture in decline" was the organic culture of the exotic Other, disintegrating before the forces of the modern world even as they wrote. But just as importantly, the "culture in decline" was their own, which paradoxically became both the enabling condition of their profession and the condition they presented themselves as attempting to solve. Tate and Ransom find the last remnants of wholeness in the spatially integrated poem and preserve these remnants as models to contemplate for the future; Sapir deploys the integral genuine culture of the Indian as a model against the spurious conditions of modern America; it is Mumford's America that is the heir of the disintegration of Melville's genuine provincial culture, and his revival of Melville's regional culture, and his work in regional planning, architecture, and social criticism, is deployed to create a new regional culture in the present.

At the same time, although both the anthropologist and the literary historian/critic deploy their versions of regional cultural/textual wholeness in order to contemplate and heal the rifts in their own (spurious) cultural moment, their ability to perceive the whole culture or text *depends* on their position outside that encompassing wholeness. To be able to see the interrelation of parts—in a culture, in a text—one needs to be both the participant *and* the observer who can stand outside of that culture or text, in a position that is in turn free of *any* encompassing horizon that might interfere with that view. To put it in Sapir's terms, one needs to be in the "cold air of fragmentary existence" to recognize the "significance of any one element of [a genuine culture] in its relation to all others." To put it in Mumford's terms, Melville's reputation and the wholeness of the culture he represents can only be salvaged and recognized as whole after they have been lost. The participant-observer, the regionalist living in a former region, or the poet-critic must have undergone Ransom's fortunate fall from poetry to prose, from tradition to modernity, from regional culture to spurious national culture, to retroactively (re)cognize or (re)construct that former wholeness.

This professionalization and institutionalization in academia was in turn facilitated by each discipline's focus on units, whether it be the unified culture captured in the monograph, or the organically unified poem. George Marcus and Michael Fischer have commented on how the monograph lent itself particularly well to the transmission of knowledge and technique in the classroom.[47] Similarly, the New Critical techniques of formal analysis provided a distinct set of tools for the teacher and student to work with, as well as distinct "texts" upon which to work. The success of both these versions of modernism is, of course, attested to by the fact that, until recently, the authority of the monograph was virtually uncontested, whereas in literary studies, the New Critical techniques of close reading became virtually synonymous with "criticism" long after its decline as a "school" in the 1950s and, as critics continue to point out, still characterize much of the work we do in the literature classroom, despite the fact that we are supposedly in the era "after the new criticism."[48]

Thus, it is clear that the literary modernist concern with poetic form, exemplified by Allen Tate and the New Criticism, is intimately tied to changes in the conception and representation of culture in anthropology in the same period. As the "armchair anthropology" practiced by Sir James Frazer gave way to the ethnographic method of Malinowski, a corresponding change in the definition of culture took place: culture as universal, evolutionary process, elements of which could be compared across time and space, was replaced by the relativist study of cultural wholes as exemplified by Malinowski's monograph, emphasizing the "difference" between distinct "cultures" and the importance of context in understanding any individual cultural trait. This shift in culture from Frazer to Malinowski, or Tylor to Sapir, I have claimed, saw an analogous development in literary modernism, as Eliot's universal Tradition of the early 1920s became Allen Tate's sectional traditions, each organically rooted to the soil of the region. This conception of organic cultural wholes, in turn, found its expression in Tate and the New Critics literary theories reifying poetic form. Thus, the cultural wholes of modernist anthropology found their analogue in the poetic icon of literary modernism, occupying structurally similar positions within the discipline, and in turn creating homologous positions of authority and professionalism for the ethnographer on one side and the poet-critic on the other, ultimately facilitating the institutionalization of both disciplines in the academy.

In examining the ways in which the formalist, aesthetic criticism of Tate and Ransom participates in the problematic of culture, we can return to the imagined narrative of literary studies of Warner and Siskin with which I began and see that the very moment that Warner and Siskin imagine literary studies as a discipline free from the problem of culture, just before the Fall into culture, was actually the moment the discipline could be said to emerge from and be structured around the problematic of culture. In this way, formalist literary criticism, aesthetics, and culture formed a common problematic in the modernist period: examining the work of anthropologist-literary critics like Sapir and interdisciplinary critics like Mumford, it is, one might argue, the moment when cultural studies really begins. Recognizing the interdisciplinary problematic of culture structuring these various fields helps us think through the current problem of culture and its supposed alternatives—a line of thought I turn to in the conclusion.

Conclusion: Composing Critical Cultures

Composing Cultures argues that "culture" formed a central problem(atic) for American modernism between 1915 and 1941—a problematic that not only shaped the literary and other artistic compositions we think of as "modernist," but also crucially shaped, in complexly parallel ways, the disciplines of anthropology, literary criticism, and American literary history as they emerged in their modern forms. As a problematic, or an orienting cluster of questions about meaning, value, aesthetics, and identity, "culture" became a central term for a variety of figures working from different disciplines, with different conceptions of what defined "culture," but nonetheless in common conversation. Each of these figures asked, in different ways and in different contexts, What is culture? What is the unit of culture? And what is the relationship between culture and aesthetic form? Questions of culture and questions of literary form are part of this problematic, as theories of the composition of cultures, how to "know" them, and the relation between cultures and peoples who "possess" them become theories of literary aesthetics, how to "read" texts, and the construction of literary canons.

Rather than a single modernist "culture concept," I have traced a complex debate over culture, with new ways to conceive of culture emerging, competing, and overlapping with older conceptions, each concept itself riven with its own tensions, complexity, and incoherencies. These debates were thoroughly interdisciplinary: in contrast to the conventional idea of an "anthropological culture concept" emerging from within anthropology, to be taken up and "applied" by artists or literary critics, the discourse of culture in the period forms an interdisciplinary (and even pre-disciplinary) debate that involved poets, linguists, philosophers, literary critics, historians, and social scientists (just to name a few). These arguments were worked out not only through their artistic production (in the case of poets and novelists), or through direct communication with interlocutors, but often through the pages of the literary journals and small magazines that were crucial to the formation of modernism, where their articles and writings would appear side-by-side with other pieces that—while apparently dealing with different issues—could be seen as in dialogue with one another around this problematic. Indeed, key figures in this debate like Edward Sapir and Lewis Mumford were themselves involved in a variety of disciplines, blurring the boundaries between social science, aesthetic theory, and literature.

The problematic of culture, I have argued, shapes modernist ideas of national, regional, or individual identity on the one hand, and aesthetic value on the other. In particular, new conceptions of culture as plural, spatial wholes—as internally coherent structures, in which "meaning" arises through the relation of elements in the structure—become particularly powerful in shaping the disciplinary debates within anthropology, literary criticism, and literary history, as new ways to "read" and understand "a culture" become new ways to understand texts. In this way, I suggest, culture and aesthetics were always intertwined. As conceived by Boasian anthropologists like Edward Sapir, culture was an aesthetic object, a harmonious, meaningful spatial structure. Similarly, for writers and critics as various as Willa Cather, Lewis Mumford, and Allen Tate, the literary text itself was seen as a meaningful, spatial structure, the integrity of which was itself a reflection of the whole culture from which it emerged. Questions of the boundaries or "units" of a spatialized culture—the cosmopolitan globe, the nation, the geographic region, or the individual—become questions of the boundedness of the literary text, and of the status of "national," "regional," or cosmopolitan literature. While some critics like Van Wyck Brooks imagined culture as coextensive with the State, and argued for both a "national" culture and a literature that would map it, others—both progressive and reactionary—imagined the "unit" of culture as the geographic region on the one hand, and the transnational circulation of ideas and people on the other, with culture in both cases bypassing the space of the nation-state. The contours of this debate, I argue, are crucial in recovering the origins of American Studies, in order to think through current debates over the nationalist origins of the field and calls for making American Studies "transnational." Finally, imagining culture, and its synecdochic embodiment the text, as a spatial, aesthetic object in turn authorized a model of professional decoder of that object, one who could reveal the system of meaning within the "complex whole," and then translate its workings to those without: the poet-critic and the participant-observer.

This way of looking at the debates over culture and their role in shaping modernist ideas of national, regional, and individual identity on one hand, and ideas of aesthetics and the poetic text on the other, has implications both for our understanding of the history of literary studies, and for current debates over the role of culture in the field. In both cases, the history of this problematic reveals how approaches and concepts that seem to be at odds or to be mutually exclusive, are in fact undergirded by common assumptions and arguments, or are even mutually constitutive. It has been common for accounts of the history of literary studies, for example, to oppose the practice of literary history and American Studies to the rise of literary criticism: the former, these accounts go, grounded in philology and empiricist epistemologies, and barely interested in issues of aesthetics and language, gave rise in the 1920s to figures like V. L. Parrington and others, and through them to American Studies; the latter, grounded in linguistics and traditions of textual interpretation, gave rise to rigorous literary criticism that takes poetic language as its object of interest, as exemplified by the New Criticism.

But as my examination has shown, anthropologists like Sapir were intensely interested in language and poetry, and developed theories of both culture and language as spatial structures; these spatial conceptions of culture as a meaningful whole were taken up by key figures in the rise of American Studies, such as Lewis Mumford, both to think about the relationship between individual texts and regional culture, and to describe the way a literary text "means." Mumford's approach, I have argued, shares many assumptions about culture and textual meaning with critics like Tate and Ransom, who in turn were also very interested in anthropological understandings of regional culture. Thus, rather than two diametrically opposed traditions—American literary history and American Studies on the one hand, and literary criticism and the New Criticism on the other—we have two disciplines that emerge from a common problematic of culture.

Similarly, attending to the problematic of culture in the period also serves to complicate the politics often attached with particular phases of a discipline, both in literary studies and in anthropology, which are then seen to be rooted in particular conceptions of "culture." Practitioners of cultural studies, as my reference to Grossberg's anthology *Cultural Studies* suggests, see themselves as countering a modernist, conservative conception of high "Culture" as universal, hierarchic, and exclusionary; within literary studies, that conservative model is associated with the reactionary politics of the New Criticism.[1] In contrast, cultural studies counters with a progressive or radical model of culture that troubles the distinction between high and low, and that opens the canon to and includes the perspectives of groups hitherto marginalized—women, racial minorities, the working class, the GLBT communities, and so on; they replace, in short, a model of "Culture" with a model of multiculturalism, or cultural pluralism.

As this study has shown, however, there is no easy connection between a theory of cultural pluralism and progressive politics: Tate and Ransom, I have shown, also draw on models of cultural pluralism to undergird both their political regionalism and their poetic theory, just as Walter Benn Michaels has shown that nativist modernists also ground their reactionary arguments in theories of cultural "difference." And while postmodern critics find suspect the modernist privileging of "unity," be they models of a unified culture or a unified poetic text, as critics such as John Guillory have argued, multicultural attempts to open the canon to, or create alternative canons for, subcultures of race, gender, and sexual orientation are themselves founded on ideas of "unity": instead of one unified culture, reflected by a single master canon, the fragmentation of the larger culture is reconstituted as multiple unit*ies*, multiple subcultures unified by their own canons.[2] Cultural pluralism, in other words, was and can be deployed for both progressive and reactionary purposes. Nor, as I will argue below, do current attempts to think beyond the limits of multiculturalism by turning to ideas of transnationalism, borderlands, contact zones, or hybridity escape from the conceptual and political challenges posed by the idea of bounded cultures. My point in this project is not to rescue the New Critics, or equate progressives and conservatives, either in the modernist period or now. Rather, it is to suggest that their progressivism or conservatism is not necessarily grounded in one theory of culture or another (or in an attention to formalist aesthetics): to overlook the *multiple* ways in which new conceptions of culture could be deployed is to miss the complexity of the debate over culture (and the corollary debates over aesthetics and literary canons), and the variety of political and aesthetic positions it made available—both in the modernist period I examine, and today.

In the same vein, postmodern anthropologists have been quick to distance themselves from their modernist predecessors, citing the complicity of the anthropological project with imperialist expansion. For them, the very concept of culture as a bounded, synchronic, spatial "whole," grounded in a specific place, and made accessible to the "scientifically" trained metropolitan anthropologist, was itself a tool of the imperial State to "incarcerate" the Other. But as I have shown, for Boasians such as Sapir, the modernist conception of culture as meaningful whole, grounded in the region on the one hand, and a transnational movement of labor and ideas on the other, was mobilized precisely to counter the imperialism of the nation-state that would "arrogate culture to itself" in the name of national culture, as well as to combat the connection between race and culture deployed to support racism and nativism.[3] As in the case of literary studies, the attempt by postmodern anthropologists to assert a break from what is seen as a problematic past—a past whose faults they also claim to transcend or correct through new theoretical approaches—results in an oversimplification of that past, and in the process valuable genealogies are lost. As Ira Bashkow has said, in the context of his own attempts to revisit Boasian anthropology as a way to think through the crisis in the field, "Notwithstanding its sustained attack against the metanarrative of progress, postmodern anthropology has tended to emphasize the inadequacies of earlier anthropology while accentuating its own disjuncture from it. In so doing, it covertly perpetuates the very notion of progress that it rightly calls in to question."[4] But if, he goes on to add, we indeed believe that history (including disciplinary history) is not simply an upward trajectory of progress, then it behooves us to look carefully at the complexity of those histories to help us understand present dilemmas.

Taking Bashkow's admonishment to heart, I suggest that reexamining the modernist problematic of culture not only allows us to understand our disciplinary (pre)histories in their complexity but also sheds light on current debates over the problem of culture. Returning to Warner and Siskin's argument with which I began, the authors argue for "stopping cultural studies" by imagining a time "before culture," when literary studies was "restricted" to either formalist aesthetics or literary history.[5] This supposed contrast, between formalist aesthetics and cultural studies' practice of situating a text within a broader concept of "culture" and history, has been the standard opening move for proponents of cultural studies as well: in this narrative, formalism, typified in the Americanist tradition by the New Criticism, "severs [the poem] from both author and reader[,] ... disentangling it from any social or historical context."[6] In this way, aesthetic form becomes a "knowledge or practice of cultivation *segregated* from the driving forces of human development—labor and politics." This, the argument goes, "divert[s] culture into the ideal realm of ethics and taste" rather than "subsuming it within culture as a whole way of life."[7] And more recently, this narrative has also been taken up by those who suggest a (re)turn to issues of aesthetic form, either—as in the case of Warner and Siskin—as part of a broader turn *from* "culture" and the problems it raises as a central concept in literary studies, or, in the case of critics like Russ Castronovo or Jonathan Loesberg, as a corrective to cultural studies itself.

But, as I have argued, even in the moment proposed as the epitome of this separation of "culture" and "form"—the modernist period and the rise of the New Criticism—culture was always a "problem," or more precisely a problematic, or a set of orienting questions and concerns about meaning and form that were worked out both in anthropological theories of culture (which were also theories of form) and in critical theories of literary form (which were also theories of culture). Far from the conventional contrast between culture as a "whole way of life" and aesthetic form, for modernist anthropologists like Sapir, this "anthropological" idea of culture was itself already an aesthetic concept, in its formulation as a "whole," meaningful spatialized object. And conversely, Tate's and Ransom's concepts of aesthetic form arose from the same problematic as Sapir's theories of culture, as their conception of the poem as a meaningful, spatial structure was itself a working out, in another disciplinary register, of the problematic addressed in their (and Sapir and Mumford's) theories of regional culture.

Attending to this history, then, reveals the ways in which, rather than being in tension, conceptions of culture and aesthetic form in literary studies each shape the other. Warner and Siskin suggest the metaphor of the bungee cord to describe the relation between literary studies and culture, the cord stretching as critics exceed the bounds of disciplinarity under the siren call of culture (and cultural studies), only to be snapped back to literary studies, specialization, and disciplinarity. (The opposition Warren and Siskin construct between the two approaches is captured in the violence of their image, however tongue-in-cheek, of "the upward flight" of the reverse bungee jump ending "in a collision with the bottom of the platform, a jarring return to the solidity of disciplinarity" ["Stopping, "103]). Instead, I offer the metaphor of the Möbius strip, that closed three-dimensional loop in which one might begin traveling along on one "side" of the strip, but end up seamlessly on the other, and then back again, as what seemed like two sides are revealed to be one.[8]

Conceptions of culture have a form and are already aesthetic; those formal features in turn shape ideas of literary or textual form. Literary form in turn implies ideas about the form of culture. Thus, several critics have noted that new historicists tended to read "culture" in the way New Critics read a poem, as rife with tension and ambiguity, but that nonetheless formed a bounded "whole" within which everything had meaning in relation to everything else. Greenblatt famously credited Clifford Geertz for his model of culture; Geertz in turn called the work of the anthropologist most like the work of the literary critic, and looked to modernist New Critics for his model of the poetic text.[9] My study, then, could be seen to move back another step along this Möbius strip, revealing the New Critics in turn in dialogue with modernist anthropologists, and in that dialogue developing both models of culture and models of the text. By the same token, critics today who propose a turn to the aesthetic as a corrective to the problems of culture should be mindful that this in many ways might be a *re*turn to the problematic in a different register.

To be fair, Warner and Siskin do not conclude that literary studies should return to an examination of aesthetic form, but their recommendation of what to "start" after "stopping" cultural studies in turn reveals the interpenetration of form and culture. They conclude that literary studies, in order to escape the "Teflon category" of culture, should (re)turn its attention to its "original" purpose, as English departments emerged in the eighteenth century: to "mediate society's relation to the dominant technologies for reading and writing" (105). Whereas for the eighteenth century that new technology was print, now it is "new technologies—electronic, digital, algorithmic—that are now saturating our society," in which "all the familiar forms of literary study—novels, newspapers, poems, plays—are being transformed" (105). But as they themselves argue, the idea of "culture" as a "totalizing" concept, as part of "narratives in which everything a society does contributes to its transition from nature into . . . *being* a culture" (102) (and setting aside their telescoping of this long and complex history), arises both with the advent of these "new technologies" of reading and writing, and with the idea of literature as a special subset of these forms of print. By their own claim, literary studies was to "mediate" between "society" and these new forms. In invoking literary studies' role as "mediator" between "society" and these "technologies," they bring "culture" back in, if only in another name. The function is the same: to think about how these new technologies of reading and writing "mean" in the context of the "society" they both are a product of, and produce. And to do so requires us to contemplate what we mean by "society," by what (new) categories we make sense of the new kinds of reading and writing these technologies enable, what it means to "mediate" between them, what "meaning" itself means. This sounds a lot like culture, and the work of cultural studies. In their attempt to return to one side of the Möbius strip, they find themselves already moving to the other—and finding that they really are the same side.

And as with the modernists I have examined here, these new technologies are producing ideas of reading, authorship, interpretation, and aesthetics that fit nicely (but not at all coincidentally) with shifting conceptions of culture. Where postmodern literary critics and anthropologists counter conceptions of culture as "whole," "unified," and bounded (and their aesthetic corollaries, the bounded, unified text) with ideas of hybridity, transnationalism, and permeable borders, the modes of reading and authorship enabled by these new technologies are celebrated in the same terms: undoing the hierarchy between author and reader, enabling liberatory, egalitarian collaborations between multiple readers/authors, the bounds of "the text" are dissolved by the hypertextual networks of the transnational World Wide Web.[10]

Reexamining the complexities of the modernist debates over culture and aesthetics also proves illuminating for current debates within American Studies, in which narratives of disciplinary history, conceptions of culture and nation, modernist unities versus postmodernist pluralities, and, most recently, the reemergence of the aesthetic, are all in play. As I suggested in chapter 3, the current search for a way to redefine the field of American Studies takes as its starting point the argument that the modernist beginnings of the field were grounded in an attempt to define a homogenous, unified American "culture"—what Pease and Weigman call the creation of an "imaginary homogeneity out of discrepant life worlds," to create an "isomorphism of the sovereign people, U.S. territory, and national culture."[11] In contrast to this nationalist, Cold War perspective, the "new" American Studies has struggled to reconstitute itself from a postcolonial, transnational perspective that accounts for the counter-narratives of racial and ethnic minorities, women, and the working class in an age of globalism.

To challenge this model of national sovereignty upon which their discipline has supposedly been based, critics have attempted to construct models that move above and below the nation-state, that are both more local and more transnational. Wai Chee Dimock, for example, argues eloquently for a "non-sovereign" history, a history that is "offbeat, off-key, off-center." "Its unorthodox paths," she describes, "jump from the micro to the macro, and bypass the default center, going over and under the jurisdiction of the nation. Its scale is both smaller and larger: operating subnationally on the one hand, as a grass-roots phenomenon, and internationally on the other hand, as a cross-border phenomenon, and in this way, bringing into relief a practice of democracy significantly different from the nation-bound variety, at once dispersed and energized by a multicentric network."[12] Significantly, it is in this spirit that critics like Dimock and Castronovo have argued for an aesthetic "turn" in American Studies and literary studies: as I discuss in chapter 3, both suggest the aesthetic as a way of bypassing the nation. As Dimock puts it, the aesthetic "is both local and global," a way for a global community "to individuate each of its members even as it affirms its integrative common ground"; in the process, the aesthetic "invokes a map that predates the nation-state, one that allows for multilateral ties, more complex and far-flung than those dictated by territorial jurisdictions."[13]

Reexamining modernist debates over culture and aesthetics, as I have here, reveals a more complex picture of the rise of American Studies, and the relationship between concepts of culture, nation and aesthetic form. Sapir and Mumford, I have suggested, both mobilized a conception of culture as meaningful whole, grounded in the region, precisely as a way to bypass the nation-state; this conception of culture—which is also an aesthetic structure—anticipates Dimock's desire to "go over and under the jurisdiction of the nation." Mumford's transposition of an aesthetic of regional culture as an aesthetic of the text, to see *Moby-Dick* as first and foremost a "regional" and "modern" novel rather than a "national" one, echoes Dimock's argument for the aesthetic as both "local" and "global." It is fitting, in this context, that Dimock describes the perspectives afforded by this nonsovereign history as "oceanic"—a term that certainly fits Mumford's account of *Moby-Dick*.[14] Mumford and Sapir's aesthetic conception of culture reveals the way in which culture and the aesthetic have always been intertwined; their deployment of this concept in opposition to the state both complicates New Americanist accounts of their own disciplinary history, and provides a potential "usable past" for the current transnational turn in the field.[15]

My primary purpose in this project has been to uncover the contours of the modernist debates over culture and aesthetics in order to complicate our current debates over the problem of culture, rather than to "solve" that problem: in uncovering the complexity of those disciplinary histories, I hope to open a space to think through the problem of culture, to see what is usable in these pasts, to see whether our proposed disjunctions or breaks from disciplinary pasts really are breaks, or if our turns—to culture, to aesthetics, to the transnational—are in some sense returns, which reveal dynamics from which we can learn. In closing, however, I would like to offer a few thoughts on what I would like to call "critical culturalism."

A common denominator that runs through the problem of culture for critics like Warner and Siskin who advocate a return to literary studies, and for critics within American Studies wanting to resist ideas of national culture, is the problem of boundedness. As Susan Hegeman points out, culture's close association with "nation"—and in particular the political boundaries of the nation-state—is the source of much of the discomfort with culture within American Studies, whose scholars look to reconfigure the discipline around ideas of transnationalism, hybridity, and globalism. This is similar to the critique of culture's boundedness with which anthropologists themselves, as Bashkow has noted, have struggled for over thirty years.

Siskin, Warner, and others, on the other hand, are not disturbed by culture's boundedness, but rather the opposite: they are disturbed by culture's tendency, in the hands of cultural studies scholars, to imperially cross, blur, and erase (disciplinary) boundaries, to be all-encompassing. They want not to transcend boundaries, but to *reassert* them, in particular the boundaries around "the literary." I have already argued that Siskin and Warner's conception of "literary studies" prior to the incursion of cultural studies is itself a misunderstanding of the history of the discipline, and that the idea of the self-contained aesthetic text-object was itself undergirded by a concept of culture as a self-contained aesthetic object (for which its literary texts, conceived as spatial forms, would be a synecdoche). Here, I want to point to the hinge of boundaries on which these inverse complaints turn: from one point of view, culture establishes boundaries that need to be permeated; from the other, culture permeates boundaries that need to be policed.

The juxtaposition, it seems to me, is striking: culture on the one hand as restrictive and exclusive, and culture as dangerously amorphous and invasive on the other; incarcerating on the one hand, yet anarchic on the other. Again, returning to modernist debates over culture proves instructive. Anthropologists like Handler and Bashkow have reminded us that for Boas, Sapir, and Benedict, the "boundaries" drawn around the "whole" structures of meaning were not fixed, but permeable and changing: "centrally concerned with diffusion ... of people, objects, images, and ideas between localities," to a large extent "their interest in drawing boundaries around cultures was precisely to gauge the historical traffic across them."[16] Thus, Sapir's concern with the structural harmony and integrity of genuine culture "is not antithetical to the diffusionist view that cultural boundaries are porous; to the contrary, it presumes it," and the interest for Sapir and others in the structure of "genuine culture" was precisely in how cultures "integrated" changing elements into the system.

Further, these boundaries were seen as plural, with "cultures appearing to have different boundaries when looked at from different viewpoints."[17] As I have shown, in the hands of thinkers like Sapir and Mumford, the boundedness of culture—in their case, the spatial conception of culture as regional—was strategic, to contrast with the boundedness of culture at the level of the state; both, however, imagined culture simultaneously as regional *and* transnational. Cather, likewise, saw regional culture as both enabled by (in the case of her vision of cosmopolitan Nebraska or Jewett's New England) and at times threatened by (in the case of *The Professor's House*) transnational flow. The force of the boundaries they draw depends on the possibility of alternative boundaries, of alternative ways to order the elements they consider (including as "disorder," "progress," and the like).

Thus, the problem with boundaries, Handler argues, is not the concept of boundaries themselves, but the reification of these boundaries by the critics who then use these reified versions to critique the idea of bounded culture in favor of hybridity, transnationalism, "border" identities, and so on. At the same time, these versions of hybridity and transnationalism actually depend on the very ideas of boundedness they critique: any "hybrid" or "trans" version of culture depends, in order to count as "hybrid," on being able to trace particular elements back to the previous original "whole" from which the hybrid versions are constituted.

Taken together, the twin objections around boundedness, I would suggest, reveal one way to begin to negotiate the problem of culture: that is, to remind ourselves at every turn that the boundaries of culture, taken in the semiotic sense as a shared system of "meaning" through which we interpret and order the world—the sense shared by the figures in this study, and drawn upon by cultural studies and anthropologists today— are provisional and relational, themselves compositions that are *both*, in the moment of their representation or composition, "real" in that they designates shared structures of meanings among members of a group, *but also in the same moment* are provisional and heuristic, the "bounds" of which can at any moment be composed in a different way, with the same elements held in a different order, to create a different set of meanings shared by a different group (including some of the same members, but now seen within different boundaries). To remind ourselves, in fact, any one composition of culture derives its (momentary) force *as* a composition only by contrast to the other possible configurations that are temporarily bracketed from view.

The solution to the problem of culture, then, is not to "forget" or "stop" culture (if that were even possible). In popular discourse, culture is everywhere, and even within literary studies "culture" remains a keyword, despite the sense that it is a problem, and amid calls to "stop" it or "turn" from it. Instead, the "solution" might be to work toward what I would call a "critical culturalism." I borrow and modify this term from Douglas Powell, who in a similar way tries to recover "regionalism"—a term that has come under related critiques—by offering "critical regionalism," a "kind of critical intersection where these coexisting and overlapping revisions of regionalism can find common ground." A "region," he argues, "is not a thing in itself, a stable and bounded object of study":

> My assertion here is that just as "community" is for Raymond Williams "a warmly persuasive word to describe an existing set of relationships, or the warmly persuasive word to describe an alternative set of relationships" (*Keywords* 76), region is always at some level an attempt to persuade as much as it is to describe. Because the "set of relationships" intersecting at any one point on the landscape is potentially unsummarizable by any one account, all versions of region are necessarily partial and hence an attempt to persuade, at the very least, of the validity of their own particular definitions. Attempts at metadescription therefore need to be as much about the representational practices and politics that inform constructions of region as they do about the definition themselves.[18]

Similarly, culture is a composition, composed to describe this "set of relationships," or "an alternative set of relationships," always partial and requiring provisional awareness of their partiality and the way they are composed. To say the term "culture" is already to fall into the "trap," to begin to draw boundaries by drawing relations between elements, to derive meanings that are always mediations, to call into being a community that then could be said to have already been there. But it need not be a trap if we are continually aware, when we deploy the term, that culture is never simply "itself"; it is always relational and provisional. As Handler has put it, "Once we have exorcised all the demons of our modern(ist) anthropological realm... we are left with an experiential given: the world, as we know it, seems orderly, at least some of the time." We carry about with us, he says, "ordering schemes, which are sedimented out of history... and which allow [us] to respond to (to interpret, to learn about, to understand) the ordering schemes of the other humans [we] encounter"; in turn, these ordering schemes "seem to elicit or trigger alternative ordering schemes from others who encounter them."[19] The key is to recognize the particular "ordering scheme"—of a culture, or of a text—being deployed at any particular moment, and the power and politics involved in that move, while also recognizing that other "ordering schemes" might be deployed as well (never without their own power dynamics).

Winfried Fluck, referring to how one might regard a text, but not at all coincidentally echoing the compositional terms of what I am calling "critical culturalism," describes this stance as an "aesthetic attitude," the "capacity of any system of signification to draw attention to itself as a form of expression and to refer to itself as a sign, thus drawing our attention to the *organizing and patterning* principles by which the object is constituted." This aesthetic moment, applied to either a textual composition or culture, "opens up the possibility of a new interpretation of the world."[20] These aesthetic moments—composing cultures, or composing texts—are precisely provisional, momentary, not the only possible compositional order, but useful for the moment in which they are invoked.

Notes

Introduction

1. William B. Warner and Clifford Siskin, "Stopping Cultural Studies," *Profession* (2008): 94.

2. Analysts have, for example, attributed the events leading up to the 2008 financial crisis at least in part to "Wall Street's culture of risk." See, for example, Bethany McLean and Joe Nocera, *All the Devils Are Here* (New York: Penguin, 2010); or anthropologist Karen Zouwen Ho's examination of Wall Street's "cultural production of liquidation" in *Liquidation: An Ethnography of Wall Street* (Durham, NC: Duke UP, 2009). Conversely, culture is also credited with corporate success. Tony Hsieh, the founder and CEO of the online retailer Zappos.com—which was recently sold to Amazon.com for $1.2 billion—writes in his autobiography/self-help/business manual that "a company's culture and a company's brand are really just two sides of the same coin.... Your culture is your brand" (Tony Hsieh, *Delivering Happiness: A Path to Profits, Passion and Purpose* [New York: Business Plus, 2010], 151). Accordingly, Zappos compiled what it calls the "Zappos Culture Book" that identifies ten core values that "formally define Zappos culture" (154). To ensure that future employees are able to preserve that culture (and brand), the Human Resources department evaluates employees according to their "culture fit" (153). In a line that might warrant its own citation in a new version of Raymond Williams's *Keywords*, Hsieh rhetorically asks, "What's the best way to build a brand for the long term? In a word: culture" (152).

3. As one *New York Times Magazine* columnist put it, the emphasis on diversity and "postmodern cleverness" in the 1990s was "so successful... that we find it hard to say what our true shared culture is." As culture becomes a matter of individual choice, "somewhere in the recesses of our mind we're haunted by the realization that the more we make our separate peace with our culture, the less sustenance that culture has to offer us all. What exactly do we belong to?" (Richard Todd, "Fragmented We Stand," *New York Times Magazine*, 28 October 2001, 15).

4. See, for example, Frans de Waal, *The Ape and the Sushi Master: Cultural*

Reflections of a Primatologist (New York: Basic Books, 2001); Frans de Waal and Peter L. Tyack, eds., *Animal Social Complexity: Intelligence, Culture, and Individualized Societies* (Cambridge, MA: Harvard UP, 2003); and Kevin N. Laland and Bennett G. Galef, eds., *The Question of Animal Culture* (Cambridge, MA: Harvard UP, 2009).

5. Lawrence Grossberg, Cary Nelson, and Paula A. Treichler, eds., introduction to *Cultural Studies* (New York: Routledge, 1992), 4.

6. Ibid.

7. Susan Hegeman, *The Cultural Return* (Berkeley: U of California P, 2012), 7.

8. For "culture" as "incarceration," see Arjun Appadurai, "Putting Hierarchy in Its Place," *Cultural Anthropology* 3, no. 1 (1988): 36–47. Other major examples (among many) of the anthropological critique of culture are Lila Abu-Lughod, "Writing Against Culture," in *Recapturing Anthropology: Working in the Present*, ed. R. Fox (Santa Fe, NM: School of American Research Press, 1991), 137–62; James Clifford and George Marcus, eds., *Writing Culture: The Poetics and Politics of Ethnography* (Berkeley: U of California P, 1986); and Renato Rosaldo, *Culture and Truth: Remaking Social Analysis* (Boston: Beacon, 1989). For a valuable taxonomy of the main lines of critique, see Robert Brightman, "Forget Culture: Replacement, Transcendence, Relexification," *Cultural Anthropology*, 10, no. 4 (1995): 509–46.

9. See Brightman, "Forget Culture"; Richard G. Fox and Barbara J. King, "Introduction: Beyond Culture Worry," in *Anthropology beyond Culture*, ed. Richard G. Fox and Barbara J. King (New York: Berg, 2002), 1–36; Michel-Rolph Trouillot, "Adieu, Culture: A New Duty Arises," in *Anthropology beyond Culture*, 37–60.

10. Walter Benn Michaels, *Our America: Nativism, Modernism, Pluralism* (Durham, NC: Duke UP, 1995).

11. Jonathan Loesberg, "Cultural Studies, Victorian Studies, and Formalism," *Victorian Literature and Culture* 27 (1999): 540; Christopher Castiglia and Russ Castronovo, "A 'Hive of Subtlety': Aesthetics and the End(s) of Cultural Studies," *American Literature* 76, no. 3 (2004): 425–527. For an overview, see Marjorie Levinson, "What Is New Formalism?" *PMLA* 122, no. 2 (2007): 558–569.

12. Susan Hegeman, "Culture, Patriotism, and the Habitus of a Discipline; or, What Happens to American Studies in a Moment of Globalization?" *Genre* 38 (Winter 2005): 454.

13. See Russ Castronovo, *Beautiful Democracy: Aesthetics and Anarchy in a Global Era* (Chicago: U of Chicago P, 2007); Wai Chee Dimock, "Aesthetics at the Limit of the Nation: Kant, Pound and the Saturday Review," *American Literature* 76, no. 3 (2004): 525–47; and Dimock, *Through Other Continents: American Literature across Deep Time* (Princeton, NJ: Princeton UP, 2008).

14. Doug Mao, "The New Critics and the Text-Object," *ELH* 63, no. 1 (1996): 226. Mao calls this characterization of New Criticism "the most popular form of attack" through which "every major movement in literary theory since the late fifties has fortified its own position" (226).

15. Allen Tate, "New England Culture and Emily Dickinson" (1932), in *The Recognition of Emily Dickinson: Selected Criticism since 1890*, ed. Caesar R. Blake and Carlton F. Wells (Ann Arbor: U of Michigan P, 1965), 160–61. Hereafter cited parenthetically in the text as "New England Culture."

16. Matthew Arnold, *Culture and Anarchy* (New Haven, CT: Yale UP, 1994), 5.

17. For a cogent summary of Boas's theoretical innovations and institutional

impact, see George Stocking, "Introduction: The Basic Assumptions of Boas' Anthropology," in *The Shaping of American Anthropology, 1883–1911: A Franz Boas Reader*, ed. George Stocking (New York: Basic Books, 1974), 1–20.

18. Edward Sapir, "Emily Dickinson, a Primitive," *Poetry: A Magazine of Verse* 26 (1925): 98. Hereafter cited parenthetically in the text as "Primitive."

19. Richard Handler, "Anti-Romantic Romanticism: Edward Sapir and the Critique of American Individualism," *Anthropological Quarterly* 62 (October 1988): 1.

20. Van Wyck Brooks, *New England: Indian Summer, 1865–1915* (New York: Dutton, 1940), 328. Hereafter cited parenthetically in the text as "Indian Summer."

21. Van Wyck Brooks, *The Flowering of New England, 1815–1865* (New York: Dutton 1936), i. Hereafter cited parenthetically in the text as "Flowering."

22. Van Wyck Brooks, "On Creating a Usable Past," *Dial* 64 (11 April 1918), 337.

23. Van Wyck Brooks, "Toward a National Culture," *Seven Arts*, March 1917, 535.

24. The classic texts, to which the emergence of "cultural studies" itself is often traced, are Raymond Williams, *Culture and Society, 1780–1950* (New York: Columbia University Press, 1958), and *Keywords: A Vocabulary for Culture and Society* (New York: Oxford UP, 1976). Williams has famously called "culture" "one of the two or three most complicated words in the English language" (*Keywords*, 76).

25. Edward Burnett Tylor, *Primitive Culture* (1871), reprinted as *The Origins of Culture* (New York: Harper and Row, 1958), 1.

26. George Stocking, "The Ethnographic Sensibility of the 1920s and the Dualism of the Anthropological Tradition," in *Romantic Motives: Essays on Anthropological Sensibility*, ed. George Stocking (Madison: Wisconsin UP, 1989), 212, 220. See also Stocking, "Introduction."

27. As the editors of *Cultural Studies* suggest, the anthropological version of culture "[leads] one to commit oneself in advance to a moral evaluation of modern society . . . to a revolutionary line of political action or, at the least, a major project of social reconstruction" (5).

28. Ann Douglass, for example, argues that the boundary crossing and free play that for her characterized the 1920s, evinced most strongly in the emergence of the Harlem Renaissance, came to an end with the New Critics' supposed renunciation of culture and biography in literary criticism, and their division of art into high and low, "undoing the philosophical, critical, and temperamental assumptions that had made possible a black and white, illiterate and literate, self-consciously American and mongrel age a decade earlier" (*Terrible Honesty: Mongrel Manhattan in the 1920s* [New York: Farrar, Strauss and Giroux, 1996], 468).

29. Christopher Douglas, *A Genealogy of Literary Multiculturalism* (Ithaca, NY: Cornell UP, 2009), 5.

30. Michaels, *Our America*.

31. Susan Hegeman, *Patterns for America: Modernism and the Concept of Culture* (Princeton, NJ: Princeton UP, 1999).

32. Marc Manganaro, *Culture, 1922: The Emergence of a Concept* (Princeton, NJ: Princeton UP, 2002).

1 / Van Wyck Brooks and Edward Sapir

1. For an account of Brooks's experiences in California and London, see Casey Nelson Blake, *Beloved Community: The Cultural Criticism of Randolph Bourne, Van Wyck*

Brooks, Waldo Frank and Lewis Mumford (Chapel Hill: U of North Carolina P, 1990), 107–11.

2. Van Wyck Brooks, *America's Coming-of-Age* (New York: B. W. Heubsch, 1915), 7. Hereafter cited parenthetically in the text as *Coming-of-Age*.

3. Van Wyck Brooks, "The Culture of Industrialism," *Seven Arts*, April 1917, 655. Hereafter cited parenthetically in the text as "Industrialism."

4. Van Wyck Brooks, "On Creating a Usable Past," *Dial* 64 (11 April 1918): 337.

5. Edward Sapir, "Civilization and Culture," *Dial* (20 September 1919): 233, 236. Hereafter cited parenthetically in the text as "Civilization."

6. Edward Sapir, "Culture, Genuine and Spurious," *American Journal of Sociology* 29 (1924), reprinted in *The Selected Writings of Edward Sapir in Language, Culture and Personality*, ed. David Mandelbaum (Berkeley: U of California P, 1951), 322, emphasis added. Hereafter cited parenthetically in the text as "Genuine."

7. George Stocking, "The Ethnographic Sensibility of the 1920s and the Dualism of the Anthropological Tradition," in *Romantic Motives: Essays on Anthropological Sensibility*, ed. George Stocking (Madison: Wisconsin UP, 1989), 220.

8. This series of discussions resulted in the collection of essays published as *Civilization in the United States: An Inquiry by Thirty Americans* (1922), in which each contributor analyzed a particular aspect of "American civilization," such as "The City," "The Small Town," "Business," and "The Family." Parson's contribution was "Sex," while Lowie wrote "Science."

9. For Sapir's literary and music criticism and the relation between his anthropological theory and his artistic practice, see Richard Handler, "The Dainty Man and the Hungry Man: Literature and Anthropology in the Work of Edward Sapir," in *Observers Observed: Essays on Ethnographic Fieldwork*, ed. George Stocking (Madison: U of Wisconsin P, 1983), 208–32.

10. Edward Sapir, "A Symposium of the Exotic," *Dial* 73 (November 1922): 568–71; T. S. Eliot, *The Waste Land*, ibid., 481–85.

11. As Michael North puts it, in his work tracing the connections between diverse disciplines and figures in the modernist period, "The difficulty . . . is getting them to stop somewhere—and it soon becomes clear, after concerted study of a very concentrated time span, that this is what conventional disciplinary boundaries are for. . . . However, disciplinary boundaries also impoverish our sense of a period, and this seems to be an especially acute problem when it comes to relations between literary modernism and other aspects of modern culture" (*Reading 1922: A Return to the Scene of the Modern* [New York: Oxford UP, 1999], 9).

12. Richard Brodhead, *The Culture of Letters: Scenes of Reading and Writing in Nineteenth Century America* (Chicago: U of Chicago P, 1993), 139.

13. Louis Menand, *The Metaphysical Club* (New York: Farrar, Straus and Giroux, 2001), 381. For a detailed history of immigration and nativism in the late nineteenth and early twentieth centuries, see John Higham, *Strangers in the Land: Patterns of American Nativism, 1860–1925* (New Brunswick, NJ: Rutgers UP, 1988).

14. Wallace Rice, "Immigration Past and Present," *Dial* 57 (1 November 1914): 337; "Laxative Literature," *Dial* 58 (10 June 1915): 451.

15. While Brooks, with his patrician Dutch and English background that stretched back into the seventeenth century, might have seen himself as a child of "old America" hearing the "thunder" of those "alien wants," many of the key figures in the

reconceptualization of culture in the period were themselves "aliens," immigrants, children of immigrants, or members of ethnic minorities. Franz Boas was a German-born Jew who immigrated to the United States as an adult in 1886; Sapir was the son of an Eastern European Jewish cantor, who emigrated from Prussia to the United States when he was six. Lewis Mumford was half-Jewish and educated in New York City public schools among a heavily immigrant population; Horace Kallen emigrated from Germany to America with his Orthodox Jewish family when he was five. While his family genealogy was more like Brooks's, Randolph Bourne was born with severe physical deformities that, coupled with an attack of spinal tuberculosis as a child, left him a hunchback and a dwarf.

16. Lewis Mumford, "The Status of the State," *Dial* 67 (26 July 1919): 59–62; Franz Boas, "Nationalism," *Dial* 66 (8 March 1919): 232–37; Thorstein Veblen, "The Passing of National Frontiers," *Dial* 64 (25 April 1918): 387–90.

17. Lewis Mumford, "Wardom and the State," *Dial* 67 (4 October 1919): 303–5.

18. David Goldberg, *Discontented America: The United States in the 1920s* (Baltimore, MD: Johns Hopkins UP, 1999), 66–67.

19. V. L. Parrington, *Main Currents of American Thought*, vol.3 (New York: Harcourt Brace, 1927), 259.

20. See, for example, Elsie Clews Parsons, "A Pilgrim Interprets the Promised Land," *Dial* 64 (31 January 1918): 107–9; and especially Randolph Bourne, "Transnational America," *Atlantic Monthly*, July 1916; and Horace Kallen, "Democracy vs. the Melting Pot," *Nation* (1916), reprinted in *Culture and Democracy* (New York: Boni and Liveright, 1924), 59–118.

21. Carl H. Grabo, "Americanizing the Immigrants," *Dial* (31 May 1919): 539.

22. William Aspenwall Bradley, "The Folk Culture of the Kentucky Highlands," *Dial* 64 (31 January 1918): 95–98; Ernest A. Boyd, "The Irish Renaissance—Renascent," *Dial* 67 (26 July 1919): 53–55; Brodhead, 139.

23. Warren Susman, "Culture and Civilization: The Nineteen-Twenties," in *Culture as History: The Transformation of American Society in the Twentieth Century* (New York: Pantheon Books, 1984), 111.

24. Bronislaw Malinowski, "The Problem of Meaning in Primitive Languages," in *The Meaning of Meaning: A Study of the Influence of Language upon Thought and of the Science of Symbolism*, ed. I. A. Richards and C. K. Ogden (1923; London: Kegan Paul, Trench, Trubner, 1947), 296–336; Edward Sapir, "An Approach to Symbolism," *Freeman* 7 (1923): 572–73.

25. T. S. Eliot, "The Metaphysical Poets," in *Selected Prose of T. S. Eliot*, ed. Frank Kermode (New York: Harcourt, Brace, 1975), 64.

26. Susan Hegeman, *Patterns for America: Modernism and the Concept of Culture* (Princeton, NJ: Princeton UP, 1999), 77.

27. Blake, *Beloved Community*, 2.

28. Matthew Arnold, *Culture and Anarchy* (New Haven, CT: Yale UP, 1994), 5.

29. Van Wyck Brooks, "Toward a National Culture," *Seven Arts*, March 1917, 535. Hereafter cited parenthetically in the text as "National Culture."

30. Hegeman, *Patterns*, 72.

31. Van Wyck Brooks, "Young America" (1916), in *Van Wyck Brooks: The Early Years*, ed. Claire Sprague (New York: Harper and Row, 1968), 166.

32. Ibid., 168.

33. Brooks, "Usable Past," 171, emphasis in original.

34. See Regna Darnell, *Edward Sapir: Linguist, Anthropologist, Humanist* (Berkeley: U of California P, 1990).

35. David Mandelbaum, letter to Jean Sapir (3 January 1956: Sapir Family Documents). Quoted in Darnell, *Edward Sapir*, 151.

36. On the relationship among Sapir's anthropology, his literary criticism, and the aesthetics and politics of American modernism, see Richard Handler, "Anti-Romantic Romanticism: Edward Sapir and the Critique of American Individualism," *Anthropological Quarterly* 62 (October 1988): 1–13; Handler, "The Dainty Man and the Hungry Man"; Marc Manganaro, *Culture, 1922: The Emergence of a Concept* (Princeton, NJ: Princeton UP, 2002); and Hegeman, *Patterns*.

37. Edward Burnett Tylor, *Primitive Culture* (1871), reprinted as *The Origins of Culture* (New York: Harper and Row, 1958), 1.

38. Ibid., 6–7.

39. See Curtis Hinsley, *Savages and Scientists: The Smithsonian Institution and the Development of American Anthropology, 1846–1910* (Washington, DC: Smithsonian Institution Press, 1981).

40. Franz Boas, "The Occurrence of Similar Inventions in Areas Widely Apart," in *The Shaping of American Anthropology: A Franz Boas Reader*, ed. George Stocking (New York: Basic Books, 1974), 62.

41. Boas, "Museums of Ethnology and Their Classification," in *Shaping of American Anthropology*, 46. For the Mason-Boas debates, see Ira Jacknis, "Franz Boas and Exhibits: On the Limitations of the Museum Method of Anthropology," in *Objects and Others: Essays on Museums and Material Culture*, ed. George Stocking (Madison: U of Wisconsin P, 1985), 75–111.

42. Hegeman, *Patterns*, 38–39.

43. Sapir once wrote of Boas's reticence to generalize from particulars to theory: "It is clear that Dr. Boas' unconscious long ago decreed that scientific cathedrals are only of the future, that for the time being spires surmounted by the definitive cross are unseemly, if not indeed sinful, that only cornerstones, unfinished walls, or even an occasional isolated portal are strictly in the service of the Lord" (Sapir, "Franz Boas," *New Republic* 57 [23 January 1929]: 278–79).

44. Stocking, "Ethnographic Sensibility," 216. Handler calls "Culture, Genuine and Spurious" the "first rigorous definition of the Boasian conception of culture.... Sapir's contribution to [the culture concept's] elaboration is incontestable, as is his influence on colleagues working on the same problems" ("Dainty Man," 224, n. 3).

45. For the complex relationship between his historical diffusion and later spatial conceptions of culture, see Hegeman, *Patterns*, 38–41.

46. Edward Sapir, "The Grammarian and His Language," in *Selected Writings*, 153, emphasis added.

47. Edward Sapir, *Language: An Introduction to the Study of Speech* (New York: Harcourt Brace, 1921), 56.

48. Parrington, *Main Currents of American Thought*, 259.

49. Edwin L. Wade, "The Ethnic Art Market in the American Southwest, 1880–1980," in *Objects and Others*, 169.

50. T. C. McLuhan, *Dream Tracks: The Railroad and the American Indian, 1890–1930* (New York: Abrams, 1985), 18. For example, one of the most popular tourist

destinations was to see the Hopi ritual known as the "Moki Snake Dance," and thus the Santa Fe railroad published a handbook giving an "account of that unparalleled dramatic pagan ceremony of the Pueblo Indians of Tusayan" (Wade, "Ethnic Art Market," 169). For a detailed analysis of the role of "ethnographic tourism"—including the Moki Snake Dance—in Anglo-American modernism, see Carey Snyder, "When the Indian Was in Vogue: D. H. Lawrence, Aldous Huxley, and Ethnological Tourism in the Southwest," *Modern Fiction Studies*, 53, no. 4 (Winter 2007): 692–96.

51. McLuhan, *Dream Tracks*, 43.

52. Stocking, "Ethnographic Sensibility," 220.

53. Austin's "A Land with Little Rain" appeared in the *Atlantic Monthly* in 1903 and was followed by a series of stories and articles, including *The Basket Woman* (1904), *Lost Borders* (1909), and *The Arrow Maker* (1911).

54. It should be noted that American modernist constructions of the unchanging Indian vanishing before modernity was precisely a construction—one that masked both the ongoing economic and cultural struggles of existing Native American peoples and the role of Native Americans as active agents in both the performance of ethnographic tourism and the production of modernist art.

55. See, for example, Brodhead, *Cultures of Letters*; and Amy Kaplan, "Nation, Region, Empire," *Columbia History of the American Novel*, ed. Emory Elliott et al. (New York: Columbia UP, 1991): 240–66.

2 / Possessing Culture

1. Willa Cather, "Nebraska: The End of the First Cycle," *Nation* 117 (5 September 1923): 237. Hereafter cited parenthetically in the text as "Nebraska."

2. Edward Sapir, "Culture Genuine and Spurious," in *The Selected Writings of Edward Sapir in Language, Culture and Personality*, ed. David Mandelbaum (Berkeley: U of California P, 1951), 316. Hereafter cited parenthetically in the text as "Genuine."

3. Randolph Bourne, "Morals and Art from the West," *Dial* 65 (14 December 1918): 557; Granville Hicks, "The Case against Willa Cather," (1933), in *Willa Cather and Her Critics*, ed. James Schroeter (Ithaca, NY: Cornell UP, 1967), 139–47.

4. Willa Cather, "Prefatory Note," *Not Under Forty* (New York: Knopf, 1936), v.

5. See for example, Phyllis Rose, "Modernism: The Case of Willa Cather," in *Modernism Reconsidered*, ed. Robert Kiely (Cambridge, MA: Harvard UP, 1983), 123–46; and Guy Reynolds, "Willa Cather as Progressive: Politics and the Writer," in *The Cambridge Companion to Willa Cather*, ed. Marilee Lindeman (New York: Cambridge UP, 2005), 19–35.

6. Don Fowler, *A Laboratory for Anthropology: Science and Romanticism in the American Southwest, 1846–1930* (Albuquerque: U of New Mexico P, 2000).

7. Willa Cather, *The Song of the Lark* (New York: Houghton, Mifflin, 1915), 306. Hereafter cited parenthetically in the text as *Song*.

8. David Harrell, for example, argues that "at some early point Cather must have begun to associate [the Cliff Dwellers] with her concept of the Kingdom of Art"; in *The Song of the Lark*, "Cather introduces this theme and explicates it, but not until 'Tom Outland's Story' does she develop it fully" (*From Mesa Verde to The Professor's House* [Albuquerque: U of New Mexico P, 1992], 140). Hermione Lee similarly suggests that Indian artifacts stand "at the heart of *The Song of the Lark* and *The Professor's House*"

as "silent lessons in the creation of communal, functioning domestic art forms" (*Willa Cather: Double Lives* [New York: Pantheon Books, 1989], 89).

9. Rose, 145.

10. Sharon O'Brien, *Willa Cather: The Emerging Voice* (New York: Oxford UP, 1987), 414. O'Brien is representative here of the way that Cather's *interpretations* of Indian culture are taken by some critics as attributes of Indian culture itself. Judith Freyer, for example, suggests that Cather's theory of art emulates the "Navajos, who lavish exhaustless patience upon their blankets, belts and ceremonial robes," but "have no wish to decorate or master nature in the European tradition, to arrange and re-create" ["Desert, Rock, Shelter, Legend: Willa Cather," in *The Desert Is No Lady: Southwestern Landscapes in Women's Writing and Art*, ed. Vera Norwood and Janice Monk (New Haven: Yale UP, 1987), 43]. It is part of my project to show that Cather's point in *The Professor's House* is that Indian art is precisely *about* "arranging" and "re-creating" nature—that is, about culture.

11. Susan Rosowski and Bernice Slote, for example, suggest that changes between Cather's description of Mesa Verde in 1916 and the "Cliff City" in 1925 are about "eliminating conventions and sharpen[ing] emphases" to "heighten effect" ("Willa Cather's 1916 Mesa Verde Essay: The Genesis of *The Professor's House*," *Prairie Schooner* 58, no. 4 [Winter 1984]: 89).

12. Letter to Elizabeth Shepley Sergeant, May 21, 1912. Quoted in Lee, 88.

13. As Cather later wrote, this story of Dick Wetherill's discovery became the basis for Tom Outland's discovery of Cliff City in the short story "The Blue Mesa," written in 1923 and turned into "Tom Outland's Story" in *The Professor's House*. See Willa Cather, "On *The Professor's House*," in *Willa Cather on Writing* (New York: Knopf, 1962), 31. Hereafter cited parenthetically in the text as *On Writing*.

14. Edith Lewis, *Willa Cather Living: A Personal Record* (New York: Alfred A. Knopf, 1953), 95. Hereafter cited parenthetically in the text as *Living*.

15. Harrell, 27. For Cushing's promotion of Zuni art and life to an Eastern metropolitan audience, see Curtis Hinsley, "Zunis and Brahmins: Cultural Ambivalence in the Gilded Age," in *Romantic Motives: Essays on Anthropological Sensibilities*, ed. George Stocking (Madison: U of Wisconsin P, 1989), 169–207. For Cushing's role both in the development of the anthropological concept of culture and in late-nineteenth-century American literary realism, see Brad Evans, *Before Cultures: The Ethnographic Imagination in American Literature, 1865–1920* (Chicago: U of Chicago P, 2005).

16. Willa Cather to S. S. McClure, 22 April 1912. Cited in O'Brien, 404.

17. Cather met Austin in New York's literary circuit around 1910, and the two shared an admiring, if competitive, relationship until a falling out in the late 1920s. See Janis Stout, *Through the Window, Out the Door: Women's Narratives of Departure, From Austin and Cather to Tyler, Morrison, and Didion* (Tuscaloosa: U of Alabama P, 1998).

18. Christopher Schedler, "Writing Culture: Willa Cather's Southwest," in *Willa Cather and the American Southwest*, ed. John N. Swift and Joseph R. Urgo (Lincoln: U of Nebraska Press, 2002), 110–23. Schedler similarly argues that Cather's conception of culture shifts from an evolutionary model to a relative model from *The Song of the Lark* to *The Professor's House*. My argument differs from Schedler's in several key ways. First, Schedler's exclusive focus on evolutionary, progressive models in *Song of the Lark* neglects the strong elements of romantic antimodernism in Cather's cultural theory. Neglecting these interpenetrating traditions of culture "flattens out"

the crucial complexity of debates, and Cather's role in them. Second, I demonstrate how the complexly interrelated forms of imperial "possession" these versions of culture enable—territorial, epistemological, aesthetic—exposes the problematic (and enabling) elements of modernist anthropological theory that are the focus of the postmodern critique. Finally, I emphasize the *formal*, spatial elements of the theory of culture as "whole" articulated in *The Professor's House*, and its role in modernist anthropological theory and literary criticism.

19. Lewis H. Morgan, *Ancient Society* (New York: Henry Holt, 1877), vi–vii; Curtis Hinsley, *Savages and Scientists: The Smithsonian Institution and the Development of American Anthropology, 1846–1910* (Washington, DC: Smithsonian Institution Press, 1981), 133–37.

20. Willa Cather, *My Ántonia* (1918; New York: Vintage Classics, 1994), 272.

21. *The Kingdom of Art: Willa Cather's First Principles and Critical Statements 1893–1902*, ed. Bernice Slote (Lincoln: U of Nebraska P, 1966), 342. For antimodernist fascination with the "primitive" throughout fin de siècle American culture, see T. J. Jackson Lears, *No Place of Grace: Antimodernism and the Transformation of American Culture, 1880–1920* (New York: Pantheon Books, 1981).

22. Willa Cather, "Mesa Verde Wonderland Is Easy to Reach," *Denver Times*, 31 January 1916, 7. Hereafter cited parenthetically in the text as "Wonderland."

23. Matthew Arnold, *Culture and Anarchy* (New Haven, CT: Yale UP, 1994), 5. Hereafter cited parenthetically in the text as *Anarchy*.

24. This same ambivalence toward Indian achievements also marks Cather's 1916 account of Mesa Verde. While the "harmony" of Indian architecture is contrasted favorably to American "ugliness," Cather suggests that this harmony may come at a price too high to pay. Mesa Verde architecture is a "successful evasion of ugliness," but "perhaps an indolent evasion"; later she remarks that "the mesa people may have been somewhat enslaved by their strongholds, and their temper may have been softened by their comparative comfort and their attention to order and detail" ("Wonderland," 7). "They seem not to have struggled to overcome their environment" and "went on gravely and reverently repeating the past, rather than battling for anything new." In the end she suggests that "the most plausible theory as to their extinction is that the dwellers on the Mesa Verde were routed and driven out by their vulgar, pushing neighbors of the plains" who—she adds with grudging respect—"were less comfortable, less satisfied, and consequently more energetic" (7).

25. The identification of the pioneer with the artist is made even more explicitly in novels like *O Pioneers!*, where Cather argues that a "pioneer should have imagination, should be able to enjoy the idea of things more than the things themselves" (Willa Cather, *O Pioneers!* [New York: Vintage, 1992], 28).

26. Willa Cather, *The Professor's House* (1925; New York: Vintage, 1990), 179. Hereafter cited parenthetically in the text as *Professor's*.

27. Cather was said to have considered Bourne "the best reviewer in the business" (James Woodress, *Willa Cather: A Literary Life* [Lincoln: U of Nebraska P, 1987], 301). Sapir was also aware of and engaged with Bourne's work, as evidenced by his eulogy upon Bourne's sudden death in the influenza epidemic of 1918 ("Randolph Bourne," *Dial* [11 January 1919], 45). Sapir clearly had met Bourne: he states that "long before [he] had met Randolph Bourne," he knew from Bourne's writing that "he was one of those extraordinarily fine-grained men that one meets but rarely in a lifetime."

Interestingly, Sapir, like Cather, particularly appreciated Bourne's literary acumen: Sapir lauds "his exquisite sensibility to the esthetic in literature, to the nuances of thought and feeling and expression. One knew instinctively that if anything passed by him with his approval or sympathy, it was indeed something genuine" (Richard Handler, "Anti-Romantic Romanticism: Edward Sapir and the Critique of American Individualism," *Anthropological Quarterly* 62 [October 1988]: 4).

28. Janis Stout, introduction to *Willa Cather and Material Culture: Real-World Writing, Writing the Real World*, ed. Janis Stout (Tuscaloosa: U of AL P, 2005), 5 n. 4.

29. See Woodress, 264–65. Harrell argues that Cather's depiction of the Cliff City follows in important ways the park brochure she read while there, which was written in part by Fewkes; Fewkes published several other works on Mesa Verde and on Indian pottery design that Cather may have read. Fewkes's methodological relationship to Boas and Sapir, however, is complex. On the one hand, as Stocking notes, Fewkes supported Boas's "culture history" (as opposed to biology) as a legitimate science in an institutional battle over the role of anthropology within the National Research Council in 1919 (George Stocking, "The Scientific Reaction against Cultural Anthropology," *Race, Culture and Evolution*, 290). On the other hand, critics such as Curtis Hinsley have argued that Fewkes represented "the trait list school" in American anthropology, believing that only through "persistent observation" and the amassing of discrete units of data could one "assemble a coherent picture of the external forms of other cultures," while any "deeper understanding" from within through imagination or intuition is impossible ("Cushing and Fewkes in the American Southwest," in *Observers Observed: Essays on Ethnographic Fieldwork*, ed. George Stocking [Madison: U of Wisconsin P, 1983), 67–68]. This tension—of the relationship of collection to selection, of part to whole, of realism to composition—occupies, I argue later, the work of both Sapir and Cather.

30. See Guy Reynolds, "Louise Pound and Willa Cather: An Intellectual Network," *Willa Cather Pioneer Memorial Newsletter* 39, no. 4 (1996): 69–72.

31. Willa Cather, "The Novel Démeublé," (1922), in *Willa Cather on Writing*, 37. Hereafter cited parenthetically in the text as *On Writing*.

32. James Clifford, "On Ethnographic Allegory," in *Writing Culture: The Poetics and Politics of Ethnography*, ed. James Clifford and George Marcus (Berkeley: U of California P, 1986), 112–13.

33. Cather more explicitly emphasized the effort required to achieve the simplicity of nature in "On the Art of Fiction": "Millet had done hundreds of sketches of peasants sowing grain, some of them very complicated and interesting, but when he came to paint the spirit of them all into one picture, 'The Sower,' the composition is so simple that it seems inevitable. All the discarded sketches that went before made the picture what it finally became, and the process was all the time one of simplifying, of sacrificing many conceptions good in themselves for one that was better and more universal" (in *On Writing*, 102). This last note of universalism also appears in Cather's essay on Jewett, where, after praising Jewett for capturing "life itself"—the particularity of New England life and language—she concludes that the "Pointed Firs" will be a "message to the future, a message in a universal language . . . the one message that even the scythe of Time spares." This movement from the particularism and relativism of regional culture to the universal raises an important tension in theories of regional culture

that I pursue later in chapters 3 and 4, with regard to Lewis Mumford, Allen Tate, and John Crowe Ransom.

34. See Walter Benn Michaels, *Our America* (Durham, NC: Duke UP, 1995). Michaels brilliantly analyzes Cather's construction, through Tom's relation to the Cliff Dwellers, of an "American" cultural identity that is both something with which one is born, but which one still must be achieved. My argument here is deeply indebted to Michaels's work. While Michaels is interested in the idea of culture as "pure," where the purity or authenticity of one's culture is guaranteed by the purity of one's racial genealogy, I am interested here in culture as "whole," as an aesthetic object, and the implications of this model for both literary criticism and for theories of artistic, national, and regional identity.

35. The first was E. K. Brown and Leon Edel, *Willa Cather: A Critical Biography* (New York: Knopf, 1953).

36. Cleanth Brooks, *The Well-Wrought Urn: Studies in the Structure of Poetry* (1942; New York: Harcourt, 1975), 195. The path that leads from Cather and Sapir in the 1920s, to Brooks in the 1940s, leads through the New Criticism of Allen Tate, John Crowe Ransom, and Robert Penn Warren (with whom Brooks edited the *Sewanee Review* and wrote such canonical New Critical texts as *Understanding Poetry* in 1938).

37. Ibid, 166.

38. Joseph Frank, "Spatial Form in Modern Literature," in *The Idea of Spatial Form* (1945; New Brunswick: Rutgers UP, 1991). Susan Hegeman has also argued that a "spatial" conception of culture connects American anthropology and modernism in the 1920s, but centers her argument around the shift from viewing the past as distant in developmental time, to viewing it as contemporaneous in time but separated in space from the metropole, and therefore accessible and appropriable to the modern(ist) anthropologist/artist (*Patterns for America* [Princeton, NJ: Princeton UP, 1999). She explicitly distinguishes her theory from Joseph Frank's formal definition of the "spatiality of modernism" (Hegeman, 224 n. 15). My argument, in contrast, seeks to make precisely this connection between the modernist culture concept and the modernist reading of texts as spatial compositions.

39. Frank, 57.

40. Ibid, 58.

41. Ibid, 15.

3 / Cultures, Canons, and Cetology

1. See especially Kermit Vanderbilt, *American Literature and the Academy: The Roots, Growth, and Maturity of a Profession* (Philadelphia: U of Pennsylvania P, 1986); David Shumway, *Creating American Civilization: A Genealogy of American Literature as an Academic Discipline* (Minneapolis: U of Minnesota P); and most recently, Elizabeth Renker, *The Origins of American Literature Studies: An Institutional History* (New York: Cambridge UP, 2007).

2. While the disciplinary history of American Studies is the subject of heated disagreement, a number of canonical histories have begun with V. L. Parrington's *Main Currents of American Thought: An Interpretation of American Literature from the Beginnings to 1920* (New York: Harcourt Brace, 1927). See, for example, Gene Wise, "Paradigm Dramas in American Studies: A Cultural and Institutional History of the Movement," *American Quarterly* 31 (1979): 293–337. For a critical reading of Wise's

narrative, and its use of history to position the field's "futures," see Donald Pease and Robyn Wiegman, "Futures," in *The Futures of American Studies*, ed. Pease and Wiegman (Durham, NC: Duke UP, 2002), 1–44.

3. Carl Van Doren, "Contemporaries of Cooper," in vol. 1 of *Cambridge History of American Literature*, ed. William Peterfield Trent, John Erskine, Stuart P. Sherman, and Carl Van Doren (New York, G. P. Putnam's Sons, 1917), 322–23.

4. Lionel Trilling, "Reality in America," in *The Liberal Imagination* (New York: Viking Press, 1950), 11.

5. Michael Zimmerman, "Herman Melville in the 1920s: A Study of the Origins of the Melville Revival, with an Annotated Bibliography," PhD diss., Columbia University, 1963, 111.

6. Paul Lauter, "Melville Climbs the Canon," *American Literature* 66 (1994): 6. See also William Spanos, *The Errant Art of Moby-Dick: The Canon, the Cold War, and the Struggle for American Studies* (Durham NC: Duke UP, 1995).

7. Clare Spark, *Hunting Captain Ahab: Psychological Warfare and the Melville Revival* (Kent, OH: Kent State UP, 2001).

8. As she puts it, "Melville has remained canonical through the whole period of canon-busting" (Myra Jehlen, introduction to *Herman Melville: A Collection of Critical Essays*, ed. Jehlen [Englewood Cliffs, NJ: Prentice Hall, 1994], 2–3).

9. The biographies are Hershel Parker's *Herman Melville: A Biography*, vol. 1, 1891–51 (Baltimore, MD: Johns Hopkins UP, 1996), and vol. 2, 1851–91 (Baltimore, MD: Johns Hopkins UP, 2002); Laurie Robertson-Lorant, *Melville: A Biography* (Boston: U of Massachusetts P, 1997); Elizabeth Hardwick, *Herman Melville* (New York: Penguin, 2000); and Andrew Delbanco, *Melville: His Work and World* (New York: Random House, 2006). The best sellers related to Melville are Nathaniel Philbrick's *In the Heart of the Sea: The Tragedy of the Whale Ship Essex* (New York: Viking, 2000) and Tim Severin's *In Search of Moby-Dick: The Quest for the White Whale* (New York: Da Capro Press, 2001). The musicals are Rinde Eckert's "And God Created Great Whales"; Laurie Anderson's multimedia production of "Moby-Dick: Songs and Stories from *Moby-Dick*" (performed in 1999–2000); Julian Rad and Hilary Adam's play *Moby-Dick* (first performed in 2003, and nominated for three Drama Desk awards in 2004); and Peter Westergaard's opera *Moby Dick: Scenes from an Imaginary Opera* (first performed in 2004). The latest dramatic adaptation I am aware of is Morris Panych's *Moby-Dick*, playing at the Stratford Shakespeare Festival in 2008. The graphic novels are Will Eisner, *Moby-Dick* (New York: Nantier Beall Minoustchine Publishing, 2001), and Marvel Comic's *Marvel Illustrated: Moby Dick* (New York: Marvel Books, 2009). When one pays even a little attention, Melville and in particular *Moby-Dick* pop up everywhere in popular culture. Several commentators also noted the uptick in Melville references after the 9/11 attacks and the beginning of the Iraq War, with—depending on the commentator—George Bush, Osama bin Laden, and Saddam Hussein playing the roles of Captain Ahab and the whale.

10. Van Wyck Brooks, "On Creating a Usable Past," *Dial* 64 (11 April 1918): 337.

11. Raymond Weaver, *Herman Melville: Mariner and Mystic* (New York: George H. Doran, 1921), 18. Hereafter cited parenthetically in the text as "*Mariner*."

12. Raymond Weaver, "Centennial of Herman Melville," *Nation* 109 (2 August 1919): 145–46. Frank Jewett Mather, "Herman Melville," *Review* 1 (9, 16 August 1919): 276–78, 298–301. Reprinted in *Moby-Dick as Doubloon, The Recognition of Herman Melville:*

Selected Criticism Since 1846, ed. Hershel Parker (Ann Arbor: U of Michigan P, 1967), 155–70.

13. This point was made as early as Zimmerman, "Herman Melville in the 1920's," 28, and more recently in Lauter, "Melville Climbs the Canon," 7–8.

14. Van Wyck Brooks, "A Reviewer's Notebook," *Freeman* 4 (26 October 1921): 166. Melville was often included in documentary articles about the South Seas, such as John Church's "A Vanishing People of the South Seas," *National Geographic* 36, no.4 (October 1919): 275–306, and even more frequently in articles giving an overview of South Seas literature, like H. T. Craven's "Tahiti from Melville to Maugham," *Bookman* 50 (November 1919): 262–67.

15. Robert Morss Lovett, "The South Sea Style," New York *Asia* 21 (April 1921): 316–20, 366–68, cited in *Checklist of Melville Reviews*, ed. Kevin J. Hayes and Hershel Parker (Evanston, IL: Northwestern UP, 1991), 276. One result of the Melville revival was to establish *Moby-Dick* as Melville's true masterpiece by the end of the decade. As Charles Anderson shows, between 1846 and 1922, 37 editions of *Typee* had been published (19 American and 18 British), and only 18 editions of *Moby-Dick* (11 American and 7 British); between 1922 and 1938, these relative numbers reversed, with a stunning 54 editions of *Moby-Dick* (34 American and 20 British) and 22 of *Typee* (15 American and 7 British). See Charles R. Anderson, *Melville in the South Seas* (New York: Columbia UP, 1939), 439. Part of my claim here revolves around this shift from *Typee* to *Moby-Dick*, as many of the attributes ascribed to Melville himself, and embodied in his "autobiographical" and "ethnological" *Typee*, are carried over into interpretations of *Moby-Dick* by the end of the decade. In *Moby-Dick*, these attributes—the fusion of "realism" and "romance," material fact and metaphysical speculation—become not just features of Melville's life, but poetic features of the text.

16. Mather, "Herman Melville," 158; Anderson, *Melville in the South Seas*, 5.

17. In what would become a tradition of reading Melville's novels autobiographically, Weaver does not give either *Typee* or *Moby-Dick* a separate chapter of analysis, but rather treats each novel as a source for the biography. He thus presents his discussion of *Moby-Dick* first, folded into an account of Melville's whaling experiences; he then discusses *Typee*, but as an account of Melville's time on Nukahiva. It is significant for my argument that by 1929 Mumford breaks with this precedent, giving a relatively brief account of Melville's experiences both aboard the whaling vessels and in the Typee valley, and devotes an entire chapter to an analysis of *Moby-Dick* itself. In this way he takes up many of the elements that Weaver attributes to Melville's life and makes them qualities of the text itself, making *Moby-Dick* (along with Melville) not only a masterpiece, but the embodiment of culture.

18. Since Weaver seems to have lifted several phrases straight out of Jewett's centenary essay on Melville, it is worth quoting in full here. Like Weaver, Mather emphasizes Melville's "sympathy," noting that "there is no condescension in the observer's attitude. Melville was one of the earliest literary travelers to see in barbarians anything but queer folk. He intuitively understood them, caught their point of view, respected and often admired it. Thus *Typee* in a peculiar sense is written from the inside" (Mather, "Herman Melville," 158).

19. James G. Frazer, *The Belief in Immortality and the Worship of the Dead*, vol. 2, *The Belief among the Polynesians* (London: MacMillan, 1922), 328–74. Frazer cites Melville as "a runaway American sailor [who] spent more than four months as a captive

in the tribe, and published an agreeable narrative of his captivity; but never having mastered the language, he was not able to give much exact information concerning the custom and beliefs of the natives" (330). Nonetheless, Frazer frequently cites Melville—along with missionaries, colonial officials and explorers—for a variety of details of everyday life: clothing, fire making, architecture, polyandry, tattooing, and burial customs and beliefs.

20. Weaver's contrasting of Melville's account of the South Seas with the accounts of missionaries and explorers was turned on its head by the end of the 1930s, as critics like Anderson showed that Melville relied heavily on precisely those missionary and explorer accounts for material in *Typee*, and his apparent four-month stay turned out to be only one month. Anderson groups Melville with precisely those travelers and "armchair" anthropologists from whom Weaver wants to distance him, and turns instead to the work of "competent ethnologists, anthropologists, and archeologists" who worked on the island from September 21, 1920, to June 21, 1921—presumably conducting fieldwork much like Malinowski did, as I detail later.

21. Bronislaw Malinowski, *Argonauts of the Western Pacific: An Account of Native Enterprise and Adventure in the Archipelagoes of Melanesian New Guinea* (1922; Prospect Heights, IL: Waveland Press, 1984). Hereafter cited parenthetically in the text as "*Argonauts*."

22. See especially George Stocking, "The Ethnographer's Magic: Fieldwork in British Anthropology from Tylor to Malinowski," in *Observers Observed: Essays on Ethnographic Fieldwork*, ed. George Stocking (Madison: U of Wisconsin P, 1983), 70–120; and James Clifford, "On Ethnographic Authority" and "On Ethnographic Self-Fashioning," in *The Predicament of Culture: Twentieth-Century Ethnography, Literature, and Art* (Cambridge, MA: Harvard UP, 1988), 21–54, 92–114.

23. See Marc Manganaro, *Myth, Rhetoric, and the Voice of Authority: A Critique of Frazer, Eliot, Frye and Campbell* (New Haven, CT: Yale UP, 1992), and *Culture, 1922: The Emergence of a Concept* (Princeton, NJ: Princeton UP, 2002), esp. chaps. 1–3.

24. Michael North, *Reading 1922: A Return to the Scene of the Modern* (New York: Oxford UP, 1999), 6.

25. Stocking, "Ethnographer's Magic," 19–20.

26. See Julia Liss, "Patterns of Strangeness: Franz Boas, Modernism, and the Origins of Anthropology," in *Prehistories of the Future: The Primitivist Project and the Culture of Modernism*, ed. Elazar Barkan and Ronald Bush (Stanford, CA: Stanford UP, 1995), 114–30.

27. Clifford, "On Ethnographic Authority," 28.

28. Willa Cather, *The Song of the Lark* (New York: Houghton, Mifflin, 1915), 303.

29. Van Wyck Brooks, *America's Coming-of-Age* (New York: B. W. Heubsch, 1915), 4. Hereafter cited parenthetically in the text as *Coming-of-Age*.

30. Alfred North Whitehead, *Science and the Modern World* (New York: Macmillan), 291, emphasis in original.

31. Van Wyck Brooks, "Our Awakeners," in *Van Wyck Brooks: The Early Years*, ed. Claire Sprague (New York: Harper and Row, 1968), 206; Edward Sapir, "Culture Genuine and Spurious," *The Selected Writings of Edward Sapir in Language, Culture and Personality*, ed. David Mandelbaum (Berkeley: U of California P, 1951), 316. All further references will be abbreviated "Genuine" and given in the text.

32. Again, I want to emphasize that Malinowski's and Weaver's desire for a new

mode of knowledge is part of a broader dissatisfaction with what many intellectuals argued was the incomplete or fragmentary knowledge provided by abstract and materialist science. In *Science and the Modern World*, Whitehead argues that there is "a general danger inherent in modern science," whose methods of analysis "fixes attention on a definite group of abstractions [and] neglects everything else." Citing the English Romantic poets like Wordsworth and Shelley as precedents for opposing the "abstract analysis of science" with "full concrete experience" (118), he argues for a new kind of scientific training in which, in addition to traditional scientific analysis,

> the centre of gravity . . . should lie in intuition without an analytical divorce from the total environment. Its object is immediate apprehension with the minimum of eviscerating analysis. The type of generality, which above all is wanted, is the appreciation of variety of value. I mean an aesthetic growth. There is something between the gross specialized values of the mere practical man, and the thin specialized values of the mere scholar. Both types have missed something; and if you add together the two sets of values, you do not obtain the missing elements. What it wanted is an appreciation of the infinite variety of vivid values achieved by an organism in its proper environment. (286)

This desire for "something between" the "mere practical man" and the "mere scholar," I am arguing, lies behind both Weaver's account of Melville and Malinowski's methodological approach to culture.

33. Clifford, "On Ethnographic Authority," 37.

34. Letter to B. Seligman, 21 June 1918, quoted in *Man and Culture: An Evaluation of the Work of Bronislaw Malinowski*, ed. Raymond Firth (London: Routledge, 1964), 6.

35. Bronislaw Malinowski, *A Diary in the Strict Sense of the Term* (London: Routledge, 1967), 140 [1 December 1917], 236 [26 March 1918]), quoted in Stocking, "Ethnographer's Magic," 101. Frazer, in his preface to *Argonauts*, likewise compares Malinowski's method to the creation of literary characters. The "man of science," he suggests, "is too apt to examine man in the abstract"; in contrast, Malinowski's method, in taking "full account of the complexity of human nature," is more like "the presentation of human nature in the greater artists, such as Cervantes and Shakespeare," whose "characters are solid, being drawn not from one side only but from many"(*Argonauts*, ix).

36. Stocking, "Ethnographer's Magic," 106–8.

37. Clifford, "On Ethnographic Authority," 29.

38. Stocking, "Ethnographer's Magic," 109.

39. Bronislaw Malinowski, "Myth in Primitive Psychology," in *Magic, Science and Religion and Other Essays* (New York: Free Press, 1948), 103.

40. Between 1919 and 1921, there were four new editions of *Typee* (one English, three American), three new editions of *Oomo* (one English, two American), one of *White Jacket* (1919), and four of *Moby-Dick* (two English, two American). See Zimmerman, "Herman Melville in the 1920s," 190–97.

41. Van Wyck Brooks, "A Reviewer's Notebook," *Freeman* 4 (26 October 1921): 166. Hereafter cited parenthetically in the text as "'Notebook' (date)."

42. This was the thesis of Brooks's *The Ordeal of Mark Twain* (New York: E. P. Dutton, 1920).

43. Van Wyck Brooks, *The Wine of the Puritans* (London: Sisley's, 1908), 17.

44. Van Wyck Brooks, "Amor Fati," in *Emerson and Others* (New York: E. P. Dutton, 1927), 161.

45. For the relationship among Mumford, Brooks, Bourne, and other members of the *Seven Arts* group, see Casey Nelson Blake, *Beloved Community: The Cultural Criticism of Randolph Bourne, Van Wyck Brooks, Waldo Frank and Lewis Mumford* (Chapel Hill: U of North Carolina P, 1990).

46. George Santayana hyperbolically called *The Golden Day* "the best book about America, if not the best American book [he had] ever read" (quoted in Donald Miller, *Lewis Mumford: A Life* [New York: Weidenfeld and Nicolson, 1987], 253), while Brooks called it "the culmination of the whole critical movement in this country during the past ten years" ("Book Reviews," *New England Quarterly* 1 [1928]: 84). While my focus here is Mumford, Melville, and the culture concept, it is worth noting Mumford's key role in so many disciplines taking shape in the late 1920s. While Mumford is best remembered today for his architectural criticism, his work in *The Golden Day* and *Herman Melville*, in terms of both subject matter and methodology, makes him a key figure in the history of Americanist criticism, American Studies, and cultural studies—a role that has been largely overlooked. Leo Marx has written of Mumford's "uniqueness," noting his "seminal work" in American architectural history and criticism (*Sticks and Stones; A Study of American Architecture and Civilization* [New York: Boni and Liveright, 1924] and *The Brown Decades: A Study of the Arts in America, 1865–1895* [New York: Harcourt, Brace, 1931]), in urban studies and the history of cities (*The Culture of Cities* [New York: Harcourt, Brace, 1938] and *The City in History: Its Origins, Its Transformations, Its Prospects* [New York: Harcourt Brace, 1961]), in American literary and cultural history (*The Golden Day* [1926] and *Herman Melville* [1929]), and in the history and criticism of technology (*Technics and Civilization* [New York: Harcourt, Brace, 1934] and *The Myth of the Machine* [New York: Harcourt, Brace, 1967, 1970]). See "Lewis Mumford: Prophet of Organicism," in *Lewis Mumford: Public Intellectual*, ed. Thomas P. Hughes and Agatha C. Hughes (New York: Oxford UP, 1990), 164. In precisely this interdisciplinarity, and in his method of "reading" the various elements of a culture—literature, architecture, philosophy, technology, economics—as symbolic systems of meaning, Mumford anticipates many of the methods of today's "cultural studies" and "cultural history."

47. Lewis Mumford, *Herman Melville* (New York: Harcourt, Brace, 1929), 365–66. Hereafter cited parenthetically in the text as *Melville*.

48. Lewis Mumford, *The Golden Day: A Study in American Culture and Experience* (New York: Boni and Liveright, 1926), 277. Hereafter cited parenthetically in the text as *Golden*.

49. At this point in the discussion in both *Herman Melville* and *The Golden Day*, Mumford cites Whitehead's *Science and the Modern World*, along with Victor Branford's *Science and Sanctity*, as "landmarks toward this new exploration [of the limits of the current scientific philosophy] . . . for they both suggest the ground-work of a philosophy which shall be oriented as completely toward Life as the dominant thought since Descartes has been directed towards the Machine" (*Golden*, 282). This underscores the way in which the debates over culture as a meaningful whole arises in the context of a wider interdisciplinary problematic.

50. Edward Sapir, *Language: An Introduction to the Study of Speech* (New York: Harcourt Brace, 1921), v.

51. Lewis Mumford, "Ex Libris," *Freeman* (22 February 1922): 575.

52. For an account of Spingarn and Mumford's relationship, see *Sketches from Life: The Autobiography of Lewis Mumford, the Early Years* (New York: Dial Press, 1982), esp. chap. 34; and Miller, *Lewis Mumford*, esp. chap. 13.

53. Joel Spingarn, "The New Criticism," in *Criticism in America: Its Function and Status*, ed. Irving Babbitt et al. (New York: Harcourt, 1924), 29, 24, 32.

54. Sapir, *Language*, 222.

55. Bronislaw Malinowski, "The Problem of Meaning in Primitive Languages," in *The Meaning of Meaning: A Study of the Influence of Language upon Thought and of the Science of Symbolism*, ed. I. A. Richards and C. K. Ogden (1923; London: Kegan Paul, Trench, Trubner, 1945), 300, 305.

56. Spingarn, 40.

57. Ibid., 42.

58. John Crowe Ransom, preface to *The World's Body* (1938; Port Washington, NY: Kennikat Press, 1964), x.

59. For the influence of Mumford's work on regional planning and the contemporary environmental movement, see Kirkpatrick Sale, *Dwellers in the Land: The Bioregional Vision* (Athens: U of Georgia P, 2000); and Robert Gottleib, *Forcing the Spring: The Transformation of the American Environmental Movement* (Washington, DC: Island Press, 1993). For Mumford's influence on the "new urbanism," see Emily Talen, "Beyond the Front Porch: Regionalist Ideals in the New Urbanist Movement," *Journal of Planning History* 7, no. 1 (2008): 20–47. For a history of the RPAA and Mumford's specific theoretical contributions, see Marc Lucarelli, *Lewis Mumford and the Ecological Region: The Politics of Planning* (New York: Guilford Press, 1995); and Carl Sussman, ed., *Planning the Fourth Migration: The Neglected Vision of the Regional Planning Association of America* (Cambridge, MA: MIT Press, 1976).

60. Peter Hall has called the RPAA *Survey Graphic* issue one of the most important documents in the history of city planning (*Cities of Tomorrow: An Intellectual History of Urban Planning and Design in the Twentieth Century*, 3rd ed. [Oxford, UK: Basil Blackwell, 2002]). The RPAA regional number appeared one month before a special issue that would become even more famous: the "Harlem number" of the *Survey Graphic*, which would become the *New Negro*. The intersection of Mumford's regionalism and the emergence of the New Negro movement on the pages of *Survey Graphic* points to another tantalizing node in this "matrix of modernism": Mumford's list of regional movements (Ireland, Czechoslovakia, Palestine), for example, matches the list of "nascent centers of folk-expression and self determination" to which Locke adds Harlem (Alain Locke, "Harlem," *Survey Graphic* 7 [May 1925]: 629).

61. Lewis Mumford, "Regionalism and Irregionalism," *Sociological Review* 29 (1927): 279, emphasis added.

62. Lewis Mumford, "The Theory and Practice of Regionalism," *Sociological Review* 20 (1928): 135.

63. Lewis Mumford, "The Status of the State," *Dial* 67 (29 July 1919): 59; "Wardom and the State," *Dial* 67 (4 October 1919): 303.

64. Lewis Mumford, "A Search for a True Community" (1922), in *The Menorah Treasury: Harvest of Half a Century*, ed. Leo W. Schwarz (Philadelphia: Jewish Publication Society of America, 1964), 860.

65. Mumford, "Status of the State," 60.

66. Mumford, "True Community," 865, 860.

67. Lewis Mumford, "The Regional Note," *Freeman* 7 (10 October 1923): 107.

68. Mumford, "True Community," 865.

69. Mumford, "Theory and Practice of Regionalism," 137.

70. In the centrality of this organizing idea of culture and form, and particularly in its explicit opposition to ideas of the nation-state, Mumford's and Sapir's regionalism differs from late-nineteenth-century versions of regionalism popularized by authors like Sarah Orne Jewett and others that, as critics like Amy Kaplan and Richard Brodhead have argued, served to narrate the emergence of the United States as a modern nation. See Kaplan, "Nation, Region, and Empire," in *The Columbia History of the American Novel*, ed. Emory Elliot, Cathy M. Davidson, Patrick O'Donnell, Valerie Smith, and Christopher P. Wilson (New York: Columbia UP, 1991), 240–66; and Richard Brodhead, *The Culture of Letters: Scenes of Reading and Writing in Nineteenth Century America* (Chicago: U of Chicago P, 1993). At the same time, these elements are precisely what link Mumford's and Sapir's regionalism to the Southern Agrarian regionalism of soon-to-be New Critics such as Ransom and Tate.

71. Mumford, "Regional Note," 107.

72. Lewis Mumford, "The American Rhythm," *New Republic* 35 (30 May 1923): 23.

73. As critics have pointed out, Americanists in the mid-twentieth century, starting with F. O. Matthiessen in 1941, tended to read the novel as embodying the conflict between democratic freedom and totalitarian authority, with Ishmael as the "authentic American voice of freedom" in contrast to Ahab and his "dictatorial demands for total dominance" (John Michael, *Identity and the Failure of America* [Minneapolis: U of Minnesota P, 2008], 73). For these critics, Melville's novel articulated particularly *national* values and conflicts: as Mattheissen observes, "even Melville can hardly have been fully aware of how symbolical an *American* hero he had fashioned in Ahab" (*American Renaissance*, 458, emphasis added). This emphasis on Ahab and Ishmael as part of a particularly national allegory is reflected in the titles of major critical works of the period: R. W. B. Lewis's *American Adam*, Richard Chase's *The American Novel*, and so on. More recently, even as critics have countered these celebratory versions of American exceptionalism, the national model has persisted, as New Americanists find in Ahab and Ishmael particularly American versions of imperial ideology, masculinity, and so on. See, for example, Donald Pease, "*Moby-Dick* and the Cold War," in *The American Renaissance Reconsidered*, ed. Walter Benn Michaels and Donald Pease (Baltimore: Johns Hopkins UP, 1989), 113–55; Wai Chee Dimock, *Empire for Liberty: Melville and the Poetics of Individualism* (Princeton, NJ: Princeton UP, 1987); Spanos, *Errant Art*; and David Leverenz, *Manhood and the American Renaissance* (Ithaca, NY: Cornell UP, 1989). Michael perceptively observes, "In these readings, 'America' appears personified as a single, univocal subject [as] Ahab emerges as the exemplary antihero of this negative national narrative" (78).

74. Sapir and Mumford gesture to the same touchstones for their examples of genuine culture on the one hand, and literary analogues to the wholeness of *Moby-Dick* on the other: ancient Greece, Renaissance Italy, and Elizabethan England. Sapir suggests the "Athens of the Periclean Age, the Rome of Augustus, the independent city-states of Italy in late medieval times, the London of Elizabethan days" as models of small culturally autonomous groups ("Genuine," 328); Mumford repeatedly compares Melville to Aeschylus, Dante, and Shakespeare.

75. Mumford, "Regional Note," 107.
76. Ibid., 108.
77. Lauter, 5
78. Spanos, 16.
79. Pease and Wiegman, "Futures," 16.
80. Lauter, 13; Spanos, 20.
81. See Shumway, *Creating American Civilization*, esp. chap. 6.
82. Several years later, in fact, Robert Penn Warren suggested, "The best work of Hawthorne or of Mark Twain or of Melville, are something else before they are American. By inspiration, Hawthorne and Melville are . . . of New England; then, almost by political and geographical definition only, or by a mystical hocus-pocus of definition, they are American." *Moby-Dick*, he proposes, is "quite as 'regional' as *The Scarlet Letter*," both embodying New England's "essence" ("Some Recent Novels," *Southern Review* 1 [1936]: 624–29).
83. Walter Benn Michaels, *Our America* (Durham, NC: Duke UP, 1995).
84. Janice Radway, introduction to *American Studies: An Anthology*, ed. Janice A. Radway, Kevin K. Gaines, Barry Shank, and Penny Von Eschen (Malden, MA: Blackwell, 2009), 2–3. For a lively exchange exemplifying the debate over how to narrate the ideological history of American Studies as a discipline, see Leo Marx, "On Recovering the 'Ur' Theory of American Studies"; George Lipsitz's response, "Our America"; and Amy Kaplan's counter-response, "A Call for a Truce"—all in *American Literary History* 17, no. 1 (2005): 118–34, 135–40, and 141–47, respectively.
85. John Guillory, *Cultural Capital: The Problem of Literary Canon Formation* (Chicago: U of Chicago P, 1993), 34, emphasis added.
86. Wai Chee Dimock, "Aesthetics and the Limits of the Nation: Kant, Pound, and the Saturday Review," *American Literature* 76 (2004): 526. Dimock pursues this project to bypass the nation in her more recent *Through Other Continents: American Literature across Deep Time* (Princeton, NJ: Princeton UP, 2006). See also Christopher Castiglia and Russ Castronovo, "A 'Hive of Subtlety': Aesthetics and the End(s) of Cultural Studies," *American Literature* 76 (2004): 425–27; and Castronovo, *Beautiful Democracy: Aesthetics and Anarchy in a Global Era* (Chicago: U of Chicago P, 2007).
87. Raymond Williams, *Culture and Society, 1780–1950* (New York: Columbia University Press, 1958), 295.

4 / Recovering the Whole

1. Allen Tate, "Literature as Knowledge," in *Essays of Four Decades* (Chicago: Swallow Press, 1968), 76. Hereafter cited parenthetically in the text as "Knowledge."
2. Terry Eagleton, *Literary Theory: An Introduction* (Oxford, UK: Blackwell, 1983), 48.
3. Mark Jancovich, *The Cultural Politics of the New Criticism* (Oxford, UK: Cambridge UP, 1993); see also Mark Malvasi, *The Unregenerate South: The Agrarian Though of John Crowe Ransom, Allen Tate and Donald Davidson* (Baton Rouge: Louisiana State UP, 1997).
4. Edward D. Pickering, "The Roots of New Criticism," *Southern Literary Journal* 41, no. 1 (Fall 2008): 93–108.
5. John Crowe Ransom, "The Idea of a Literary Anthropologist, and What He Might Say of the Paradise Lost of Milton," in *Selected Essays of John Crowe Ransom*,

ed. Thomas Daniel Young and John Hindle (Baton Rouge: Louisiana State UP, 1984), 323. Hereafter cited parenthetically in the text as "Literary Anthropologist."

6. Michael North, *Reading 1922: A Return to the Scene of the Modern* (New York: Oxford UP, 1999), 6.

7. Warren Susman, "Culture and Civilization: The Nineteen-Twenties," in *Culture as History: The Transformation of American Society in the Twentieth Century* (New York: Pantheon Books, 1984); James Clifford, "On Ethnographic Authority," in *The Predicament of Culture: Twentieth-Century Ethnography, Literature, and Art* (Cambridge, MA: Harvard UP, 1988).

8. Richards serves as a case study, in several of Tate's and Ransom's essays, of the complex but ultimately mistaken scientist who tries to explain poetry in terms of physiology and value, including Ransom's "A Psychologist Looks at Poetry" in *The World's Body* (Port Washington, NY: Kennikat Press, 1964), and "I. A. Richards" in *The New Criticism* (Westport, CT: Greenwood Press, 1978), and Tate's "Literature as Knowledge." In each of these cases, Tate and Ransom differentiate the early "behaviorist" Richards from the later Richards who writes *Coleridge on Imagination* in 1936, in which he comes to argue, in ways that Tate and Ransom praise, the organic nature of the poem and its status as a kind of knowledge equal to, if different from, science. Hereafter cited parenthetically in the text as *Body* and *New Criticism*.

9. Bronislaw Malinowski, "The Problem of Meaning in Primitive Languages," in I. A. Richards and C. K. Ogden, *The Meaning of Meaning: A Study of the Influence of Language upon Thought and of the Science of Symbolism* (1923; London: Kegan Paul, Trench, Trubner, 1945), 297. Hereafter cited parenthetically in the text as "Meaning."

10. Marc Manganaro, introduction to *Modernist Anthropology: From Fieldwork to Text* (Princeton, NJ: Princeton UP, 1990), 4.

11. John Crowe Ransom, "Flux and Blur in Contemporary Art," *Sewanee Review* 37, no. 3 (July 1929): 360–61, emphasis added.

12. John Crowe Ransom, letter to Allen Tate, 5 September 1926, MS, in Allen Tate Papers, Special Collections, Princeton University, Princeton, NJ.

13. John Crowe Ransom, "Wanted: An Ontological Critic," in *The New Criticism* (Westport, CT: Greenwood Press, 1978), 295. Hereafter cited parenthetically in the text as *New Criticism*.

14. Twelve Southerners, "Introduction: A Statement of Principles," in *I'll Take My Stand: The South and the Agrarian Tradition* (New York: Harper and Row, 1962), xxvi, emphasis added.

15. John Crowe Ransom, "Reconstructed but Unregenerate," in *I'll Take My Stand*, 5. Hereafter cited parenthetically in the text as "Reconstructed."

16. John Crowe Ransom, "The Aesthetics of Regionalism," in *Selected Essays*, 45, 55. Hereafter cited parenthetically in the text as "Aesthetics."

17. Edward Sapir, "Culture Genuine and Spurious," in *The Selected Writings of Edward Sapir in Language, Culture and Personality*, ed. David Mandelbaum (Berkeley: U of California P, 1951), 310. Hereafter cited parenthetically in the text as "Genuine."

18. Arjun Appadurai, "Putting Hierarchy in Its Place," *Cultural Anthropology* 3, no. 1 (1988): 36–47.

19. Allen Tate, "Hart Crane" (1930), in *Poetry Reviews of Allen Tate, 1922–1944*, ed. Ashley Brown and Frances Neel Cheney (Baton Rouge: Louisiana State UP, 1983), 99, 101, 102. Hereafter cited parenthetically in the text as "Hart Crane."

20. Langdon Hammer, *Hart Crane and Allen Tate: Janus-Faced Modernism* (Princeton, NJ: Princeton UP, 1993), 35. Hereafter cited parenthetically in the text as *Janus*.

21. Thus, critics such as Marcus Cunliffe conclude that the poem is "a remarkable achievement[;] . . . however, it is not a unified achievement" (*The Literature of the United States* [Penguin Books, 1954]), whereas R. W. Butterfield concludes that "*The Bridge* is conceptually fractured. . . . We may say that the structure looks magnificent, but that it is not safe" (*The Broken Arc: A Study of Hart Crane* [Edinburgh: Oliver & Boyd, 1969], vi, 214).

22. Crane to Waldo Frank, 19 August 1926, in *O My Land, My Friends: The Selected Letters of Hart Crane*, ed. Langdon Hammer and Brom Weber (New York: Four Walls, Eight Windows, 1997), 272; Crane to Otto Kahn, 19 September 1926, *Selected Letters*, 276.

23. While my focus in this chapter is not on Crane's poem itself, critics have argued that Crane's vision of American "culture" in *The Bridge* also draws on the versions of cultural pluralism that I have been tracing, in which the emphasis on wholeness and difference produces a version of pluralist nativism. See Jared Garner, "'Our Native Clay': Racial and Sexual Identity and the Making of *The Bridge*," *American Quarterly* 44, no. 1 (March 1992): 24–50.

24. Allen Tate, introduction to *Hart Crane's "White Buildings"* (New York: Liveright, 1972), x. Hereafter cited parenthetically in the text as *White Buildings*.

25. Tate to Donald Davidson, 14 May 1926, reprinted in *The Literary Correspondence of Donald Davidson and Allen Tate*, ed. John Tyree Fain and Thomas Daniel Young (Athens: U of Georgia P, 1974), 166.

26. Van Wyck Brooks, "The Culture of Industrialism," *Seven Arts* (April 1917): 655.

27. Allen Tate, "Tension in Poetry," in *Essays of Four Decades*, 63; Tate, "The Profession of Letters in the South," in *Essays*, 523.

28. Allen Tate, "American Poetry since 1920," in *Poetry Reviews*, 79. Hereafter cited parenthetically in the text as "American."

29. T. S. Eliot, "Tradition and the Individual Talent," in *Selected Prose of T. S. Eliot* (New York: Harcourt, Brace, 1976), 5, 4. Hereafter cited parenthetically in the text as "Tradition."

30. T. S. Eliot, "The Function of Criticism," in *Selected Prose of T. S. Eliot* (London: Faber & Faber, 1975), 72, emphasis in original. Hereafter cited parenthetically in the text as "Function."

31. Van Wyck Brooks, "On Creating a Usable Past," *Dial* 64 (11 April 1918), 337, emphasis in original.

32. Willa Cather, *The Song of the Lark* (New York: Houghton, Mifflin, 1915), 306.

33. Marc Manganaro, *Myth, Rhetoric, and the Voice of Authority: A Critique of Frazer, Eliot, Frye and Campbell* (New Haven, CT: Yale UP, 1992), 69–70.

34. Ibid., 69.

35. Twelve Southerners, "Introduction," ix.

36. Allen Tate, "Remarks on Southern Religion," *I'll Take My Stand*, 157. Hereafter cited parenthetically in the text as "Remarks."

37. Allen Tate, *Jefferson Davis: His Rise and Fall; A Biographical Narrative* (New York: Minton, Balch, 1929), 301.

38. *Literary Correspondence*, 230.

39. Ibid., 406.

40. Allen Tate, "The Fallacy of Humanism," in *The Critique of Humanism: A Symposium*, ed. C. Hartley Grattan (New York: Brewer and Warren, 1930), 129–66. Hereafter cited parenthetically in the text as "Fallacy." Lewis Mumford also contributed an essay, entitled "Toward an Organic Humanism," to the symposium.

41. This, in turn, sheds some light on Tate's objection to the title of *I'll Take My Stand* as being a "special plea." What for Tate is powerfully sectional in the Fugitive poets and others like them was that they "steadily refuse to issue any special plea," as did those who were attempting to construct a national identity ("American," 82). A "special plea," then, indicated a false unity that could be forced only through a conscious program, rather than allowing the unity to naturally "take care of itself." Thus, objecting to the title as a "special plea," in Tate's use of the term, implies that the work was not sectional *enough*: it seemed to base the Twelve Southerners' unity on the conscious promotion of a cause, rather than on the unconscious "good fortune of some deeper agreement" through which, according to the "Introduction," "the book was expected to achieve its unity" (ix).

42. Joseph Frank, "Spatial Form in Modern Literature," in *The Idea of Spatial Form* (1945; New Brunswick, NJ: Rutgers UP, 1991), 31–66.

43. James Clifford, "On Ethnographic Allegory," in *Writing Culture: The Poetics and Politics of Ethnography*, ed. James Clifford and George Marcus (Berkeley: U of California P, 1986), 111.

44. Clifford, *Predicament of Culture*, 34.

45. Clifford, "On Ethnographic Authority," 113–15.

46. Lewis Mumford, *Herman Melville* (New York: Harcourt, Brace, 1929), 183. Indeed, according to Mumford, Melville had the "fortune to pronounce a valedictory on many ways of life and scenes that were becoming extinct.... He lived among the South Sea Islanders when they were still pretty much as Captain Cook found them, just before the perversion and decimation by our exotic Western civilization. He recorded life on a man-of-war half a generation before the sail gave place to steam, wood to armour-plate, and grappling-irons to long-range guns. He described life on a sailing packet before steam had increased the speed, the safety, and the pleasant monotony of transatlantic travel: and finally, he recorded the last heroic days of whaling" (184).

47. George E. Marcus and Michael M. J. Fisher, *Anthropology as Cultural Critique: An Experimental Moment in the Human Sciences* (Chicago: U of Chicago P, 1986), 21.

48. Vincent B. Leitch, *American Literary Criticism from the Thirties to the Eighties* (New York: Columbia UP, 1988), 25.

Conclusion

1. Lawrence Grossberg, Cary Nelson, and Paula A. Treichler, eds., introduction to *Cultural Studies* (New York: Routledge, 1992), 4.

2. John Guillory, *Cultural Capital: The Problem of Literary Canon Formation* (Chicago: U of Chicago P, 1993), 34.

3. Edward Sapir, "Culture, Genuine and Spurious," in *The Selected Writings of Edward Sapir in Language, Culture and Personality*, ed. David Mandelbaum (Berkeley: U of California P, 1951), 329.

4. Ira Bashkow, "A NeoBoasian Conception of Cultural Boundaries," *American Anthropologist* 106, no. 3 (2004): 444.

5. William B. Warner and Clifford Siskin, "Stopping Cultural Studies," *Profession* (2008): 94–107.

6. Terry Eagleton, *Literary Theory: An Introduction* (Minneapolis, U of Minnesota P, 1983), 47, 48.

7. Ian Hunter, "Aesthetics and Cultural Studies," *Cultural Studies*, 348.

8. A Möbius strip is defined as a three-dimensional object with only one side and one edge. The easiest way to picture it (or make one) is to take a strip of paper, twist it one-half turn, and connect the ends to form a loop.

9. See Stephen Greenblatt, *Renaissance Self-Fashioning: From More to Shakespeare* (Chicago: U of Chicago P, 1980); Clifford Geertz, "Notes on a Balinese Cockfight" and "Ideology as a Cultural System," in *The Interpretation of Cultures* (New York: Basic Books, 1973), 412–53, 193–233.

10. The connection between postmodern and poststructuralist theories of the text (which are also theories of culture) and the possibilities offered by new technologies of reading and writing were already articulated in George P. Landow, *Hypertext: The Convergence of Contemporary Critical Theory and Technology* (Baltimore: Johns Hopkins UP, 1991).

11. Donald Pease and Robyn Wiegman, "Futures," in *The Futures of American Studies*, ed. Pease and Wiegman (Durham, NC: Duke UP, 2002), 16.

12. Wai Chee Dimock, "World History according to Katrina," *States of Emergency: The Objects of American Studies* (Chapel Hill: U of North Carolina P, 2009), 146.

13. Wai Chee Dimock, "Aesthetics and the Limits of the Nation: Kant, Pound, and the *Saturday Review*," *American Literature* 76 (2004): 526.

14. Dimock, "World History," 154.

15. Some Americanists have likewise recently begun looking to late nineteenth and early-twentieth-century anthropology as a "usable past" for the field. See Michael Elliot, "Cultural Anthropology and the Routes of American Studies, 1851–1942," in *A Concise Companion to American Studies*, ed. John Carlos Rowe (Malden, MA: Blackwell, 2010), 36–58.

16. Bashkow, 445.

17. Ibid., 446.

18. Douglas Reichert Powell, *Critical Regionalism: Connecting Politics and Culture in the American Landscape* (Chapel Hill: U of North Carolina P, 2007), 21.

19. Richard Handler, "Afterword: Mysteries of Culture," *American Anthropologist* 106, no. 3 (September 2004): 493.

20. Winfried Fluck, "Aesthetics and Cultural Studies," in *Aesthetics in a Multicultural Age*, ed. Emory Elliott, Louis Freitas Caton, Jeffrey Rhyne (New York: Oxford UP, 2002), 87, 88, emphasis added.

Index

aesthetic form: of American Studies, 188–89; and cultural studies, 185–86; culture as, 4, 5, 18, 43, 51, 59, 117–18, 181; in literary studies, 186–87; of poetry, 6, 121–22, 160; regionalism and, 21, 59, 89, 115, 156; and whole way of life, 186

aesthetic object: culture as, 48, 54, 74, 150, 182, 190; *Moby-Dick* as, 120, 122, 128; space and, 83; whole cultures as, 54, 128, 137–38, 141, 205n34; work of art as, 38

aesthetic(s): anthropology and, 58; attitude, 193; Crocean, 121–23; of culture, 59, 84, 114, 119, 133, 182; as global and local, 133, 189; knowledge as, 101; in literary studies, 22, 61, 84, 140; in modernist art, 51; and the nation, 4, 133, 189; regionalism and, 157; and Southwest Indian art, 60; Spingarn's theory of, 114, 121–23

agrarianism, Southern: culture, 153–55; politics, 138–39; writers/writings, 21, 150, 153, 176

American culture, 16, 32–33, 89; as an oxymoron, 52, 124; definitions of, 2, 11; as divided, 33–34, 88, 91–92; as fragmented and spurious, 55, 72, 85, 127–28; homogeneity of, 158, 188; immigration and, 11, 28–29, 131; material-ideal fusion of, 111; Melville revival and, 90; and national culture, 56, 127; values of, 129, 130–31, 167

Americanization, 29, 31, 128

American modernism, 8, 25, 97, 133, 201n54; problem of culture in, 4, 23, 53, 181

American Renaissance, 86, 112

American Renaissance (Matthiessen), 4, 86, 112, 131

American Southwest: Cather's trips to, 61–63; Pueblo Indians of, 50–51, 62–63; tourism and exploration, 50–51, 63, 200n50

American Studies, 183, 213n84; aesthetics and, 188–89; critics, 3–4, 190; homogeneity of, 132; Melville studies and, 86–87; nationalist origins of, 6, 133–34, 182, 190; rise of, 130–31

America's Coming of Age (Brooks), 9, 24–25, 119; focal center theory, 38, 109, 116; highbrow/lowbrow dualism, 19, 24, 108, 111; immigration in, 29; living culture, 37–39; notion of divided America, 19, 33–34, 42; organic culture in, 35, 53; "usable past" concept, 88. *See also* Brooks, Van Wyck

Ancient Society (Morgan), 65

Anderson, Charles, 93, 207n15, 208n20

anthropology: and aesthetic objects, 48–49, 74; comparative form of, 146; cultural pluralism and, 16–17, 156; and culture rescue and decline, 178–79; evolutionary approaches, 12–13

anthropology (continued):
literary circles and, 25–26; literary modernism and, 13, 53, 176, 179; modernist, 23, 51, 81–82, 143–44, 175–76, 179; New Criticism and, 20, 22, 179, 187; participant-observer methodology, 14–15, 56, 97–98; postmodern, 3, 84, 184–85; of Pueblo Southwest, 49–50; selection process in, 74–75. *See also* Boas, Franz; ethnology; literary anthropologist; Malinowski, Bronislaw; Sapir, Edward
Argonauts of the Western Pacific (Malinowski), 88, 90, 96–97, 144; ethnographic knowledge and experience, 98–99; ethnography in literary terms, 104, 209n35; myth and cultural heroes, 105; participant-observation in, 102–3, 106, 134, 148; scientific objectivity, 101–2, 106; whole culture in, 106–7, 146, 177. *See also* Malinowski, Bronislaw
Arnold, Matthew, 41, 61, 65, 136–37; *Culture and Anarchy*, 37; definition of culture, 6, 69, 166; high Culture theory, 11, 16, 19, 34, 36; standard of perfection, 45–46
art: and economy, 138, 142; Melville's, 106, 107, 110, 118; organic/living culture and, 38–40, 42, 90, 92, 109; "primitive," 68–69, 123; Southwest Indian, 50–51; themes in Cather's writings, 60, 64, 66–70, 77; and tradition, 169
artisan guilds, 111–12
art object, 20, 48, 61, 123
assimilation, 2, 17; tradition and, 172–73; universalist, 143, 155
Austin, Mary, 63, 201n53; *The American Rhythm*, 51, 128

Bashkow, Ira, 185, 190
Birth of a Nation, The (Griffith), 29
Boas, Franz, 8, 27, 158, 200n43; employment, 97–98; ethnic background, 199n15; and museum display, 46–47; redefinition of culture, 28, 147; students of, 12, 14, 51
boundaries, 190–92, 198n11
Bourne, Randolph, 31, 33, 59, 126, 139, 158; connection to Sapir and Cather, 72, 203n27; physical deformities, 199n15
Bridge, The (Crane), 215n21, 215n23; Tate's criticism of, 21–22, 141, 160–68, 173–75

Brodhead, Richard, 23, 28, 52, 212n70
Brooks, Cleanth, 17, 82, 123
Brooks, Van Wyck: on Arnoldian culture, 36–37; background, 33, 198n15; characterization of Whitman, 37–38, 40; connection to Sapir, 27, 205n36; cultural metaphors, 35, 38, 119; definition of culture, 23, 24–25; on experience, 35–36, 38, 41, 54; on highbrow/lowbrow division, 19, 33–34, 37, 42, 44, 99–100, 111; on immigration, 29; literary achievements, 24; living culture theory, 35, 37–40, 42; on Melville, 90, 107–13, 134; national culture theory, 9, 25, 39–42, 56, 111, 182; on organic culture and art, 39, 42, 90, 92, 109; view of Dickinson, 9–10
Brooks, Van Wyck, works: "Amor Fati," 112; *The Flowering of New England, 1815–1865*, 10; *New England: Indian Summer, 1865–1915*, 9–10; "On Creating a Usable Past," 41, 108; "Reviewer's Notebook," 88–89, 108–10, 113; "The Culture of Industrialism," 33–34, 36; "Toward a National Culture," 10, 33, 35–36, 39–41; *Wine of the Puritans*, 110–11. *See also America's Coming of Age* (Brooks)

canon formation, 10; critics of, 16; culture and, 6, 89, 133; Melville revival and, 18, 20, 87–88, 98
Castronovo, Russ, 4, 133, 186, 189
Cather, Willa: *Alexander's Bridge*, 61; composition theory, 75; criticism of, 59–60; literary achievements, 59–60; Mesa Verde essay, 60, 76, 202n11; *My Ántonia*, 59, 70; "Nebraska: The End of the First Cycle," 57–58; "On the Art of Fiction," 111–12, 204n33; *O Pioneers!*, 59, 70, 203n25; on Sarah Orne Jewett, 75–76, 78, 204n33; social connections, 72; trips to the American Southwest, 61–63, 72; use of art/artifacts in writings, 60, 64, 66–70, 77, 202n10. *See also Professor's House, The* (Cather); *Song of the Lark, The* (Cather)
civilization, American, 11, 27, 67, 130–31, 158; division in, 19, 25, 44, 109, 111, 118
Civil War, 38, 125, 155, 172
Clifford, James, 75, 103, 105, 176
Coleridge, Samuel Taylor, 38, 109

INDEX / 221

concerted textual program, 23, 28, 32, 33
corporate culture, 2, 195n1
Crane, Hart. See Bridge, The (Crane)
critical culturalism, 22, 190, 192–93
Croce, Benedetto, 121–23
cultivation: artistic, 61, 68–70, 83; individual, 35, 69, 84, 117
cultural pluralism: anthropological versions of, 16–17, 156; Brooks's model of, 23, 169; and language theory, 145–46; modernist versions of, 57; and nativism, 17, 56, 132, 215n23; as problematic, 55; progressive and reactionary politics and, 159–60, 184; Sapir's model of, 26, 47, 158; Tate's version of, 141, 166, 184
cultural studies, 188, 197n24, 210n46; aesthetics of, 3, 9, 22, 84, 185; and anthropology, 84; boundaries of, 190–91; high and low culture and, 184; interdisciplinarity of, 2, 84, 133, 180; and New Criticism, 138–40; stopping or ending of, 1, 3, 185, 187. See also literary studies
cultural wholes: as an aesthetic object, 54, 128, 137–38, 141, 205n34; and anthropology, 3, 176, 179; difference in, 146; ethnographers and, 177; in evolutionary terms, 12–13, 45; Malinowski on, 106–7, 155, 177, 179; Melville's embodiment of, 21, 89, 122, 128; poetry and, 148–49; and possession, 77; Sapir's theory of, 25, 74, 118, 123, 158; Tate and Ransom on, 136–37, 140–41, 162, 168; and unity, 15, 55–56, 133. See also whole, culture as meaningful; wholeness
culture: anthropological versions of, 13, 14, 53, 88, 179, 181, 197n27; as a body, 102, 148; boundedness of, 15, 56, 74, 79, 88, 184, 190–91; as a composition, 75–77, 192; in decline, 178; interdisciplinary debate over, 13–14, 20, 23, 28, 53; metaphors, 35, 38, 119, 186; modernist conceptions of, 5, 15, 155, 185; new conceptions of, 13, 58, 119, 132, 137, 182, 184; popular usage of term, 1–2, 195n3; practices, 12–13; and the self, 8, 35, 68; as a structure, 150–51. See also American culture; genuine culture; organic culture; spatialization of culture
"Culture, Genuine and Spurious" (Sapir), 25, 47, 53, 117–18, 124; aesthetic form of culture, 61, 89; American civilization in, 43–44, 47, 49; figure of the Indian in, 20, 72, 156–57; language and structure, 48; solution of genuine culture, 19

Dial, The, 25, 29–32, 43; contributors to, 27–28, 53, 113
Dickinson, Emily, 6–10
difference, 140, 175, 179, 184
Dimock, Wai Chee, 4, 133, 188–89, 213n86
Douglas, Christopher, 16–17
Douglass, Ann, 16, 18, 197n28

"economic man," 100–101, 103
Edelman, Lee, 161
Eliot, T. S., 158, 160–61; on organic wholes, 169–70; "The Function of Criticism," 169, 173, 176; universal Tradition, 141, 163, 166, 168–70, 174–75, 179; The Waste Land, 27, 144, 162, 164, 170–71
environmentalism, 56, 158
ethnology: classification of culture in, 45–46; display practices in museums, 46–47, 65; evolutionary narratives in, 64, 66; field methods, 98; Melville's influence on, 95. See also anthropology
European civilization, 45, 65, 171
European literature, 170
evolution: cultural, 45–46; stages of, 64–65
evolutionary progress, 12–13, 65–66, 68, 202n18
experience: aesthetic, 152; Brooks on, 35–36, 38, 41, 54; child's, 67–68; and culture, 14; in ethnographic methodology, 97–99, 102–5, 148; and imagination, 21, 93–95, 103, 105–6, 112, 120; Melville's South Sea, 88, 90, 92, 114, 116, 134; poetic, 140, 176–77

Fewkes, Jesse Walter, 72, 204n29
Fluck, Winifried, 193
formlessness, 53, 110, 126
form of culture, 9–10, 18, 85, 212n70; Brooks on, 39–40, 119; and form of poetry, 141; and literary form, 187; Melville revival and, 88, 110, 114, 126; separation in, 186
Frank, Joseph, 82–83, 175, 205n38
Frazer, James, 95, 102, 146, 179, 207n19; The Golden Bough, 170
Freyer, Judith, 202n10

Geertz, Clifford, 187
genre, meaning of, 28
genuine culture, 17; and aesthetic objects, 48; of the American Indian, 20, 44–45, 49–51, 130, 159; in Cather's writings, 72–73, 78–80; definition of, 25–26, 46, 118, 157; imperialism and, 79; Melville's embodiment of, 88–89, 114, 118, 212n74; solution of, 19; structure of, 48–49, 191; in the U.S., 79–80; as whole, 49, 54, 72, 74, 114. *See also* "Culture, Genuine and Spurious" (Sapir)
Golden Bough, The (Frazer), 170
Greek and Roman cultures, 172
Guillory, John, 132, 184

Hammer, Langdon, 161–62, 166, 171, 174–76
Handler, Richard, 9, 43, 190–93
Harlem Renaissance, 5, 98, 197n28
Harrell, David, 201n8, 204n29
Hegeman, Susan, 3, 17, 33, 190; spatial concept of culture, 18, 205n38
Herder, Johann Gottfried, 11–12
Herman Melville: Mariner and Mystic (Weaver), 88, 90–92, 105, 113. *See also* Weaver, Raymond
hierarchy: in culture concepts, 12, 25, 34, 36, 106; Eliot's, 175; evolutionary, 64
highbrow/lowbrow division: Brooks on, 19, 33–34, 37, 42, 44, 99–100, 111; Melville's embodiment of, 108, 109, 110
high Culture, 12, 23–24, 134, 162; Arnoldian, 11, 16, 19, 34, 36
Hinsley, Curtis, 204n29
historicism, 142, 155
humanism, 142, 172–73
hybridity, 188, 190–91

identity: American, 2, 11, 79–80, 164, 167–68; cultural, 3, 17–18, 205n34; Southern, 171
I'll Take My Stand: The South and the Agrarian Tradition, 21, 153, 170, 216n41
immigration, 28; and American culture, 11, 29, 131
imperialism, 3, 52, 126, 185; and aesthetics, 78, 84; U.S., 31, 51, 87
Indian culture: art and artifacts, 50, 60–61, 63, 202n10; as genuine culture, 20, 44–45, 49–51, 130, 159; possession of, 79; Pueblo, 62–63, 156

individuality, 35–37; and tradition, 173–74
industrialism, 158; culture and, 31, 36, 91; science and, 137, 148, 153
international culture, 41–42
internationalism, 31, 52

Jancovich, Mark, 138
Jehlen, Myra, 87
Jewett, Sarah Orne, 75–78, 212n70

Kallen, Horace, 57, 131, 199n15
Kaplan, Amy, 52, 212n70
knowledge: as aesthetic, 101, 185; ethnographic experience and, 98–99, 102–3, 107; poetry and, 124, 137, 138, 151; and science, 106, 142, 145, 147–48, 150, 209n32

labor crisis, 30–32
language: and meaning, 138, 140, 143–44, 147, 149–50; and poetry, 82–83, 136–39; and reality, 32; scientific, 148, 155; as a structure, 48, 49, 73; translation of native, 122, 145, 149; as whole, 145–46, 150–51. *See also* poetry
Lauter, Paul, 16, 130–31
Lee, Hermione, 201n8
Lewis, Edith, 62, 72
literary anthropologist, 141–43, 152, 155
literary criticism, 3–6, 84, 139, 205n34; modernist, 7, 19, 48, 175; Mumford's, 89, 117–20; and New Criticism, 183, 197n28; rise of, 15, 56, 183
literary modernism, 59, 72, 144, 198n11; anthropology and, 13, 53, 176, 179
literary studies: aesthetic form/ turn in, 22, 61, 140, 185–87, 189; anthropology and, 9, 84; and culture relation, 186–87; history of, 183; institutionalization of, 86, 130; as a mediator, 187–88; New Criticism and, 179; problem of culture in, 1, 3–7, 179–80, 186–87, 190, 192
living culture, 35, 37–40, 42
Lowie, Robert, 27, 118

Malinowski, Bronislaw, 13, 97, 208n32; on cultural wholes, 106–7, 155, 177, 179; on ethnographic experience and knowledge, 98–99, 103, 148; language theories, 122, 140, 143–50; Melville and, 97, 101, 104, 106; *Myth in Primitive Psychology*, 106; participant-observer methodology, 99–97, 101–3, 106, 134, 148, 176; on "Primitive Economic Man," 100; "The Problem of Meaning in Primitive Language," 98, 143, 145–46, 149. See also *Argonauts of the Western Pacific* (Malinowski)

Mandelbaum, David, 43

Manganaro, Marc, 97, 146, 170; circuits of culture, 17, 18

Mao, Doug, 196n14

material-ideal division, 91, 92, 101, 103, 106; fusion, 110–12, 207n15

Mather, Frank Jewett, 90, 93, 95, 207n18

Matthiessen, F. O., 4, 212n73; *American Renaissance*, 86, 112, 131

melting pot ideal, 31

Melville, Herman, 207n19, 208n20; canonization of, 20, 86, 113; critical reception of, 86–87, 92–93; editions of works, 108, 207n15, 209n40; embodiment of wholeness, 21, 89; as a hero of culture, 105–7, 108, 112, 114, 130, 134; *Oomo*, 93, 109; regionalism of, 125, 127–30; similarities to Malinowski, 97, 101, 104, 106; South Sea experiences, 88, 92–96, 134. See also *Moby-Dick* (Melville); *Typee* (Melville)

Melville revival, 20–21, 98, 108; Brooks's contribution to, 35, 90, 107–13, 134; contributors to, 15, 88–89, 90, 206n9; critics, 130–31; and problem of culture, 133; and rise of American studies, 86–87, 130–31. See also *Moby-Dick* (Melville); Mumford, Lewis; Weaver, Raymond

Mesa Verde, 204n29; Cather's accounts of, 60, 62, 67, 72, 202n11, 203n24

Michaels, Walter Benn, 79, 132, 184; on cultural identity, 3, 17–18, 205n34

minority literatures, 17

Moby-Dick (Melville): as an aesthetic object, 120, 122, 128; Brooks's critique of, 109–10, 112; canonization of, 113, 115, 137, 160; critical attention of, 108, 212n73; dramatic adaptations of, 206n9; as literary form, 89; as a masterpiece, 20, 130, 207n15; Mumford's analysis of, 113–16, 119–22, 128–30, 177, 207n17; new readings of, 87–88; regionalism/ universalism of, 89, 115, 128–30, 177, 189; unity of, 129, 134; Weaver's critique of, 91, 94, 108, 207n17; wholeness of, 21, 116, 118, 212n74

modernism: critics of, 5, 16, 52, 161–62; history of, 56; international, 147; poetic unity and, 176; spatiality of, 82, 205n38; transnational, 97, 98. See also American modernism; literary modernism

multiculturalism, 2, 5, 132, 184

Mumford, Lewis: on aesthetic form, 120–21; connection to Sapir, 118–19; construction of culture, 117–19, 122; ethnic background, 199n15; *The Golden Day*, 113, 115, 117–18, 125, 210n46; Herman Melville, 21, 89, 113–17, 121–26, 216n46; literary achievements, 113, 119; on regionalism and wholeness of *Moby-Dick*, 125, 128–30, 134, 177, 189; regional planning interests, 124–27; on science and imagination, 115–16; on the state, 30, 126

museums, American, 46–47, 65

myth, 105–7, 160–61

national culture: and American studies, 4, 189–90; Brooks's theory of, 9, 25, 39–42, 56, 111, 182; in Cather's writings, 79–81, 84; imperialism of, 52; Mumford's concept of, 126–28, 130; pluralism and, 12; and the state, 15–16; Tate's version of, 167

nation-state, 29, 52, 188–90; culture and, 19, 133; homogeneity of, 132; regional culture and, 124, 127, 129, 212n70

nativism, 56, 185, 215n23

naturalism, 82

New Americanists, 87, 132–33, 189, 212n73

New Criticism, 196n14; cultural pluralism and, 138, 159–60; cultural studies and, 138–40; literary criticism and, 61, 183, 197n28; modernist anthropology and, 20, 22, 61, 187; and poetic language and form, 136–39, 179; and poetic unity, 160–62, 165, 175; progressivism, 184; reading methods, 4, 88, 179; rise of, 19, 131, 147, 186; Spingarn on, 121. See also Ransom, John Crowe; Tate, Allen

New England culture, 7, 10, 75–76, 127

North, Michael, 97–98, 198n11

O'Brien, Sharon, 60, 202n10
Ogden, C. K., 32, 98, 143–44
organic culture: in Melville's art, 106, 108, 112–13; as whole, 54, 56; and works of art, 39, 42, 92, 109

Paradise Lost (Milton), 110, 141–42, 165
Parrington, V. L., 31, 50, 78–79, 183
Parson, Elsie Clews, 27, 51, 118
Pearce, Roy Harvey, 142–43, 155
perfection, 6, 37, 45–46, 69
Pickering, Edward, 139
pioneers, 58, 70
Platonic idealism, 149–50
pluralism, 12, 41, 131; poetic, 140; Ransom's theory of, 141, 154–55, 158–59; regionalism and, 155, 159, 174, 184; Tate's version of, 163, 170–71, 174; and tradition, 170–71, 174. See also cultural pluralism
poet-critic, 15, 56, 141, 176–79, 183
poetry: aesthetic form of, 6, 121–22, 160; American, 128; Fugitive, 174; and historical context, 142; and knowledge, 124, 138, 151; language and, 56; meaning of culture for, 6–10, 186; modern, 82–83, 165, 175; New Critical practices of, 21, 84; psychological responses to, 144, 150, 214n8; and science, 124, 140, 147–48, 150; and space, 54, 156–57, 175; structure of, 149, 151–53, 161; unity in, 141, 163–66, 174, 176–77, 179. See also *Bridge, The* (Crane)
possession: of culture, 2, 61, 63, 77–78, 81, 83; imperial, 84; of Indian culture, 79; of the pioneer, 70; self-, 20, 69, 81
Powell, Douglas, 192
Professor's House, The (Cather), 58, 85; Cliff Dwellers in, 60, 62, 70–73, 76–79, 205n34; compared to Keats's Grecian urn, 81–82; Indian art/artifacts in, 64, 66, 202n10; Professor St. Peter's narrative, 78; regional and national culture concepts in, 79–81, 83; whole culture concept in, 20, 74, 83, 202n18
progressivism, 184; evolutionary, 66, 68. See also reactionary and progressive critics

race, 3, 84, 158, 185; and cultural identity, 3, 17–18

Ransom, John Crowe: on cultural wholes, 136–37, 140–41, 154, 157; *The New Criticism*, 4, 140, 149, 152, 154, 159; pluralism theory, 141, 154–55, 158–59; poetry theories, 21, 136–40, 143, 147–50, 153–56; on regionalism and aesthetic form, 16, 156–58, 186; Southern agrarian writings, 138–39, 150, 152–55; "The Aesthetics of Regionalism," 157–58; "The Idea of a Literary Anthropologist," 141–43, 151, 155; "The Mimetic Principle," 143, 147; "The Tense of Poetry," 143, 151–53; "Wanted: An Ontological Critic," 143, 148–49, 151–52, 154; *The World's Body*, 140, 143, 147, 149, 151
reactionary and progressive critics, 16, 21, 135; and cultural pluralism, 159–60, 184; and culture as whole, 139–40; and unit of culture, 5, 78–79
regional culture: in Cather's works, 79–81, 191; and difference, 140; of *Moby-Dick*, 89, 115, 128–30, 131, 134, 177, 189; and nation-state, 124, 127, 129, 212n70; Sapir's version of, 52–53, 56, 127; and the state, 15–16; and textual meaning, 183; and unity, 22, 128–29, 167; universalism and, 204n33
regionalism, 21, 41, 52, 56; and aesthetic form, 21, 59, 89, 115, 156; Cather on, 20, 59; "critical," 192; in Melville's works, 89, 115, 125–30; Mumford's, 127–28, 130, 158, 191, 211n60, 212n70; Ransom's aesthetics and, 16, 156–58, 186; Sapir's, 191, 212n70; Sarah Orne Jewett's, 75–76, 212n70
Regional Planning Association of America (RPAA), 125, 211n60
Richards, I. A., 136, 150, 214n8; *The Meaning of Meaning* (with Ogden), 32, 98, 143–45, 149; *Practical Criticism*, 32, 119, 144

"salvage ethnography," 75, 177
Santayana, George, 210n46
Sapir, Edward: academic and literary achievements, 8, 27, 43, 118–19; on American Indian culture, 20, 44–45, 49–51, 157; "Civilization and Culture," 25, 27, 30–31, 42–43, 53, 118; connection to Bourne, 72, 203n27; connection to

Brooks, 27; critique of Dickinson, 8–9; cultural pluralism concept, 26, 47, 158; on culture as meaningful whole, 19, 54, 83, 89, 185–86; definition/concepts of culture, 23–26, 45–46, 54–55, 132–33, 189; on geography of culture, 52, 124; *Language: An Introduction to the Study of Speech*, 49, 121; link to Boas, 43, 200n43; on national culture, 127; regional culture theory, 52–53, 56, 127; regionalism, 191, 212n70; on structure of language, 48, 49, 73, 183; theory of the integral self, 9. *See also* "Culture, Genuine and Spurious" (Sapir); genuine culture

Schedler, Christopher, 64, 66, 202n18

science: and culture, 136; and imagination, 115–16; knowledge and, 106, 142, 145, 147–48, 150, 209n32; modern, 100; objective, 101–2; and poetry, 124, 140, 147–48, 150

Seven Arts, 25, 26–27, 33, 113

Shumway, David, 16

Siskin, Clifford, 1–5, 179–80, 185–87, 190

Song of the Lark, The (Cather), 57, 60–61, 84–85, 202n18; artistic cultivation in, 20, 66–70, 81, 83; Cliff Dwellers, 63–64, 67, 69, 73, 76, 100; Indian pottery, 63–66, 71; symbol of eagle in, 69–70

sovereignty, 52, 133, 188

Spanos, William, 87, 130–31

Spark, Clare, 87

spatialization of culture, 5, 15, 17, 54, 205n38; as an aesthetic object, 18, 48, 73, 83, 118; Cather's use of, 20, 155; in whole culture context, 47, 134, 137, 175

Spingarn, Joel, 114, 121–23

state, the: American identity and, 79; critiques of, 30, 53, 126; culture and, 16, 56, 182; power of, 31, 54, 126; unity of, 22. *See also* national culture; nation-state

Stocking, George, 47, 98, 104, 105, 204n29; on the classical period (1920s), 12, 26

Stout, Janis, 72

Susman, Warren, 32

Tate, Allen: "American Poetry Since 1920," 167, 171, 174; critique of I. A. Richards's works, 119, 136, 144, 214n8; on cultural wholes, 136–37, 140, 163, 165, 168; definition of culture, 6–8; essay on Dickinson, 6–8, 9; "Function of Criticism," 169–70, 173, 176; "Literature as Knowledge," 136; "Long View" of history, 172; pluralism concept, 166–67, 170–71, 174, 184; "Remarks on the Southern Religion," 170–71; review of *The Bridge* (Crane), 21–22, 141, 160–68, 173–75; review of *White Buildings* (Crane), 164, 166; sectionalism, 169, 171, 174–75; "The Fallacy of Humanism," 172, 174; theory of poetry, 21, 136–39, 141, 165; version of tradition, 167–68, 171–74, 176

totality, 151, 171, 175; integrated, 116, 118

Trachtenberg, Alan, 139

tradition: American, 166–68, 171; Eliot's universal, 141, 166, 169–70, 174–75, 179; pluralism and, 170–71, 174; Tate's version of, 167–68, 171–74, 176

transnationalism, 184, 188, 190–91

transnational movement, 75, 79–80, 84, 185

Trilling, Lionel, 86

Twain, Mark, 109

Tylor, Edward Burnett, 46, 61, 68–69; *Primitive Culture*, 12, 45, 65

Typee (Melville), 93, 95, 106, 108–9, 207n15, 208n20, 209n40; Weaver's treatment of, 88, 92, 94, 96–98, 103, 106, 207nn17–18

unit of culture, 5, 124, 141; of America, 166; Brooks's theory of, 40, 56, 111, 182; in Cather's writings, 79, 84; debates over, 18, 23–24; false, 163. *See also* national culture; regional culture

unity: of America, 127–28, 132, 167–68; canons and, 184; cultural wholes and, 15, 55–56, 133; false, 22, 127, 168, 173–74, 216n41; formal, 48, 130, 160, 168; genuine, 15, 55; in poetry/poetic, 9, 141, 163–66, 176–77; regional and national, 22, 128–29, 167; of self, 9; of tradition and culture, 161–63, 164, 167–68

universalism: and culture, 36, 156, 170; Eliot's, 141, 166, 169–70, 174–75, 179; hierarchical, 140; in *Moby-Dick*, 129–30; and pluralism, 155

Wade, Edwin, 50

Warner, William B., 1–5, 179–80, 185–87, 190

Warren, Robert Penn, 213n82

way of life: and aesthetic form, 186; of the artist, 39; in Cather's culture concepts, 61, 64–66, 68–69, 71–73, 77; of Native Americans, 44–45, 158; in New England, 75–76, 114; Southern agrarian, 139, 153–54, 171; whole, 7, 12, 21, 92, 137–38, 140–41

Weaver, Raymond, 21, 99, 101, 134, 209n32; assessment of Melville, 88, 91–92, 104, 208n20; description of *Moby-Dick*, 94; on Melville as a cultural hero, 105–8, 114; on Melville's experiences with the Typees, 90, 92–96, 98, 103, 106, 207nn17–18

Whitehead, Alfred North, 32, 119; *Science and the Modern World*, 100, 209n32, 210n49

Whitman, Walt, 36; Brooks's characterization of, 37–38, 40; Melville and, 111; *Specimen Days*, 38

whole, culture as meaningful, 14, 85, 137, 140, 210n49; Cather's concept of, 20, 72; Malinowski's version of, 106–7; modernist conception of, 185; Mumford's accounts of, 114, 117, 130, 189; Sapir's concept of, 19, 54, 83, 89, 185–86. *See also* cultural wholes

wholeness: of America, 168; of the art object, 20, 123; ethnographers and, 177; of genuine culture, 49, 54, 72, 74, 114; individual elements of, 47; language as, 145–46, 150–51; living or organic, 169–70; of Melville and *Moby-Dick*, 21, 89, 113, 116, 130, 178, 212n74; region as a, 125; Sapir on, 25, 46, 54; textual, 16, 178; unity and, 15, 55–56. *See also* cultural wholes

whole poem, 82, 122, 141, 143, 174; irreducibility of, 148–49; stability of, 151, 154

Williams, Raymond, 11, 133, 192

Young Americans, 25, 33, 159; critique of the state, 30, 53, 126; founders of, 9; intellectual circles, 27; rise of, 4. *See also* Bourne, Randolph; Mumford, Lewis

Cultural Frames, Framing Culture

Books in this series examine both the way our culture frames our narratives and the way our narratives produce the culture that frames them. Attempting to bridge the gap between previously disparate disciplines, and combining theoretical issues with practical applications, this series invites a broad audience to read contemporary culture in a fresh and provocative way.

Nancy Martha West
Kodak and the Lens of Nostalgia

Raphael Sassower and Louis Cicotello
The Golden Avant-Garde: Idolatry, Commercialism, and Art

Margot Norris
Writing War in the Twentieth Century

Robin Blaetz
Visions of the Maid: Joan of Arc in American Film and Culture

Ellen Tremper
I'm No Angel: The Blonde in Fiction and Film

Naomi Mandel
Against the Unspeakable: Complicity, the Holocaust, and Slavery in America

Debra Walker King
African Americans and the Culture of Pain

Jon Robert Adams
Male Armor: The Soldier-Hero in Contemporary American Culture

Rachel Hall
Wanted: The Outlaw in American Visual Culture

Stephanie L. Hawkins
American Iconographic: "National Geographic," Global Culture, and the Visual Imagination

Stephanie Harzewski
Chick Lit and Postfeminism

Samuel Chase Coale
Quirks of the Quantum: Postmodernism and Contemporary American Fiction

Eric Aronoff
Composing Cultures: Modernism, American Literary Studies, and the Problem of Culture

www.ingramcontent.com/pod-product-compliance
Lightning Source LLC
Chambersburg PA
CBHW011746220426
43667CB00019B/2913